BUSINESS IN LITERATURE

REVISED EDITION

Edited by

Charles A. Burden
Professor of Management
Georgia State University

and

Valerie E. Mock

1988

Business Publishing Division
Georgia State University
College of Business Administration
Atlanta, Georgia

Published by

Business Publishing Division
College of Business Administration
Georgia State University
University Plaza
Atlanta, Georgia 30303-3093
Telephone: 404/651-4253

Revised Edition

©1988 by the College of Business Administration, Georgia State University

First edition published in 1977 by David McKay Company, Inc.
and reprinted in 1980 by Longman Inc.

All rights reserved, including the right to reproduce this publication,
or portions thereof, in any form without prior permission from the publisher.

92 91 90 89 88   5 4 3 2 1

Georgia State University, a unit of the University System of Georgia,
is an equal educational opportunity institution and an equal
opportunity/affirmative action employer.

Printed in the United States of America

Library of Congress Cataloging-in-Publication Data

Business in literature. — Rev. ed. / edited by Charles A. Burden,
Valerie E. Mock.
p. cm.
Bibliography: p.
ISBN 0-88406-206-6
1. Business—Literary collections. 2. Organization—Literary
collections. I. Burden, Charles A. II. Mock, Valerie E.
PN6071.B86B8   1988
808.8'0355—dc19   88-19915
                                CIP

Book design and cover design by Patton H. McGinley, Jr.

Phototypesetting by Donald E. Dedmon

CONTENTS

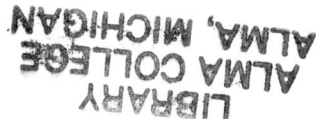

Acknowledgments — xi

Introduction — xix

1 ORGANIZATION AS A DETERMINANT OF STYLES OF LIFE — 1

POEMS

Written in London, September, 1802 / William Wordsworth	3
Empire Builders / Archibald MacLeish	3
"Ace" Shaw / Edgar Lee Masters	6
Departmental / Robert Frost	7
Calling to United Work / Ilya Ivanovich Sadofief	8
a salesman is an it that stinks Excuse / e e cummings	9
Little Boxes / Malvina Reynolds	10
The Unknown Citizen / W. H. Auden	11

Drug Store / Karl Shapiro	12
Poem / Alan Dugan	13
The Computer's First Christmas Card / Edwin Morgan	14
Hospital Visit / Sterling Eisiminger	15
On a Shaker Slat-Back Rocker / Sterling Eisiminger	15
Bureau 2 / Josephine Miles	16
Bohemia / Dorothy Parker	17
Clothes Make the Man / Jack Conway	17
Life Cycle of Common Man / Howard Nemerov	19
Life in the Ashtray / Terrill Shepard Soules	20
Trading on Gravity / Barri Armitage	21
The Importance of Garbage Collectors / Vivian Lowe	22
Why We Are Late / Josephine Miles	23
A Summer Morning / Richard Wilbur	24

FICTION

From *Digging for Gold: A Story of California* / Horatio Alger	25
The Japanese Quince / John Galsworthy	31
Song of the Shirt, 1941 / Dorothy Parker	34

ESSAYS

That Aristocracy May Be Engendered by Manufactures / Alexis de Tocqueville	43
The House of Morgan / John Dos Passos	47
Just Singin' the Office Workers' Summer Blues / Ellen Goodman	51

VIEWPOINTS

The Drive for Power / J. Bronowski — 53

2 ORGANIZATION AS AN INFLUENCE ON VALUES — 55

POEMS

The Hangman at Home / Carl Sandburg	58
I Am a Union Woman / Aunt Molly Jackson	59
pity this busy monster,manunkind / e e cummings	60
I Paint What I See / E. B. White	61
At the Florist's / Jacques Prévert	62
Three Poems—Robert Whitmore / Arthur Ridgewood M.D. / Giles Johnson, Ph.D. / Frank Marshall Davis	63
Boy-Man / Karl Shapiro	65
Office Love / Karl Shapiro	66
What *Was* Her Name? / John Ciardi	67
Limited / Carl Sandburg	67
Transcontinent / Donald Hall	68
Theorem / Carl Sandburg	68
The Development / Marge Piercy	69
The Purist / Ogden Nash	70
Systems / JoAllen Bradham	70
Parrot as Per Tech Specs / JoAllen Bradham	72
The Truck / John Stone	72
The News / John Godfrey Saxe	74
Delayed Decision / John Dickson	74

Apostrophe to Man / Edna St. Vincent Millay   76
Art / Anonymous   76

FICTION

The Man Higher Up / O. Henry   78
Quality / John Galsworthy   90
The Catbird Seat / James Thurber   97

ESSAYS

Letters 105 and 106 / Montesquieu   107
Life Without Principle / Henry David Thoreau   111
The Business Illusion of Managing Emotions /
   Ellen Goodman   123

VIEWPOINTS

The Inhumane Businessman / Russell Kirk   126

3 ORGANIZATION AS FULFILLMENT   135

POEMS

The Worldling / Voltaire   138
Composed Upon Westminster Bridge,
   September 3, 1802 / William Wordsworth   142
Hard Times Cotton Mill Girls / Anonymous   143
In the Factory / Ilya Ivanovich Sadofief   144
The Tired Worker / Claude McKay   145
Stevedore / Leslie M. Collins   145

A Lone Striker / Robert Frost	146
Two Tramps in Mud Time / Robert Frost	148
Happiness / Carl Sandburg	150
Richard Cory / Edwin Arlington Robinson	151
Richard Cory / Paul Simon	151
Fish Crier / Carl Sandburg	152
Chicago / Carl Sandburg	153
A Valedictory to Standard Oil of Indiana / David Wagoner	154
The Woman at the Washington Zoo / Randall Jarrell	156
Secretary / Ted Hughes	157
Plan / Rod McKuen	157
The Report / Jon Swan	158
For Granted / Julie Porosky	161
Retirement / Naomi H. Barnard	162
What's That Smell in the Kitchen? / Marge Piercy	162
Town Life / Jay Parini	163
I'll Go to Crazy Ruby's / Dorie LaRue	166
Typists / P. K. Page	167

FICTION

Wakefield / Nathaniel Hawthorne	168
Bartleby, the Scrivener / Herman Melville	176

ESSAYS

From *Second Discourse* / Jean-Jacques Rousseau	214
From *An Inquiry Into the Nature and Causes of the Wealth of Nations* / Adam Smith	215
On American Leisure / Irwin Edman	217

VIEWPOINTS

The Effects of the Industrial Revolution on
    Women and Children / Robert Hessen   226
Report of a Special Task Force to the
    Secretary of Health, Education, and Welfare   234
Exporting the Technological Revolution /
    Robert Gilpin   235

4 ORGANIZATION AS A RELIGION   239

POEMS

The World Is Too Much With Us /
    William Wordsworth   242
The Latest Decalogue / Arthur Hugh Clough   242
To a Locomotive in Winter / Walt Whitman   243
Cassandra / Edwin Arlington Robinson   244
John Henry / Anonymous   246
The Hammer / Carl Sandburg   250
The Iron Messiah / Vladimir Timofeevich Kirillov   251
Portrait of a Machine / Louis Untermeyer   252
Prayers of Steel / Carl Sandburg   253
The Heavenly Factory / Vasili Vasilievich Kazin   253
Why Wait for Science / Robert Frost   254
A Projection / Reed Whittemore   254
Appalachian Suicide / Jesse Stuart   256
Name Us a King / Carl Sandburg   262
Dirge / Kenneth Fearing   263

The Daily Grind / Fenton Johnson	264
Investment / Norman Nathan	265
Back Through the Looking Glass to This Side / John Ciardi	266
Success / Alice Rose George	267
Power / Adrienne Rich	268
Owed to New York—1906 / Byron Rufus Newton	269
Printed Words / Liz Sohappy Bahe	270
Boom! Sees Boom in Religion, Too / Howard Nemerov	271
The True-Blue American / Delmore Schwartz	272

FICTION

From *L'Assommoir* / Émile Zola	274
From *The Grapes of Wrath* / John Steinbeck	286
The Laugher / Heinrich Böll	294
The Tool / Antoine de Saint-Exupéry	297

ESSAYS

The Parable of Talents / *Matthew* 25:14–30	302
Labour / Thomas Carlyle	303
Our High-tech Hardware Will Have to Learn to Live With the 'Human Factor' / Ellen Goodman	305

VIEWPOINTS

The Drive for Power / J. Bronowski	308
The Hazards of Corporate Responsibility / Gilbert Burck	310

5 EPILOGUE   323

POEMS

Lament for a Rush Hour Crowd / Mary T. Gentry   324
Prayers: 1964–1984 / Ginny Sikes   324
South-bound on 75 / Ginny Sikes   325
Interstate Billboard / Ginny Sikes   325
Macon, Ga. / Ginny Sikes   326
The Tyrant / James L. Stanford   326
My Second Job / Karen Eckert   328
The Appointment / Karen Eckert   329
Don't You Know What You Want? /
   Linda Podger-Williams   329
A Conglome**R**ation **O**f **N**icknames **Y**ou
   Most often **S**ay / Linda Podger-Williams   330
I'll Be Home at Six / Pat Brown   331
For You / Shirley Adams   332
Machine / John B. Farrow   333
Enlightenment / Bonnie Greer   334

ESSAYS

Finding Happiness in Work / Jim Wooten   336

Suggestions for Further Reading   338

Acknowledgments

We are greatly indebted to Drs. Elke Burden, Lynn Ganim, and Sterling Eisiminger for their contributions to this book. Additionally, we would like to thank Dr. Karla Stein; John Phillip Baroni; Cary Bynum, Margaret F. Stanley, and Claudia Forman of the Business Publishing Division at Georgia State University; and the colleagues and students who provided ideas and advice for this book. We would also like to thank the following authors and publishers who gave us permission to reprint material:

"Empire Builders" from *Collected Poems* 1917–1952 by Archibald MacLeish. Copyright 1952 by Archibald MacLeish. Reprinted by permission of the Houghton Mifflin Company.

"'Ace' Shaw" by Edgar Lee Masters from *Spoon River Anthology*, published by Macmillan, Inc. Copyright 1914, 1915 by William Marion Reedy; copyright 1915, 1916, 1942, 1944 by Edgar Lee Masters. Reprinted by permission of Ellen C. Masters.

"Departmental" by Robert Frost from *The Poetry of Robert Frost*, edited by Edward Connery Lathem. Copyright ©1936 by Robert Frost; copyright ©1964 by Leslie Frost Ballantine; copyright ©1969 by Holt, Rinehart and Winston. Reprinted by permission of Holt, Rinehart and Winston, publishers.

"Calling to United Work" by Ilya Ivanovich Sadofief from *Popular Poetry in Soviet Russia*, edited by George Z. Patrick. Published in 1929 by the Regents of the University of California. Reprinted by permission of the University of California Press.

"a salesman is an it that stinks Excuse" by e e cummings. Copyright 1944 by e e cummings; copyright renewed ©1972 by Nancy Andrews. Reprinted from *Complete Poems* 1913–1962 by e e cummings by permission of Harcourt Brace Jovanovich, Inc.

"Little Boxes," from the song "Little Boxes," words and music by Malvina Reynolds. Copyright ©1962 by Shroder Music Co. (ASCAP). Reprinted by permission.

"The Unknown Citizen" from *Collected Shorter Poems* 1927–1957 by W. H. Auden. Copyright 1940 and renewed ©1968 by W. H. Auden. Reprinted by permission of Random House, Inc. and Faber & Faber Ltd.

"Drug Store" from *Selected Poems* by Karl Shapiro. Copyright 1941 and renewed ©1969 by Karl Shapiro. Reprinted by permission of Random House, Inc.

"Poem" from *Collected Poems* by Alan Dugan. Copyright ©1961 by Alan Dugan; copyright ©1963, 1967, 1969 by Yale University Press. Reprinted by permission of the author.

"The Computer's First Christmas Card" by Edwin Morgan from *The Second Life*. Copyright ©1968 by Edinburgh University Press. Reprinted by permission of the publisher.

xii/ACKNOWLEDGMENTS

"Hospital Visit" and "On a Shaker Slat-Back Rocker" by Sterling Eisiminger. Copyright ©1977 by Sterling Eisiminger. Reprinted by permission of the author.

"Bureau 2" and "Why We Are Late" from *Coming to Terms* by Josephine Miles. Copyright ©1979 by Josephine Miles. Reprinted by permission of the University of Illinois Press.

"Bohemia" from *The Portable Dorothy Parker* by Dorothy Parker. Copyright 1928; copyright renewed ©1956 by Dorothy Parker. All rights reserved. Reprinted by permission of Viking Penguin, Inc.

"Clothes Make the Man" by Jack Conway from *The Nantucket Review*, no. 26, Fall 1986. Copyright ©1986 by *The Nantucket Review*. Reprinted with permission of the publisher.

"Life Cycle of Common Man" and "Boom!" by Howard Nemerov from *Collected Poems*. Copyright ©1977 by Howard Nemerov. Published by University of Chicago Press. Reprinted by permission of the author.

"Life in the Ashtray" by Terrill Shepard Soules from *The Selectric Poems*. Reprinted by permission of the author.

"Trading on Gravity" by Barri Armitage. First appeared in *Poetry*, February 1987. Copyright ©1987 by The Modern Poetry Association. Reprinted with the permission of the editor of *Poetry* and the author.

"The Importance of Garbage Collectors" by Vivian Lowe from *Sand Hills: The Augusta College Literary Magazine*, Spring 1979. Copyright ©1979. Reprinted by permission of the author.

"A Summer Morning" by Richard Wilbur. Copyright ©1960 by Richard Wilbur. Reprinted from his volume *Advice to a Prophet and Other Poems* by permission of Harcourt Brace and Jovanovich, Inc.

Excerpt from *Digging for Gold* by Horatio Alger, Jr., introduction by John Seelye. Reprinted by permission of Macmillan Company, Inc.

"The Japanese Quince" from A *Motley* by John Galsworthy. Copyright 1910, Charles Scribner's Sons. Reprinted by permission of Charles Scribner's Sons.

"Song of the Shirt, 1941" from *The Portable Dorothy Parker* by Dorothy Parker. Copyright ©1941 by Dorothy Parker; copyright renewed ©1969 by Lillian Hellman. Reprinted by permission of Viking Penguin, Inc.

"The House of Morgan" from *Nineteen Nineteen* by John Dos Passos, published by Houghton Mifflin Company. Copyright 1931 by John Dos Passos; copyright renewed ©1959 by John Dos Passos. Reprinted by permission of Elizabeth Dos Passos.

"Just Singin' the Office Workers' Summer Blues" by Ellen Goodman, *Atlanta Constitution*, 1 August 1986. Copyright ©1986 by the Boston Globe Newspaper Company/Washington Post Writers Group. Reprinted with permission.

Excerpt from *The Ascent of Man* by J. Bronowski, pp. 279–280 and 280–285. Copyright ©1973 by J. Bronowski. Reprinted by permission of Little, Brown and Co. and BBC Publications.

"The Hangman at Home" from *Smoke and Steel* by Carl Sandburg. Copyright 1920 by Harcourt Brace Jovanovich, Inc.; copyright renewed 1948 by Carl Sandburg. Reprinted by permission of the publishers.

"I Am a Union Woman" by Aunt Molly Jackson from *The World Split Open: Four Centuries of Women Poets in England and America 1552–1950*, edited by Louise Bernikow. Published by Random House.

ACKNOWLEDGMENTS/xiii

"pity this busy monster,manunkind" from *Complete Poems 1913–1962* by e e cummings. Copyright 1944 by e e cummings; copyright renewed ©1972 by Nancy T. Andrews. Reprinted by permission of Harcourt Brace Jovanovich, Inc.

"I Paint What I See" from *The Fox and the Peapack* (1938) by E. B. White. Copyright 1933 by E. B. White. Reprinted by permission of Harper & Row, Publishers.

"At the Florist's" from *Selections From Paroles* by Jacques Prévert, translated by Lawrence Ferlinghetti. Copyright 1947 by Editions du Point du Jour, Paris; copyright 1958 by City Light Books. Reprinted by permission of City Light Books.

"Three Poems" by Frank Marshall Davis from *Black Man's Verse*, edited by Dudley Randall. Copyright 1935 by Frank Marshall Davis. Reprinted by permission of Frank Marshall Davis.

"Boy-Man" from *Selected Poems* by Karl Shapiro. Copyright 1947 by Karl Shapiro. Reprinted by permission of Random House, Inc. Originally appeared in *The New Yorker*.

"Office Love" from *Selected Poems* by Karl Shapiro. Copyright ©1968 by Karl Shapiro. Reprinted by permission of Random House, Inc.

"What Was Her Name?" from *Person to Person* by John Ciardi. Copyright ©1962 by Rutgers, The State University. Reprinted by permission of the author.

"Limited" from *Chicago Poems* by Carl Sandburg. Copyright 1916 by Holt, Rinehart, and Winston, Inc.; copyright 1944 by Carl Sandburg. Reprinted by permission of Harcourt Brace Jovanovich, Inc.

"Transcontinent" by Donald Hall. Copyright ©1959 by *Saturday Review*. Reprinted by permission of *Saturday Review*.

"Theorem" from *The Sandburg Range* by Carl Sandburg. Copyright 1957 by Carl Sandburg. Reprinted by permission of Harcourt Brace Jovanovich, Inc.

"The Development" and "What's That Smell in the Kitchen" from *Circles on the Water* by Marge Piercy. Copyright ©1982 by Marge Piercy. Reprinted by permission of Alfred A. Knopf, Inc.

"The Purist" from *Verses from 1929 On* by Ogden Nash. Copyright 1935 by Ogden Nash. Reprinted by permission of Little, Brown and Company.

"Systems" and "Parrot as Per Tech Specs" from *Songs My Computer Taught Me* by JoAllen Bradham. Reprinted by permission of the author.

"The Truck" from *In All This Rain* by John Stone. Copyright ©1980 by John Stone. Reprinted by permission of Louisiana State University Press and the author.

"The News" by John Godfrey Saxe from *The Norton Book of Light Verse*, edited by Russell Baker. Copyright ©1986 by Russell Baker. Reprinted by permission of W. W. Norton & Company, Inc.

"Delayed Decision" by John Dickson. First appeared in *Poetry*, February 1987. Copyright ©1987 by The Modern Poetry Association. Reprinted by permission of the editor of *Poetry* and the author.

"Apostrophe to Man" by Edna St. Vincent Millay from *Collected Poems*. Published by Harper & Row. Copyright ©1934, 1962 by Edna St. Vincent Millay and Norma Millay Ellis. Reprinted by permission.

"Art," anonymous, from *The Norton Book of Light Verse*, edited by Russell Baker. Copyright ©1986 by Russell Baker. Reprinted by permission of W. W. Norton & Company, Inc.

xiv/ACKNOWLEDGMENTS

"The Man Higher Up" from *The Gentle Grafter* by O. Henry. Copyright 1908 by Doubleday & Company, Inc. Reprinted by permission of Doubleday & Company, Inc.

"Quality" by John Galsworthy. Copyright 1912 by Charles Scribner's Sons. Reprinted by permission of Charles Scribner's Sons from *The Inn of Tranquility* by John Galsworthy. Also reprinted by permission of William Heinemann Ltd.

"The Catbird Seat" by James Thurber from *The Thurber Carnival*. Copyright 1945 by James Thurber; copyright ©1973 by Helen W. Thurber and Rosemary Thurber Sauers. Published by Harper & Row. Originally printed in *The New Yorker*.

Letters 105 and 106 from Montesquieu from *Persian Letters*, translated by C. J. Betts (Penguin Classics 1973), pp. 192-196. Copyright by C. J. Betts, ©1973. Reprinted by permission of Penguin Books Ltd.

"Life Without Principle" by Henry David Thoreau from *The Works of Thoreau*, edited by Henry S. Canby. Copyright ©1967 by Marion G. Canby. Published by Houghton Mifflin Company, Boston.

"The Business Illusion of Managing Emotions" by Ellen Goodman, *Atlanta Constitution*, 22 September 1983. Copyright ©1983 by the Boston Globe Newspaper Company/Washington Post Writers Group. Reprinted with permission.

"The Inhumane Businessman" by Russell Kirk. Copyright ©1957 by Time, Inc. Reprinted from *Fortune* magazine (May 1957) by special permission.

"Hard Times Cotton Mill Girls," anonymous, from *The World Split Open: Four Centuries of Women Poets in England and America 1552-1950*, edited by Louise Bernikow. Published by Random House, Inc.

"In the Factory" by Ilya Ivanovich Sadofief from *Popular Poetry in Soviet Russia*, edited by George Z. Patrick. Published in 1929 by The Regents of the University of California. Reprinted by permission of the University of California Press.

"The Tired Worker" by Claude McKay from *Selected Poems of Claude McKay*. Copyright ©1981 by Twayne Publishers, Inc. Reprinted by permission of Twayne Publishers, a division of G. K. Hall & Co., Boston.

"Stevedore" by L. M. Collins was first published in *Poet Lore*, Winter 1944. Reprinted by permission of the author.

"A Lone Striker" and "Two Tramps in Mud Time" by Robert Frost from *The Poetry of Robert Frost*, edited by Edward Connery Lathem. Copyright 1936 by Robert Frost; copyright ©1964 by Lesley Frost Ballantine; copyright ©1969 by Holt, Rinehart and Winston. Reprinted by permission of Holt, Rinehart and Winston.

"Happiness" from *Chicago Poems* by Carl Sandburg. Copyright 1916 by Holt, Rinehart and Winston, Inc.; copyright 1944 by Carl Sandburg. Reprinted by permission Harcourt Brace Jovanovich, Inc.

"Richard Cory" by Edwin Arlington Robinson from *The Children of the Night*. Reprinted by permission of Charles Scribner's Sons.

"Richard Cory" by Paul Simon. Copyright ©1966 by Paul Simon. Used by permission.

"Fish Crier" and "Chicago" from *Chicago Poems* by Carl Sandburg. Copyright 1916 by Holt, Rinehart and Winston, Inc.; copyright 1944 by Carl Sandburg. Reprinted by permission of Harcourt Brace Jovanovich, Inc.

ACKNOWLEDGMENTS/xv

"A Valedictory to Standard Oil of Indiana" from *New and Selected Poems* by David Wagoner. Copyright ©1969 by Indiana University Press. Reprinted by permission of the publisher. Originally printed in *The New Yorker*.

"The Woman at the Washington Zoo" from *The Woman at the Washington Zoo* by Randall Jarrell. Copyright ©1960 by Randall Jarrell. Reprinted by permission of Atheneum Publishers.

"Secretary" from *The Hawk in the Rain* by Ted Hughes. Copyright ©1957 by Ted Hughes. Reprinted by permission of Harper & Row, Publishers, Inc.

"Plan" from *Lonesome Cities* by Rod McKuen. Copyright ©1968 by Rod McKuen. Reprinted by permission of Random House, Inc.

"The Report" by Jon Swan. Copyright ©1964 by The New Yorker Magazine, Inc. Reprinted by permission.

"For Granted" by Julie Porosky was first published in *The Green Horse for Poetry*, no. 4. Copyright ©1975 by Kerry Thomas and Richard Behm. Reprinted by permission of the author.

"Retirement" by Naomi H. Barnard from *Sand Hills: The Augusta College Literary Magazine*, Spring 1975. Copyright ©1975. Reprinted by permission of the author.

"Town Life" by Jay Parini first appeared in *Poetry*, September 1986. Copyright ©1986 by *The Modern Poetry Association*. Reprinted by permission of the editor of *Poetry* and the author.

"I'll Go to Crazy Ruby's" by Dorie LaRue from *Cotton Boll/The Atlanta Review*, vol. 1, no. 1, Fall 1985. Copyright ©1985 by Cotton Boll Press. Reprinted by permission of the publisher.

"Typists" by P. K. Page. Reprinted by permission of the author.

Excerpt from *Second Discourse* from *Rousseau First and Second Discourses* by Jean-Jacques Rousseau, translated by Roger D. and Judith R. Masters. Published by St. Martin's Press, Inc.

"On American Leisure" from *Adam and the Baby and the Man from Mars* by Irwin Edman. Copyright 1929 by Irwin Edman; copyright renewed 1957 by Meta Markel, executrix of the estate of Irwin Edman. Reprinted by the permission of Houghton Mifflin Company, Boston.

"The Effects of the Industrial Revolution on Women and Children" by Robert Hessen from *Capitalism: The Unknown Ideal* by Ayn Rand. Copyright ©1962 by the Objectivist Newsletter, Inc. Reprinted by permission of the author.

Excerpt from *Work in America*, pp. 186-187. Special Task Force, U.S. Department of Health, Education, and Welfare. Published in 1973 by MIT Press, Cambridge, Massachusetts.

"Exporting the Technological Revolution" by Robert Gilpin was first published in *Saturday Review*, 31 December 1975. Copyright ©1975 by *Saturday Review*. Reprinted by permission of the publisher.

"Cassandra" from *Collected Poems* by Edwin Arlington Robinson. Copyright 1916 by Edwin Arlington Robinson; copyright renewed 1944 by Ruth Nivison. Reprinted with permission of Macmillan Publishing Co., Inc.

"The Hammer" from *Complete Poems* by Carl Sandburg. Copyright 1950 by Carl Sandburg. Reprinted by permission of Harcourt Brace Jovanovich, Inc.

"The Iron Messiah" by Vladimir T. Kirilov from *Popular Poetry in Soviet Russia* by George Z. Patrick. Published in 1929 by The Regents of the University of California. Reprinted by permission of the University of California Press.

xvi/ACKNOWLEDGMENTS

"Portrait of a Machine" from *Long Feud* by Louis Untermeyer. Copyright 1923 by Harcourt Brace Jovanovich, Inc.; copyright renewed 1951 by Louis Untermeyer. Reprinted by permission of Harcourt Brace Jovanovich, Inc.

"Prayers of Steel" from *Cornhuskers* by Carl Sandburg. Copyright 1918 by Holt, Rinehart and Winston, Inc.; copyright renewed 1946 by Carl Sandburg. Reprinted by permission of Harcourt Brace Jovanovich, Inc.

"The Heavenly Factory" by V. V. Kazin from *Popular Poetry in Soviet Russia* by George Z. Patrick. Published in 1929 by The Regents of the University of California. Reprinted by permission of the University of California Press.

"Why Wait for Science" from *The Poetry of Robert Frost*, edited by Edward Connery Lathem. Copyright 1947; copyright renewed ©1969 by Holt, Rinehart and Winston; copyright ©1975 by Lesley Frost Ballantine. Reprinted by permission of Holt, Rinehart and Winston.

"A Projection" by Reed Whittemore from *Poems New and Selected*. Copyright 1956 and ©1967 by Reed Whittemore. Published by the University of Minnesota Press, Minneapolis.

"Appalachian Suicide" by Jesse Stuart was first published in *Esquire* 72 (December 1969). Copyright ©1969 by Esquire. Reprinted by permission of the publisher.

"Name Us a King" from *Harvest Poems* by Carl Sandburg. Copyright ©1960 by Carl Sandburg. Reprinted by permission of Harcourt Brace Jovanovich, Inc.

"Dirge" from *New and Selected Poems* by Kenneth Fearing. Copyright ©1956 by Kenneth Fearing. Reprinted by permission of Indiana University Press.

"The Daily Grind" by Fenton Johnson from *American Negro Poetry*, edited by Arna Bontemps. Published in 1970 by Hill and Wang. We have been unable to reach the copyright holder of the "Daily Grind" and would welcome any information that would help us to do so.

"Investment" by Norman Nathan. Copyright ©1970 by *Saturday Review*. Reprinted by permission of *Saturday Review*.

"Back Through the Looking Glass to This Side" by John Ciardi from *The Norton Book of Light Verse*, edited by Russell Baker. Copyright ©1978 by John Ciardi. Reprinted by permission of the University of Arkansas Press.

"Success" by Alice Rose George from *The Paris Review* 101, vol. 28 (Winter 1986). Reprinted with permission of *The Paris Review* and the author.

"Power" is reprinted from *The Dream of a Common Language, Poems 1974–77*, by Adrienne Rich, by permission of W. W. Norton & Company, Inc. Copyright ©1978 by W. W. Norton & Company, Inc.

"Owed to New York—1906" by Byron Rufus Newton from *The Norton Book of Light Verse*, edited by Russell Baker. Copyright ©1986 by Russell Baker. Reprinted by permission of W. W. Norton & Company, Inc.

"Printed Words" by Liz Sohappy Bahe from *Carriers of the Dream Wheel*, edited by Duane Niatum. Copyright ©1975 by Liz Sohappy Bahe. We have been unable to reach the author and would welcome any information that would help us to do so.

"The True-Blue American" by Delmore Schwartz from *Selected Poems: Summer Knowledge*. Published by New Directions Publishing Corporation. Copyright ©1985 by Robert Phillips. Reprinted by permission.

ACKNOWLEDGMENTS/**xvii**

Excerpt from *The Grapes of Wrath* by John Steinbeck. Copyright 1939; copyright renewed ©1967 by John Steinbeck. All rights reserved. Reprinted by permission of The Viking Press.

"The Laugher" from *18 Stories* by Heinrich Böll, translated by Leila Vennewitz. Copyright ©1966 by Heinrich Boll. Reprinted by permission of McGraw-Hill Book Company.

"The Tool" from *Wind, Sand and Stars*, by Antoine de Saint-Exupéry. Copyright 1939 by Antoine de Saint-Exupéry; copyright renewed ©1967 by Lewis Galantière. Reprinted by permission of Harcourt Brace Jovanovich, Inc.

"Our High-tech Hardware Will Have to Learn to Live with the 'Human Factor'" by Ellen Goodman. Published by the *Atlanta Constitution*, 14 January 1987. Copyright ©1987 by the Boston Globe Newspaper Company/Washington Post Writers Group. Reprinted with permission.

"The Hazards of 'Corporate Responsibility'" by Gilbert Burck. Copyright ©1973 by Time, Inc. Reprinted from *Fortune* magazine (June 1973) by special permission.

"Lament for a Rush Hour Crowd" by Mary T. Gentry. We have been unable to reach the author and would welcome any information that would help us to do so.

"Prayers: 1964–1984," "Southbound on 75," "Interstate Billboard," and "Macon, Ga." by Ginny Sikes. Printed by permission of the author.

"The Tyrant" by James L. Stanford. Printed by permission of the author.

"My Second Job" and "The Appointment" by Karen Eckert. Printed by permission of the author.

"Don't You Know What You Want?" and "A ConglomeRation Of Nicknames You Most often Say" by Linda Podger-Williams. Printed by permission of the author.

"I'll Be Home at Six" by Pat Brown. Printed by permission of the author.

"For You" by Shirley Adams. Printed by permission of the author.

"Machine" by John B. Farrow. Printed by permission of the author.

"Enlightenment" by Bonnie Greer. We have been unable to reach the author and would welcome any information that would help us to do so.

"Finding Happiness in Work," by Jim Wooten. Published by the *Atlanta Journal*, 19 November 1979. Copyright ©1979 by the *Atlanta Journal*. Reprinted by permission of the publisher.

Introduction

This anthology is about modern organizational life. It is a reflection of the way we live, the way we organize and work, as presented through the eyes of literary writers—poets and authors of fiction and essays.

The selections in this book focus on modern work, organizations, the "organization person," organizational concepts, and the influences of organizations on society. Among other things, these insights should help the reader as an individual and as part of society in deciding how to react to and influence organizations.

Although the anthology is entitled *Business in Literature*, the word *business* is not limited to commercial or industrial activities. Instead it is employed in the broader sense of an organized and purposeful activity or endeavor, as in "I'm in the education business" or "She's the best basketball player in the business." Hence, *Business in Literature* focuses on the more narrowly interpreted business activities of commercial and industrial firms, but is not restricted to those activities. Governments, religious institutions, educational systems, labor unions, and other organizations and bureaucracies are also included.

Almost everyone would agree that modern organizations exert a tremendous influence on our lives. A typical weekday finds most of us at our jobs in organizations for about half of our waking hours. When we leave our jobs, we move into organized traffic patterns and reach our zoned living quarters to watch a carefully orchestrated newscast about the successes and failures of human beings in organizing and living together in some civilized (hence, organized) fashion throughout the world. In short, a variety of public agencies, businesses, unions, educational systems, and even organized recreational activities daily influence our lives.

In this book, we are presenting literary selections that reflect the nature and extent of organizational influences. While some writers directly address bureaucracies or employees, other writers are included because they bring to mind an organizational concept or a managerial complexity. We have chosen literary writers because they, more than most people, aspire to reflect finely and articulate precisely their perceptions of what they themselves and others have experienced. This collection represents a wide range of writers and works from different countries, primarily since the industrial revolution (which is generally accepted as the beginning of the modern organizational period). We have selected each work on the basis of its presentation of an important insight into our topic.

Writers, of course, influence a society with their work, and they reflect in words the way parts of the society think, act, and feel. Some of the works included here express a positive attitude toward organizations and organized life, others a more negative one. Specific institutions and their actions are praised and criticized, and it is up to the reader not only to weigh the accuracy of the critiques, but also to consider the advantages and disadvantages of the organizations.

One might argue that literary writers often tend to be negative toward organized life because the nature of their work, writing, is an independent effort, an act of creation performed alone. The administrator, on the other hand, works with creating ideas whose realization ultimately demands the coordination of human activities. Thus the administrator tends to be more sympathetic toward organized life than does the writer. We must be aware that not all administrators and not all literary writers fit into these molds. Even more important is our recognition that there is a wide range of attitudes toward organizations on the part of administrators, writers, and the many others who are neither one nor the other. And each of these persons can make valid points about his or her contributions to society. One purpose of this book is to keep the lines of communication open among the various positions, in the belief that open communications among all of us will benefit us all.

The selections in the first chapter present views on how business and other bureaucratic organizations can influence styles of life. Selections in the second chapter show similar influences on values. Chapter 3 deals with the success and failure of organizations to bring fulfillment into our lives. In the last chapter organizations and work are treated with fear and admiration as near-mystical phenomena. To broaden the perspective, we have also included in each chapter a section called *Viewpoints*, which contains comments by nonliterary observers; these comments serve to illuminate from different angles the concerns of the literary writers. Certainly there are common threads running through the chapters; and some of the works could easily fit into more than one chapter. Finally, in this revised edition there has been added an Epilogue that includes some intriguing works by a nontraditional group of writers: organizational practitioners. These young managers, none of them professional writers, make some moving observations about modern organized life.

1
Organization as a Determinant of Styles of Life

> It couldn't be called ungentle.
> But how thoroughly departmental.
> —ROBERT FROST

Organization" comes to English from the Latin word for instrument. Considering this origin, one might think of an object made up of many parts that, when played, produces harmonious sounds.

For centuries, men and women have attempted to organize their disparate parts in ways to make life more comfortable for the participants. The ordered functioning whole, the group as a healthy, coherent organism, is an ideal that has seldom been achieved even in groups as small as the family, but it remains an ideal.

Efforts to organize people in one way or another are some of the strongest life determinants. One of the most obvious examples is the impact of any government on the lives of its citizens. On a more limited scale, labor unions have raised the salaries, pensions, and medical benefits of millions of workers, but they have also been guilty of graft that exploits those workers. Other organizations have automatically relegated women to secretarial positions, and blacks to token positions with high visibility but little responsibility. In general, the ordered whole, in which ideally a worker receives satisfaction from personal success and the success of the organization of which he or she is a part, has been a rarity both in contemporary Marxist and in democratic states.

Ironically, as economist Robert Heilbroner has noted, capitalist and socialist societies share many of the same values and goals, and this commonness has made these systems more similar than we might expect. Some shared values include: efficiency, control of nature, and increased production. "All these values," Heilbroner states, "manifest themselves throughout bourgeois and 'socialist' styles of life, both lived by the clock, organized by the factory or office, obsessed with material achievements, attuned to highly quantitative modes of thought—in a word, by styles of life that, in contrast with nonindustrial civilizations, seem dazzlingly rich in every dimension except that of the cultivation of the human person."[1]

As treated by the arts, the worker has traditionally been the oppressed while the administrator has been the oppressor. Such a reduction is, of course, an oversimplification of the organizational world, and the best writers have avoided easy dichotomies that reduce complex relationships to their lowest denominators.

In the following chapter, examine the relationship of the working person with the organization, and ask yourself in every case whether the relationship is a satisfactory one. What is your opinion of the woman in "Poem" in her mask of "business lipstick"? What do you think of the Shaker craftsman in his celibate pride? Have their respective organizations been good for these men and women? How much organization is ever desirable? What have been the shaping influences of organization as a social force? Can humans be happy as a differentiated part of an organism adapted for a specific function? Can they find satisfaction as an organ stop, or must they always dream of being magnificent pipe organs?

---

1. Robert L. Heilbroner, *An Inquiry into the Human Prospect* (New York: W. W. Norton, 1974), 77.

POEMS

William Wordsworth (1770–1850)

Written in London, September, 1802
(Composed September, 1802.—Published 1807.)

O Friend! I know not which way I must look
For comfort, being, as I am, opprest,
To think that now our life is only drest
For show; mean handy-work of craftsman, cook,
Or groom!—We must run glittering like a brook
In the open sunshine, or we are unblest:
The wealthiest man among us is the best:
No grandeur now in nature or in book
Delights us. Rapine, avarice, expense,
This is idolatry; and these we adore:
Plain living and high thinking are no more:
The homely beauty of the good old cause
Is gone; our peace, our fearful innocence,
And pure religion breathing household laws.

Archibald MacLeish (1892–1952)

Empire Builders

The Museum Attendant:

This is *The Making of America in Five Panels*:

This is Mister Harriman making America:
Mister-Harriman-is-buying-the-Union-Pacific-at-Seventy:
The Santa Fe is shining on his hair.

This is Commodore Vanderbilt making America:
Mister-Vanderbilt-is-eliminating-the-short-interest-in-Hudson:
Observe the carving on the rocking chair.

This is J. P. Morgan making America:
(The Tennessee Coal is behind to the left of the Steel Company.)
Those in mauve are braces he is wearing.

This is Mister Mellon making America:
Mister-Mellon-is-represented-as-a-symbolical-figure-in-
    aluminum-
Strewing-bank-stocks-on-a-burnished-stair.

This is the Bruce is the Barton making America:
Mister-Barton-is-selling-us-Doctor's-Deliciousest-Dentrifrice.
This is he in beige with the canary.

You have just beheld the Makers making America:
This is The Making of America in Five Panels:
America lies to the west-southwest of the switch-tower:
There is nothing to see of America but land.

*The Original Document
under the Panel Paint*:

"To Thos. Jefferson Esq. his obd't serv't
M. Lewis: captain: detached:
                              Sir:

Having in mind your repeated commands in this matter,
And the worst half of it done and the streams mapped,

And we here on the back of this bench beholding the
Other ocean—two years gone and the cold

Breaking with rain for the third spring since St. Louis,
The crows at the fishbones on the frozen dunes,

The first cranes going over from south north,
And the river down by a mark of the pole since the morning,

And time near to return, and a ship (Spanish)
Lying in for the salmon: and fearing chance or the

Drought or the Sioux should deprive you of these discoveries—
Therefore we send by sea in this writing.

                                                Above the
Platte there were long plains and a clay country:
Rim of the sky far off, grass under it,

Dung for the cook fires by the sulphur licks.
After that there were low hills and the sycamores,

And we poled up by the Great Bend in the skiffs:
The honey bees left us after the Osage River:

The wind was west in the evenings, and no dew and the
Morning Star larger and whiter than usual—

The winter rattling in the brittle haws.
The second year there was sage and the quail calling.

All that valley is good land by the river:
Three thousand miles and the clay cliffs and

Rue and beargrass by the water banks
And many birds and the brant going over and tracks of

Bear, elk, wolves, marten: the buffalo
Numberless so that the cloud of their dust covers them:

The antelope fording the fall creeks, and the mountains and
Grazing lands and the meadow lands and the ground

Sweet and open and well-drained.
                              We advise you to
Settle troops at the forks and to issue licenses:

Many men will have living on these lands.
There is wealth in the earth for them all and the wood standing

And wild birds on the water where they sleep.
There is stone in the hills for the towns of a great people . . ."

You have just beheld the Makers Making America:

They screwed her scrawny and gaunt with their seven-year panics:
They bought her back on their mortgages old-whore-cheap:

They fattened their bonds at her breasts till the thin blood
     ran from them.

Men have forgotten how full clear and deep
The Yellowstone moved on the gravel and the grass grew
When the land lay waiting for her westward people!

Edgar Lee Masters (1869–1950)

"Ace" Shaw

I never saw any difference
Between playing cards for money
And selling real estate,
Practicing law, banking, or anything else.
For everything is chance.
Nevertheless
Seest thou a man diligent in business?
He shall stand before Kings!

Robert Frost (1895–1963)

Departmental

An ant on the tablecloth
Ran into a dormant moth
Of many times his size.
He showed not the least surprise.
His business wasn't with such.
He gave it scarcely a touch,
And was off on his duty run.
Yet if he encountered one
Of the hive's enquiry squad
Whose work is to find out God
And the nature of time and space,
He would put him onto the case.
Ants are a curious race;
One crossing with hurried tread
The body of one of their dead
Isn't given a moment's arrest—
Seems not even impressed.
But he no doubt reports to any
With whom he crosses antennae,
And they no doubt report
To the higher-up at court.
Then word goes forth in Formic:[1]
"Death's come to Jerry McCormic,
Our selfless forager Jerry.
Will the special Janizary[2]
Whose office it is to bury
The dead of the commissary
Go bring him home to his people.
Lay him in state on a sepal.
Wrap him for shroud in a petal.
Embalm him with ichor of nettle.
This is the word of your Queen."
And presently on the scene
Appears a solemn mortician;
And taking formal position,

With feelers calmly atwiddle,
Seizes the dead by the middle,
And heaving him high in air,
Carries him out of there.
No one stands round to stare.
It is nobody else's affair.

It couldn't be called ungentle.
But how thoroughly departmental.

> 1. Pertaining to ants; here, the ant's language.
> 2. Member of an elite Turkish army group.

Ilya Ivanovich Sadofief (1889–1965)

Calling to United Work

Calling to united work, the factory whistles
Had startled the owl, doubt.
Again the life-giving fount
Is frothy, and afresh it seethes.

Again in the suburbs the living stream
Of creative hosts blusters:
We will file, saw, forge, and plane
The hunchback of chaos, the ribs of fate.

The communicators sing again,
Upon the rails slides the weighty crane;
From the forges come thunder and uproar,
From the boilers a shrill tempest rolls.

Factory life bubbles like a stream;
One pressure of a callous hand,
And the sharp chisel will tap
The cankers of the sterile fields.

About the throats of sooty stacks
Death circled like an evil bird of prey;
The factory with a triumphant stroke
Burned his bony frame at the stake.

Now the infidel whispers not
That the keys to life he cannot find;
The foundries, like volcanoes,
Burn the gray sorrow and woes.

The factory leads to the red carnival,
Through its fiery gates,
Those who in the Commune do not believe,
Who prayed for our peril!

There, happiness will last for ever,
And the factory—turbulent, ardent—
With the galaxy of its cupolas
Will kindle the flames of the future.

And the lifeless hand
Will never still
The moving factory fly-wheel
Christened in the bloody stream.

e e cummings   (1894–1962)

a salesman is an it that stinks Excuse

a salesman is an it that stinks Excuse

Me whether it's president of the you were say
or a jennelman name misder finger isn't
important whether it's millions of other punks
or just a handful absolutely doesn't
matter and whether it's in lonjewray

or shrouds is immaterial it stinks

a salesman is an it that stinks to please

but whether to please itself or someone else
makes no more difference than if it sells
hate condoms education snakeoil vac
uumcleaners terror strawberries democ
ra(caveat emptor)cy superfluous hair

or Think We've Met subhuman rights Before

MALVINA REYNOLDS   (1900–1978)

Little Boxes

1. Little boxes on the hillside,
   Little boxes made of ticky tacky,
   Little boxes on the hillside,
   Little boxes all the same,
   There's a green one and a pink one,
   And a blue one and a yellow one,
   And they're all made out of ticky tacky,
   And they all look just the same.

2. And the people in the houses
   All went to the university,
   Where they were put in boxes
   And they came out all the same,
   And there's doctors and lawyers,
   And business executives,
   And they're all made out of ticky tacky
   And they all look just the same.

3. And they all play on the golf course
   And drink their martinis dry,
   And they all have pretty children
   And the children go to school,
   And the children go to summer camp

    And then to the university,
    Where they are put in boxes
    And they come out all the same.

 4. And the boys go into business
    And marry and raise a family
    In boxes made of ticky tacky
    And they all look just the same.
    There's a green one and a pink one,
    And a blue one and a yellow one,
    And they're all made out of ticky tacky
    And they all look just the same.

W. H. AUDEN   (1907–1973)

The Unknown Citizen

   (To JS/07/M/378
   This Marble Monument
   Is Erected by the State)

He was found by the Bureau of Statistics to be
One against whom there was no official complaint,
And all the reports on his conduct agree
That, in the modern sense of an old-fashioned word, he was a saint,
For in everything he did he served the Greater Community.
Except for the War till the day he retired
He worked in a factory and never got fired,
But satisfied his employers, Fudge Motors Inc.
Yet he wasn't a scab or odd in his views,
For his Union reports that he paid his dues,
(Our report on his Union shows it was sound)
And our Social Psychology workers found
That he was popular with his mates and liked a drink.
The Press are convinced that he bought a paper every day
And that his reactions to advertisements were normal in every way.

Policies taken out in his name prove that he was fully insured,
And his Health-card shows he was once in hospital but left it
    cured.
Both Producers Research and High-Grade Living declare
He was fully sensible to the advantages of the Instalment Plan
And had everything necessary to the Modern Man,
A phonograph, a radio, a car and a frigidaire.
Our researchers into Public Opinion are content
That he held the right opinions for the time of year;
When there was peace, he was for peace; when there was war, he
    went.
He was married and added five children to the population,
Which our Eugenist[1] says was the right number for a parent of
    his generation,
And our teachers report he never interfered with their education.
Was he free? Was he happy? The question is absurd:
Had anything been wrong, we should certainly have heard.

1. A specialist who works to improve the biological characteristics of the human race.

KARL SHAPIRO   (1913–   )

Drug Store

*I do remember an apothecary,
And hereabouts 'a dwells*

It baffles the foreigner like an idiom,
And he is right to adopt it as a form
Less serious than the living-room or bar;
    For it disestablishes the café,
Is a collective, and on basic country.

Not that it praises hygiene and corrupts
The ice-cream parlor and the tobacconist's
Is it a center; but that the attractive symbols
    Watch over puberty and leer
Like rubber bottles waiting for sick-use.

Youth comes to jingle nickels and crack wise;
The baseball scores are his, the magazines
Devoted to lust, the jazz, the Coca-Cola,
   The lending-library of love's latest.
He is the customer; he is heroized.

And every nook and cranny of the flesh
Is spoken to by packages with wiles,
"Buy me, buy me," they whimper and cajole;
   The hectic range of lipstick pouts,
Revealing the wicked and the simple mouth.

With scarcely any evasion in their eye
They smoke, undress their girls, exact a stance;
But only for a moment. The clock goes round;
   Crude fellowships are made and lost;
They slump in booths like rags, not even drunk.

Alan Dugan (1923–   )

Poem

The person who can do
accounts receivable as fast
as steel machines and out-
talk telephones, has wiped
her business lipstick off,
undone her girdle and belts
and stepped down sighing from
the black quoins of her heels
to be the quiet smiler with
changed eyes. After long-
haired women have unwired
their pencil-pierced buns, it's an
event with pennants when
the Great Falls of emotion say
that beauty is in residence,
grand in her hotel of flesh,

and Venus of the marriage manual,
haloed by a diaphragm,
steps from the shell *Mercenaria*
to her constitutional majesty
in the red world of love.

EDWIN MORGAN (1920–)

THE COMPUTER'S FIRST CHRISTMAS CARD

```
      JOLLYMERRY
      HOLLYBERRY
      JOLLYBERRY
      MERRYHOLLY
      HAPPYJOLLY
      JOLLYJELLY
      JELLYBELLY
      BELLYMERRY
      HOLLYHEPPY
      JOLLYMOLLY
      MARRYJERRY
      MERRYHARRY
      HOPPYBARRY
      HEPPYJARRY
      BOPPYHEPPY
      BERRYJORRY
      JORRYJOLLY
      MOPPYJELLY
      MOLLYMERRY
      JERRYJOLLY
      BELLYBOPPY
      JORRYHOPPY
      HOLLYMOPPY
      BARRYMERRY
      JARRYHAPPY
      HAPPYBOPPY
      BOPPYJOLLY
      JOLLYMERRY
      MERRYMERRY
      MERRYMERRY
      MERRYCHRIS
      AMMERRYASA
      CHRISMERRY
      ASMERRYCHR
      YSANTHEMUM
```

Sterling Eisiminger (1941–)

Hospital Visit

You may think I've been stony, O'Hare,
you who forecast my death a year ago
shocked now by this Medusan head,
but I have heard every word you have said.

For months aspiring that a hand or foot,
I wasn't even sure I had, could reach
the cord to your adamant pump,
I surely ruptured more ducts in this scotched
brain of mine trying to contact those limbs.
Then you took the case and soldered the shunt.
Suddenly these brazen hands were reaching for you—
you who joked of necrophilia.
Horribly, I'm not sure you didn't try;
I heard just your heaving over me
and the faint cracking of a lubricant.

And now your administrators,
Who know me only through your polished shield,
are suing to win the court's injunction
"to enjoin the continuing trespass."
And once I thought I had no cause to live—
I live to thwart the wallet of Perseus
And charge a static curse.

On a Shaker[1] Slat-Back Rocker

Built for the millennium,
it's guarded by a ribbon now.
Its lantern-jawed maker,
one of hundreds once,
dead one hundred years,
was forbidden to touch the sisters,

---

1. A celibate religious group popular in the United States in the nineteenth century.

buy or borrow books of the world,
lean a chair against a wall,
or sit with his feet on the rounds.
Moreover, he was not
to fix his mark upon his work
or turn a piece superfluous,
for, he was told, good spirits
do not dwell where there is dirt.

Yet all things considered,
we see this joiner
of the willowy aesthetic
pleased beneath his daily cross.
Unaware he sought
a spin-off of his ardor,
he made what others only seek.

Formerly a bedroom chair,
it has a lean spirit
and the legs of a girl,
the sensual confession
of its celibate maker.
Of this world or another,
we fail to imagine
one better than this
in a Shaker museum
in up-state New York.

Josephine Miles (1911–1985)

Bureau 2

Skunks fight under the house and keep us
Wakeful, they are down from the hills in the drought.
Lots of colloquial remedies, mothballs, tomato juice
Leave them unmoved. Call the S P C A.
Call the Bureau of Health, call the P G & E[1] where they rest

---

1. Pacific Gas and Electric.

Past the meter box, call the Animal Shelter,
Call commercial exterminators; all reply
With a sigh, and a different number to call
Next month or next year when they're not so busy.
Asking around, getting the number finally
Number of the chief health officer of the county,
Mr. Simms. His secretary answers,
What makes you think Mr. Simms will speak to you?
What makes you think Mr. Simms is interested in skunks?
Mr. Simms is animal health officer of this whole county
And his chief interest is wolves.

Dorothy Parker (1893–1967)

Bohemia

Authors and actors and artists and such
Never know nothing, and never know much.
Sculptors and singers and those of their kidney
Tell their affairs from Seattle to Sydney.
Playwrights and poets and such horses' necks
Start off from anywhere, end up at sex.
Diarists, critics, and similar roe
Never say nothing, and never say no.
People Who Do Things exceed my endurance;
God, for a man that solicts insurance!

Jack Conway (1887–1952)

Clothes Make the Man

Clothes make the man, Jack,
and that's a fact.
They make coats for blokes,
what's got maids,
and got it made too,
you chump.

They make hats for cats like us, Jack
Shoes for dudes,
what's feeling in the mood for being cool.
Rags for fags and hags,
what watches soap operas all the time.
And they got pants what dance all by themselves, Jack,
that is if you ain't got no rhythm.

Got clothes made in Milan,
Japan, Iran,
even got designer sheets for "de Klan,"
you got that man?

They got avant-garde leotards,
debonair underwear,
even got some risque, sashays.
Got them high heels for Lucille,
And obscene jeans for Geraldine,
You know what I mean, Jack,
the kind she likes to wear.

They got it all,
from Presidents to malcontents;
hip,
slick,
double-knits.
Get that in your head.
Ain't no cop a cop,
No priest a priest,
nun a nun,
or bum a bum,
without his threads.

Clothes make the man, Jack,
until your dead,
and then we all just naked again.

Howard Nemerov (1920–   )

Life Cycle of Common Man

Roughly figured, this man of moderate habits,
This average consumer of the middle class,
Consumed in the course of his average life span
Just under half a million cigarettes,
Four thousand fifths of gin and about
A quarter as much vermouth; he drank
Maybe a hundred thousand cups of coffee,
And counting his parents' share it cost
Something like half a million dollars
To put him through life. How many beasts
Died to provide him with meat, belt and shoes
Cannot be certainly said.
                         But anyhow,
It is in this way that man travels through time,
Leaving behind him a lengthening trail
Of empty bottles and bones, of broken shoes,
Frayed collars and worn out or outgrown
Diapers and dinnerjackets, silk ties and slickers.

Given the energy and security thus achieved,
He did . . .? What? The usual things, of course,
The eating, dreaming, drinking and begetting,
And he worked for the money which was to pay
For the eating, et cetera, which were necessary
If he were to go on working for the money, et cetera,
But chiefly he talked. As the bottles and bones
Accumulated behind him, the words proceeded
Steadily from the front of his face as he
Advanced into the silence and made it verbal.
Who can tally the tale of his words? A lifetime
Would barely suffice for their repetition;
If you merely printed all his commas the result
Would be a very large volume, and the number of times

He said "thank you" or "very little sugar, please,"
Would stagger the imagination. There were also
Witticisms, platitudes, and statements beginning
"It seems to me" or "As I always say."

Consider the courage in all that, and behold the man
Walking into deep silence, with the ectoplastic
Cartoon's balloon of speech proceeding
Steadily out of the front of his face, the words
Borne along on the breath which is his spirit
Telling the numberless tale of his untold Word
Which makes the world his apple, and forces him to eat.

TERRILL SHEPARD SOULES (1946–   )

Life in the Ashtray

I live in the ashtray with Mother.
Working nine jobs as I do, I
really relish that
bimonthly half-hour off.

During which I pay bills
and pound out novels.

I sort the day's screams,
o.k. the night's dreams,
wax fresh babies,
mail free rabies,
inoculate poets,
prevent against forests,
blight troths,
blind mouths,
oil gulls.

Yes, those new businesses
that bright new mayor snagged
make us all walk
just that much taller.

Mother has it as how I mismanage,
fritter, you could say, my
precious half-hour off.
"Budget your blood!"
"Budget your blood!"
Mother thinks about blood a lot.

But she knows goddamned well,
the creaky old stinkbomb,
how strict these days
the budget banks are with their budgets.

She'd yammer less, I suppose,
if we could just swing a move
to a more expensive ashtray.

BARRI ARMITAGE (1937–   )

Trading on Gravity

Voluntary or not, the pull
begins with the eyes.
At Livingstone's Lounge
in the changing light of the jukebox,
you draw me out to dance.

We marry, cart our groceries
and dressers up three flights.
Each morning we throw off blankets
and rise—boomerangs flying
out to others, back to bed.

Children add weight
or weightlessness. We kiss
scraped elbows and knees,
hike down Granger's Gorge,
join Booster Clubs.

Mirrors keep finding
more sags. We cheer
in concrete stadiums,
cross country, walk its edge
as surf tosses up, drags out.

Years tug at the balance,
news wears. We brace
teeth and foundations, pull
together, pull back, pull muscles.
Paint peels, fruit falls.

Earth covers our losses:
the great ones, boxed and buried,
and the small—100,000 pieces
a minute—flaking skin,
salt, saliva, lint.

Our donations increase:
more hair in the drain,
more sweat at tennis. But tonight
as I roll close, your touch makes again
the moment earth becomes air.

VIVIAN LOWE (1925–)

The Importance of Garbage Collectors

They are my alarm clock
And rouse me from my spot in a warm bed,
In a warm house
With their shouts—the shouts
Of erratic cymbaleers crashing
Lids on cans, cursing angry dogs—
And I sense the cold rattle
Of trash-pickers' bones,
The raw flesh of hands.

I shiver, then hide inside a crazy quilt
Until the trovers dutifully return
The morning to the half-asleep
And rumble off with remnants
Of parties—old foil, broken bottles—
To fill pits and build new plots
For more warm houses,
Warm beds and spots.

JOSEPHINE MILES (1911–1985)

Why We Are Late

A red light is stuck
At the corner of LeConte and Euclid.
Numbers of people are going in and out of the 7 Palms Market,
Some sitting with beer at La Vals.[1]
Lots lugging bags to the Laundromat—Open—
A couple thumbing rides up the hill, fog curling in over
    the newsracks,
Low pressures.

You can tell it is about five or six o'clock
And we are coming home from a meeting not bad, not good,
Just coming along, and stop at the red light.
Time stands there, we in the midst of it,
The numberless years of our lives.
A late green light later
May let us get home.

---

1. A pizza restaurant popular with students in Berkley, California.

Richard Wilbur (1921–)

A Summer Morning

Her young employers, having got in late
From seeing friends in town
And scraped the right front fender on the gate,
Will not, the cook expects, be coming down.

She makes a quiet breakfast for herself.
The coffee-pot is bright,
The jelly where it should be on the shelf.
She breaks an egg into the morning light,

Then, with the bread-knife lifted, stands and hears
The sweet efficient sounds
Of thrush and catbird, and the snip of shears
Where, in the terraced backward of the grounds,

A gardener works before the heat of day.
He straightens for a view
Of the big house ascending stony-gray
Out of his beds mosaic with the dew.

His young employers having got in late,
He and the cook alone
Receive the morning on their old estate,
Possessing what the owners can but own.

FICTION

Horatio Alger (1832–1899)

From Digging for Gold: A Story of California

Grant did not write his mother that he was coming home; he wanted to surprise her. He landed in New York and took the train the same day for Woodburn. He arrived early one morning and went at once to the house where his mother was boarding.

Mrs. Tarbox's face lighted up with amazement and joy when she saw Grant.

"O Grant, can it really be you?" she exclaimed, as she embraced him.

"I don't think it is anybody else, Mother," returned Grant, with a smile.

"How you have grown!"

"Yes, Mother; I am three inches taller than when I went away."

"I have good news for you, Grant. Mr. Wilkins has engaged me as housekeeper, with a good salary."

"How much is he going to pay you?"

"Three dollars a week."

"You can't go, Mother. I want you for my housekeeper, and will pay you five dollars a week."

"I wish you could afford to do it, Grant."

"I can, Mother. As near as I can figure it out, I am worth about eight thousand dollars, and expect to be worth a good deal more within a year."

"This can't be possible! How could you—a boy of sixteen—gain so much money?"

"Partly at the mines, partly by speculating in real estate in San Francisco. But I will give you particulars hereafter. Are the Bartletts living at the farm?"

"Yes; but I hear Mrs. Bartlett wants to sell it. She and Rodney want to go to a city to live."

"And you didn't get a cent from the estate?"

"No; Mrs. Bartlett offered me twenty-five dollars."

"Which you very properly refused. No matter! You won't need to depend on that family for anything. You've got a rich son."

At this moment a buggy drove into the yard.

"That's Mr. Wilkins come for me," said Mrs. Tarbox. "Don't you think it will be best for me to accept the engagement?"

"No, Mother; I shall provide you with a home of your own, and give you enough to keep it up. I will buy back the house that used to be ours when Father was alive."

"O Grant, if you can!"

"I can. I shall be able to buy it for two thousand dollars."

"It has been offered for eighteen hundred."

"So much the better."

Here Mr. Wilkins entered the house. He was a pleasant-looking elderly gentleman, with white hair.

"Well, Mrs. Tarbox, are you ready?" he asked.

"I am very sorry to disappoint you, Mr. Wilkins; but my son Grant, who has just returned from California, wants me to have a home of my own."

"Why, why; so Grant is back—and looking stout and rugged. Have you done well, Grant?"

"Yes, Mr. Wilkins; far better than I expected. I am able to provide my mother with a home of her own, and while we appreciate your kind offer, she will be happier and more independent living so."

"I won't say a word against it, though I am disappointed. Your father was an old friend of mine, and I would like to have had his widow in my home. But I am pleased with her better prospects."

"Please don't mention my plan for her. I want to take some people by surprise."

"I'll be mum, Grant."

"Now, Mother, I think I'll take a walk. I'll be back soon."

Out in the street Grant fell in with Tom Childs.

"I am delighted to see you, Grant," said Tom, grasping his hand. "Have you just arrived?"

"Yes, Tom."

"Were you lucky?"

Grant smiled, and pulled out an elegant gold watch.

"You wrote me to get a watch that would beat Rodney's. Here it is!"

"What a beauty! What did you pay for it?"

"I bought it at Tiffany's for one hundred and twenty-five dollars."

Tom opened wide his eyes in amazement.

"A hundred and twenty-five dollars!" he ejaculated. "Then you must be rich!"

"I've got a little money."

"As much as a thousand dollars?"

"A good deal more."

"Then you've beaten Rodney both in money and a watch. I am awfully glad."

"What news is there, Tom?"

"Some bad news. You know, I told you about Abner Jones and the mortgage on his farm. It comes due in three days, and Mrs. Bartlett is going to foreclose and take possession of the farm."

"What's the amount of the mortgage?"

"A thousand dollars."

"Then she won't do it! I'll advance the money and assume the mortgage myself."

"Bully for you, Grant! Here's Mr. Jones himself coming. Tell him, and put him out of his anxiety."

Abner Jones approached with downcast eyes and sad face. He saw no way of saving the farm, and it would doubtless be sold far below its value. When he saw Grant his face brightened, for he had always liked the boy.

"Welcome home, Grant!" he said heartily. "When did you come?"

"I have just arrived."

"Did you do well?"

"Finely. How is it with you?"

"I am about to lose my home, Grant," he said sadly. "There's a mortgage on it, held by Mrs. Bartlett, that I can't pay."

"And won't she extend it?"

"No; she wants to get possession of it."

"Can't you get anybody to advance the money?"

"No; we have no capitalist in Woodburn that can command that sum in ready money."

"You forget me, Mr. Jones."

"What do you mean, Grant?" asked the farmer quickly.

"I mean that I will advance the money, Mr. Jones."

"It isn't possible that you've got so much as that, Grant?"

"I assure you that it is."

"But you'll straiten yourself."

"No; I have brought double that sum with me, and have more in California."

"Then I am saved! You have made me very happy, Grant."

"It's all right, Mr. Jones. I am making a business investment."

A few minutes later Grant met Rodney Bartlett walking with a slow dignified step, swinging a light bamboo cane.

"Good morning, Rodney!" he said, touching his hat with a smile.

"What! have you come back, Grant Colburn?" cried Rodney, in surprise.

"Yes, I arrived this morning."

"Grandpa's dead, and Ma and I have got the property."

"So I hear."

"I suppose you hurried home to see if you couldn't get some of it," sneered Rodney.

"I think my mother could get a share if she went to law."

"That's where you are mistaken. You have come on a fool's errand."

"That isn't what brought me."

"If you want a place, perhaps Ma will have you for a farm boy."

Grant smiled.

"As she has you, I don't think she will need me," he said.

"Do you think I would soil my hands by farm work? I am a gentleman."

"I am glad to hear it."

"What do you say to that watch?" and Rodney complacently produced his gold chronometer.

"It is a fair watch," said Grant, examining it.

"I should say it was! It cost sixty dollars."

"Suppose you look at mine"; and Grant produced his. Rodney had not noticed that he had one.

Rodney looked paralyzed, for he saw that it was a much finer one than his.

"Is it oroide[1]?" he gasped.

Grant laughed.

"It was bought at Tiffany's, and Tiffany doesn't sell oroide watches."

"How much did it cost?"

"A hundred and twenty-five dollars."

"I don't believe it!" said Rodney sharply.

"I can show you Tiffany's receipt," he said, and he drew a paper from his pocket.

"And you spent all your money for that watch?" ejaculated Rodney.

"No; I have more left."

Rodney walked away abruptly. All his pride in his watch had gone. He hurried back to the farm, and told his mother the astounding news.

"Ma," he said, "you must buy me a nicer watch. I don't want that farm boy to beat me."

Mrs. Bartlett would not at first believe that Rodney's story was correct. When convinced, she would not accede to her son's request.

"A sixty-dollar watch is good enough for a boy of your age," she said. "Grant Colburn will come to the poorhouse if he spends money like that. If Pa were living he could claim the guardianship of the boy and take care of his money. Do you know how much he has got?"

"He didn't tell me."

"It isn't likely he has as much as you. I hear his mother is going to be housekeeper for Mr. Wilkins."

But later in the day Mrs. Bartlett learned that this was a mistake. She was very much worried about Grant's plans, and anxious to learn how much money he had.

Meanwhile Grant called on the proprietor of their old home and bought it for eighteen hundred dollars, only paying five

---

1. An alloy containing copper used to imitate gold.

hundred down, for he could get much better interest for his money in San Francisco, and could well afford to pay six per cent interest on the balance. He bought the house just as it stood—furniture and all—as his mother had originally sold it. If the price of the property seems small, it must be remembered the Woodburn was a country village.

There was another surprise in store for the Bartletts.

On the day when the mortgage on the Jones place came due, Mrs. Bartlett, accompanied by her lawyer, called at the farm.

"Mr. Jones," she said, "I have come to foreclose the mortgage on your place."

"You can't do it, Mrs. Bartlett," replied the farmer.

Mrs. Bartlett closed her thin lips firmly, and her cold gray eyes rested on the farmer's face.

"Why can't I do it, Mr. Jones?" she asked, in an acid tone.

"Because I am going to pay it."

"But you can't do it!" she exclaimed, in dismay.

"Here is the money, ma'am. You'll find it correct. Now, I'll thank you to cancel the mortgage, Mr. Lawyer."

"Have I got to take the money?" asked Sophia Bartlett.

"Certainly," said the lawyer.

"Where did you get it? I didn't know you had any," she asked sharply.

"I am not obliged to tell; but I will do so to satisfy you. The money is kindly advanced by Grant Colburn."

"That boy!" ejaculated Mrs. Bartlett furiously.

"Yes; he has been to me a friend in need."

If evil wishes could have blighted him, Grant would have stood in great danger, for he had disappointed Sophia Bartlett in her cherished desire.

"It beats all how that boy has got on!" she muttered. "I wish he had never been to California."

Prosperity makes friends. Though Rodney liked Grant no better he made friendly overtures to him now that he looked upon him as rich, but Grant, though polite, was cold. He understood the value of such friendship.

Now for a few concluding words. Grant returned to California. Eventually he intends to take his mother out there, for his business interests are growing more extensive, and in five years he will be a rich man. Mrs. Bartlett has sold her farm and gone to Chicago, but her pecuniary ventures have not been successful, and Rodney is by no means a dutiful son. He is growing extravagant, and is always calling upon his mother for money, while he shows no willingness to work. The whole family is likely to end in poverty.

Giles Crosmont has returned to England with his son, leaving his California property in charge of Grant. He has invited Grant and his mother to visit him at his home in Devonshire, and, some summer, the invitation will probably be accepted. Tom Cooper has established himself in San Francisco, but his father and mother have returned with a competence to their home in Iowa.

"It was a lucky day, Mother," said Grant one day, "when I came to California to dig for gold."

"Many came out here and failed," returned his mother; "but you had good habits and the qualities that insure success."

John Galsworthy (1867–1933)

The Japanese Quince

As Mr. Nilson, well known in the City, opened the window of his dressing-room on Campden Hill, he experienced a peculiar sweetish sensation in the back of his throat, and a feeling of emptiness just under his fifth rib. Hooking the window back, he noticed that a little tree in the Square Gardens had come out in blossom, and that the thermometer stood at sixty. "Perfect morning," he thought; "spring at last!"

Resuming some meditations on the price of Tintos, he took up an ivory-backed hand-glass and scrutinised his face. His firm, well-coloured cheeks, with their neat brown moustaches, and his round, well-opened, clear grey eyes, wore a reassuring appearance of good health. Putting on his black frock coat, he went downstairs.

In the dining-room his morning paper was laid out on the sideboard. Mr. Nilson had scarcely taken it in his hand when he again became aware of that queer feeling. Somewhat concerned, he went to the French window and descended the scrolled iron steps into the fresh air. A cuckoo clock struck eight.

"Half an hour to breakfast," he thought; "I'll take a turn in the Gardens."

He had them to himself, and proceeded to pace the circular path with his morning paper clasped behind him. He had scarcely made two revolutions, however, when it was borne in on him that, instead of going away in the fresh air, the feeling had increased. He drew several deep breaths, having heard deep breathing recommended by his wife's doctor; but they augmented rather than diminished the sensation—as if some sweetish liquor coursed within him, together with a faint aching just above his heart. Running over what he had eaten the night before, he could recollect no unusual dish, and it occurred to him that it might possibly be some smell affecting him. But he could detect nothing except a faint sweet lemony scent, rather agreeable than otherwise, which evidently emanated from the bushes budding in the sunshine. He was on the point of resuming his promenade, when a blackbird close by burst into song, and, looking up, Mr. Nilson saw at a distance of perhaps five yards a little tree, in the heart of whose branches the bird was perched. He stood staring curiously at this tree, recognising it for that which he had noticed from his window. It was covered with young blossoms, pink and white, and little bright green leaves both round and spiky; and on all this blossom and these leaves the sunlight glistened. Mr. Nilson smiled; the little tree was so alive and pretty! And instead of passing on, he stayed there smiling at the tree.

"Morning like this!" he thought; "and here I am the only person in the Square who has the—to come out and—!" But he had no sooner conceived this thought than he saw quite near him a man with his hands behind him, who was also staring up and smiling at the little tree. Rather taken aback, Mr. Nilson ceased to smile, and looked furtively at the stranger. It was his next-door neighbour, Mr. Tandram, well known in the City, who had occupied the adjoining house for some five years. Mr. Nilson perceived at once the awkwardness of his position, for, being married, they had not yet had occasion to speak to one another. Doubtful as to his proper conduct, he decided at last to murmur: "Fine morning!" and was passing on, when Mr. Tandram answered:

"Beautiful, for the time of year!" Detecting a slight nervousness in his neighbour's voice, Mr. Nilson was emboldened to regard him openly. He was of about Mr. Nilson's own height, with firm, well-coloured cheeks, neat brown moustaches, and round, well-opened, clear grey eyes; and he was wearing a black frock coat. Mr. Nilson noticed that he had his morning paper clasped behind him as he looked up at the little tree. And, visited somehow by the feeling that he had been caught out, he said abruptly:

"Er—can you give me the name of that tree?"

Mr. Tandram answered:

"I was about to ask you that," and stepped towards it. Mr. Nilson also approached the tree.

"Sure to have its name on, I should think," he said.

Mr. Tandram was the first to see the little label, close to where the blackbird had been sitting. He read it out.

"Japanese quince!"

"Ah!" said Mr. Nilson, "thought so. Early flowerers."

"Very," assented Mr. Tandram, and added: "Quite a feelin' in the air today."

Mr. Nilson nodded.

"It was a blackbird singin'," he said.

"Blackbirds," answered Mr. Tandram, "I prefer them to thrushes myself; more body in the note." And he looked at Mr. Nilson in an almost friendly way.

"Quite," murmured Mr. Nilson. "These exotics, they don't bear fruit. Pretty blossom!" and he again glanced up at the blossom, thinking: "Nice fellow, this, I rather like him."

Mr. Tandram also gazed at the blossom. And the little tree, as if appreciating their attention, quivered and glowed. From a distance the blackbird gave a loud, clear call. Mr. Nilson dropped his eyes. It struck him suddenly that Mr. Tandram looked a little foolish; and, as if he had seen himself, he said: "I must be going in. Good morning!"

A shade passed over Mr. Tandram's face, as if he, too, had suddenly noticed something about Mr. Nilson.

"Good morning," he replied, and clasping their journals to their backs they separated.

Mr. Nilson retraced his steps towards his garden window, walking slowly so as to avoid arriving at the same time as his neighbour.

Having seen Mr. Tandram mount his scrolled iron steps, he ascended his own in turn. On the top step he paused.

With the slanting spring sunlight darting and quivering into it, the Japanese quince seemed more living than a tree. The blackbird had returned to it, and was chanting out his heart.

Mr. Nilson sighed; again he felt that queer sensation, that choky feeling in his throat.

The sound of a cough or sigh attracted his attention. There, in the shadow of his French window, stood Mr. Tandram, also looking forth across the Gardens at the little quince tree.

Unaccountably upset, Mr. Nilson turned abruptly into the house, and opened his morning paper.

Dorothy Parker (1893–1967)

Song of the Shirt, 1941

It was one of those extraordinarily bright days that make things look somehow bigger. The Avenue seemed to stretch wider and longer, and the buildings to leap higher into the skies. The window-box blooms were not just a mass and a blur; it was as if they had been enlarged, so that you could see the design of the blossoms and even their separate petals. Indeed you could sharply see all sorts of pleasant things that were usually too small for your notice—the lean figurines on radiator caps, and the nice round gold knobs on flagpoles, the flowers and fruits on ladies' hats and the creamy dew applied to the eyelids beneath them. There should be more of such days.

The exceptional brightness must have had its effect upon unseen objects, too, for Mrs. Martindale, as she paused to look up the Avenue, seemed actually to feel her heart grow bigger than ever within her. The size of Mrs. Martindale's heart was renowned among her friends, and they, as friends will, had gone around babbling about it. And so Mrs. Martindale's name was high on the list of all those organizations that send out appeals to buy tickets and she was frequently obliged to be photographed seated at a table, listening eagerly to her neighbor, at some function for the good of charity. Her big heart did not, as is so sadly often the case, inhabit a big bosom. Mrs. Martindale's breasts were admirable, delicate yet firm, pointing one to the right, one to the left; angry at each other, as the Russians have it.

Her heart was the warmer, now, for the fine sight of the Avenue. All the flags looked brand-new. The red and the white and the blue were so vivid they fairly vibrated, and the crisp stars seemed to dance on their points. Mrs. Martindale had a flag, too, clipped to the lapel of her jacket. She had had quantities of rubies and diamonds and sapphires just knocking about, set in floral designs on evening bags and vanity boxes and cigarette-cases; she had taken the lot of them to her jeweller, and he had assembled them into a charming little Old Glory. There had been enough of them for him to devise a rippled flag, and that was fortunate, for those flat flags looked sharp and stiff. There were numbers of emeralds, formerly figuring as leaves and stems in the floral designs, which were of course of no use to the present scheme and so were left over, in an embossed leather case. Some day, perhaps, Mrs. Martindale would confer with her jeweller about an arrangement to employ them. But there was no time for such matters now.

There were many men in uniform walking along the Avenue under the bright banners. The soldiers strode quickly and surely, each on to a destination. The sailors, two by two, ambled, paused at a corner and looked down a street, gave it up and went slower along their unknown way. Mrs. Martindale's heart grew again as she looked at them. She had a friend who made a practice of stopping uniformed men on the street and thanking them, individually, for what they were doing for *her.* Mrs. Martindale felt that this was going unnecessarily far. Still, she did see, a little bit, what her friend meant.

And surely no soldier or sailor would have objected to being addressed by Mrs. Martindale. For she was lovely, and no other woman was lovely like her. She was tall, and her body streamed like a sonnet. Her face was formed all of triangles, as a cat's is, and her eyes and her hair were blue-gray. Her hair did not taper in its growth about her forehead and temples; it sprang suddenly, in great thick waves, from a straight line across her brow. Its blue-gray was not premature. Mrs. Martindale lingered in her fragrant forties. Has not afternoon been adjudged the fairest time of the day?

To see her, so delicately done, so finely finished, so softly sheltered by her very loveliness, you might have laughed to hear that she was a working-woman. "Go on!" you might have said, had such been your unfortunate manner of expressing disbelief. But you would have been worse than coarse; you would have been wrong. Mrs. Martindale worked, and worked hard. She worked doubly hard, for she was unskilled at what she did, and she disliked the doing of it. But for two months she had worked every afternoon five afternoons of every week, and had shirked no moment. She received no remuneration for her steady services. She gave them because she felt she should do so. She felt that you should do what you could, hard and humbly. She practiced what she felt.

The special office of the war-relief organization where Mrs. Martindale served was known to her and her co-workers as Headquarters; some of them had come to call it H.Q. These last were of the group that kept agitating for the adoption of a uniform—the design had not been thoroughly worked out, but the idea was of something nurselike, only with a fuller skirt and a long blue cape and white gauntlets. Mrs. Martindale was not in agreement with this faction. It had always been hard for her to raise her voice in opposition, but she did, although softly. She said that while of course there was nothing *wrong* about a uniform, certainly nobody could possibly say there was anything *wrong* with the idea, still it seemed—well, it seemed not quite right to make the work an excuse, well, for fancy dress, if they didn't mind her saying so. Naturally, they wore their coifs at Headquarters, and if anybody wanted to take your photograph in your coif, you should go through with it, because it was good for the organization and publicized its work. But please, not whole uniforms, said Mrs. Martindale. Really, *please,* Mrs. Martindale said.

Headquarters was, many said, the stiffest office of all the offices of all the war-relief organizations in the city. It was not a place where you dropped in and knitted. Knitting, once you have caught the hang of it, is agreeable work, a relaxation from what strains life may be putting upon you. When you knit, save when you are at those bits where you must count stitches, there is enough of your mind left over for you to take part in conversations, and for you to be receptive of news and generous with it. But at Headquarters they sewed. They did a particularly difficult and tedious form of sewing. They made those short, shirtlike coats, fastened in back with tapes, that are put on patients in hospitals. Each garment must have two sleeves, and all the edges must be securely bound. The material was harsh to the touch and the smell, and impatient of the needle of the novice. Mrs. Martindale had made three and had another almost half done. She had thought that after the first one the others would be easier and quicker of manufacture. They had not been.

There were sewing machines at Headquarters, but few of the workers understood the running of them. Mrs. Martindale herself was secretly afraid of a machine; there had been a nasty story, never traced to its source, of somebody who put her thumb in the wrong place, and down came the needle, right through nail and all. Besides, there was something—you didn't know quite how to say it—something more of sacrifice, of service, in making things by hand. She kept on at the task that never grew lighter. It was wished that there were more of her caliber.

For many of the workers had given up the whole thing long before their first garment was finished. And many others, pledged to daily attendance, came only now and then. There was but a handful like Mrs. Martindale.

All gave their services, although there were certain doubts about Mrs. Corning, who managed Headquarters. It was she who oversaw the work, who cut out the garments, and explained to the workers what pieces went next to what other pieces. (It did not always come out as intended. One amateur seamstress toiled all the way to the completion of a coat that had one sleeve depending from the middle of the front. It was impossible to keep from laughing; and a sharp tongue suggested that it might be sent in as it was, in case an elephant was brought to bed. Mrs. Martindale was the first to say "Ah, don't! She worked so hard over it.") Mrs. Corning was a cross woman, hated by all. The high standards of Headquarters were important to the feelings of the workers, but it was agreed that there was no need for Mrs. Corning to scold so shrilly when one of them moistened the end of her thread between her lips before thrusting it into her needle.

"Well, really," one of the most spirited among the rebuked had answered her. "If a little clean spit's the worst they're ever going to get on them . . ."

The spirited one had returned no more to Headquarters, and there were those who felt that she was right. The episode drew new members into the school of thought that insisted Mrs. Corning was paid for what she did.

When Mrs. Martindale paused in the clear light and looked along the Avenue, it was at a moment of earned leisure. She had just left Headquarters. She was not to go back to it for many weeks, nor were any of the other workers. Somewhere the cuckoo had doubtless sung, for summer was coming in. And what with everybody leaving town, it was only sensible to shut Headquarters until autumn. Mrs. Martindale, and with no guilt about it, had looked forward to a holiday from all that sewing.

Well, she was to have none, it turned out. While the workers were gaily bidding farewells and calling out appointments for the autumn, Mrs. Corning had cleared her throat hard to induce quiet and had made a short speech. She stood beside a table piled with cut-out sections of hospital coats not yet sewn together. She was a graceless woman, and though it may be assumed that she meant to be appealing, she sounded only disagreeable. There was, she said, a desperate need, a dreadful need, for hospital garments. More were wanted right away, hundreds and thousands of them; the organization had had a cable that morning, urging and pleading. Headquarters was closing until September—that meant all work would stop. Certainly they had all earned a vacation. And yet, in the face of the terrible need, she could not help asking—she would like to call for volunteers to take coats with them, to work on at home.

There was a little silence, and then a murmur of voices, gaining in volume and in assurance as the owner of each realized that it was not the only one. Most of the workers, it seemed, would have been perfectly willing, but they felt that they absolutely must give their entire time to their children, whom they had scarcely *seen* because of being at Headquarters so constantly.

Others said they were just plain too worn out, and that was all there was to it. It must be admitted that for some moments Mrs. Martindale felt with this latter group. Then shame waved over her like a blush, and swiftly, quietly, with the blue-gray head held high, she went to Mrs. Corning.

"Mrs. Corning," she said. "I should like to take twelve, please."

Mrs. Corning was nicer than Mrs. Martindale had ever seen her. She put out her hand and grasped Mrs. Martindale's.

"Thank you," she said, and her shrill voice was gentle.

But then she had to go and be the way she always had been before. She snatched her hand from Mrs. Martindale's and turned to the table, starting to assemble garments.

"And please, Mrs. Martindale," she said, shrilly, "kindly try and remember to keep the seams straight. Wounded people can be made terribly uncomfortable by crooked seams, you know. And if you could manage to get your stitches even, the coat would look much more professional and give our organization a higher standing. And time is terribly important. They're in an awful hurry for these. So if you could just manage to be a little quicker, it would help a lot."

Really, if Mrs. Martindale hadn't offered to take the things, she would have . . .

The twelve coats still in sections, together with the coat that was half finished, made a formidable bundle. Mrs. Martindale had to send down for her chauffeur to come and carry it to her car for her. While she waited for him, several of the workers came up, rather slowly, and volunteered to sew at home. Four was the highest number of garments promised.

Mrs. Martindale did say good-by to Mrs. Corning, but she expressed no pleasure at the hope of seeing her again in the autumn. You do what you can, and you do it because you should. But all you can do is all you can do.

Out on the Avenue, Mrs. Martindale was herself again. She kept her eyes from the great package the chauffeur had placed in the car. After all, she might, and honorably, allow herself a recess. She need not go home and start sewing again immediately. She would send the chauffeur home with the bundle, and walk in the pretty air, and not think of unfinished coats.

But the men in uniform went along the Avenue under the

snapping flags, and in the sharp, true light you could see all their faces; their clean bones and their firm skin and their eyes, the confident eyes of the soldiers and the wistful eyes of the sailors. They were so young, all of them, and all of them doing what they could, doing everything they could, doing it hard and humbly, without question and without credit. Mrs. Martindale put her hand to her heart. Some day, maybe, some day some of them might be lying on hospital cots . . .

Mrs. Martindale squared her delicate shoulders and entered her car.

"Home, please," she told her chauffeur. "And I'm in rather a hurry."

At home, Mrs. Martindale had her maid unpack the clumsy bundle and lay the contents in her up-stairs sitting-room. Mrs. Martindale took off her outdoor garments and bound her head, just back of the first great blue-gray wave, in the soft linen coif she had habitually worn at Headquarters. She entered her sitting-room, which had recently been redone in the color of her hair and her eyes; it had taken a deal of mixing and matching, but it was a success. There were touches, splashes rather, of magenta about, for Mrs. Martindale complemented brilliant colors and made them and herself glow sweeter. She looked at the ugly, high pile of unmade coats, and there was a second when her famous heart shrank. But it swelled to its norm again as she felt what she must do. There was no good thinking about those twelve damned new ones. Her job immediately was to get on with the coat she had half made.

She sat down on quilted blue-gray satin and set herself to her task. She was at the most hateful stretch of the garment—the binding of the rounded neck. Everything pulled out of place, and nothing came out even, and a horrid starchy smell rose from the thick material, and the stitches that she struggled to put so prettily appeared all different sizes and all faintly gray. Over and over, she had to rip them out for their imperfection, and load her needle again without moistening the thread between her lips, and see them wild and straggling once more. She felt almost ill from the tussle with the hard, monotonous work.

Her maid came in, mincingly, and told her that Mrs. Wyman wished to speak to her on the telephone; Mrs. Wyman wanted to ask a favor of her. Those were two of the penalties attached to the possession of a heart the size of Mrs. Martindale's—people were constantly telephoning to ask her favors and she was constantly granting them. She put down her sewing, with a sigh that might have been of one thing or of another, and went to the telephone.

Mrs. Wyman, too, had a big heart, but it was not well set. She was a great, hulking, stupidly dressed woman, with flapping cheeks and bee-stung eyes. She spoke with rapid diffidence, inserting apologies before she needed to make them, and so was a bore and invited avoidance.

"Oh, my dear," she said now to Mrs. Martindale, "I'm so sorry to bother you. Please do forgive me. But I do want to ask you to do me the most tremendous favor. Please do excuse me. But I want to ask you, do you possibly happen to know of anybody who could possibly use my little Mrs. Christie?"

"Your Mrs. Christie?" Mrs. Martindale asked. "Now, I don't think—or do I?"

"You know," Mrs. Wyman said. "I wouldn't have bothered you for the world, with all you do and all, but you know my little Mrs. Christie. She has that daughter that had infantile, and she has to support her, and I just don't know *what* she's going to do. I wouldn't have bothered you for the world, only I've been sort of thinking up jobs for her to do for me right along, but next week we're going to the ranch, and I really don't know *what* will become of her. And the crippled daughter and all. They just won't be able to *live!*"

Mrs. Martindale made a soft little moan. "Oh, how awful," she said. "How perfectly awful. Oh, I wish I could—tell me, what can I do?"

"Well, if you could just think of somebody that could use her," Mrs. Wyman said. "I wouldn't have bothered you, honestly I wouldn't, but I just didn't know who to turn to. And Mrs. Christie's really a wonderful little woman—she can do anything. Of course, the thing is, she has to work at home, because she wants to take care of the crippled child—well, you can't blame her, really. But she'll call for things and bring them back. And she's so quick, and so good. Please do forgive me for bothering you, but if you could just think——"

"Oh, there must be somebody!" Mrs. Martindale cried. "I'll think of somebody. I'll rack my brains, truly I will. I'll call you up as soon as I think."

Mrs. Martindale went back to her blue-gray quilted satin. Again she took up the unfinished coat. A shaft of the exceptionally bright sunlight shot past a vase of butterfly orchids and settled upon the waving hair under the gracious coif. But Mrs. Martindale did not turn to meet it. Her blue-gray eyes were bent on the drudgery of her fingers. This coat, and then the twelve others beyond it. The need, the desperate, dreadful need, and the terrible importance of time. She took a stitch and another stitch and another stitch and another stitch; she looked at their wavering line, pulled the thread from her needle, ripped out three of the stitches, rethreaded her needle, and stitched again. And as she stitched, faithful to her promise and to her heart, she racked her brains.

ESSAYS

Alexis de Tocqueville (1805–1859)

That Aristocracy May Be Engendered by Manufactures

I have shown that democracy is favourable to the growth of manufactures, and that it increases without limit the numbers of the manufacturing classes: we shall now see by what sideroad manufacturers may possibly in their turn bring men back to aristocracy. It is acknowledged that when a workman is engaged every day upon the same detail, the whole commodity is produced with greater ease, promptitude, and economy. It is likewise acknowledged that the cost of the production of manufactured goods is diminished by the extent of the establishment in which they are made, and by the amount of capital employed or of credit. These truths had long been imperfectly discerned, but in our time they have been demonstrated. They have been already applied to many very important kinds of manufactures, and the humblest will gradually be governed by them. I know of nothing in politics which deserves to fix the attention of the legislator more closely than these two new axioms of the science of manufactures.

When a workman is unceasingly and exclusively engaged in the fabrication of one thing, he ultimately does his work with singular dexterity; but at the same time he loses the general faculty of applying his mind to the direction of the work. He every day becomes more adroit and less industrious; so that it may be said of him, that in proportion as the workman improves the man is degraded. What can be expected of a man who has spent twenty years of his life in making heads for pins? and to what can that mighty human intelligence, which has so often stirred the world, be applied in him, except it be to investigate the best method of making pins' heads? When a workman has spent a considerable portion of his existence in this manner, his thoughts are for ever set upon the object of his daily toil; his body has contracted certain fixed habits, which it can never shake off: in a word, he no longer belongs to himself, but to the calling which he has chosen. It is in vain that laws and manners have been at the pains to level all barriers round such a man, and to open to him on every side a thousand different paths to fortune; a theory of manufactures more powerful than manners and laws binds him to a craft, and frequently to a spot, which he cannot leave: it assigns to him a certain place in society, beyond which he cannot go: in the midst of universal movement it has rendered him stationary.

In proportion as the principle of the division of labour is more extensively applied, the workman becomes more weak, more narrow-minded, and more dependent. The art advances, the artisan recedes. On the other hand, in proportion as it becomes more manifest that the productions of manufactures are by so much the cheaper and better as the manufacture is larger and the amount of capital employed more considerable, wealthy and educated men come forward to embark in manufactures which were heretofore abandoned to poor or ignorant handicraftsmen. The magnitude of the efforts required, and the importance of the results to be obtained, attract them. Thus at the very time at which the science of manufactures lowers the class of workmen, it raises the class of masters.

Whereas the workman concentrates his faculties more and more upon the study of a single detail, the master surveys a more extensive whole, and the mind of the latter is enlarged in proportion as that of the former is narrowed. In a short time the one will require nothing but physical strength without intelligence; the other stands in need of science, and almost of genius, to ensure success. This man resembles more and more the administrator of a vast empire—that man, a brute. The master and the workman have then here no similarity, and their differences increase every day. They are only connected as the two rings at the extremities of a long chain. Each of them fills the station which is made for him, and out of which he does not get: the one is continually, closely, and necessarily dependent upon the other, and seems as much born to obey as that other is to command. What is this but aristocracy?

As the conditions of men constituting the nation become more and more equal, the demand for manufactured commodities becomes more general and more extensive; and the cheapness which places these objects within the reach of slender fortunes becomes a great element of success. Hence there are every day more men of great opulence and education who devote their wealth and knowledge to manufactures; and who seek, by opening large establishments, and by a strict division of labour, to meet the fresh demands which are made on all sides. Thus, in proportion as the mass of the nation turns to democracy, that particular class which is engaged in manufactures becomes more aristocratic. Men grow more alike in the one—more different in the other; and inequality increases in the less numerous class in the same ratio in which it decreases in the community. Hence it would appear, on searching to the bottom, that aristocracy should naturally spring out of the bosom of democracy.

But this kind of aristocracy by no means resembles those kinds which preceded it. It will be observed at once, that as it applies exclusively to manufactures and to some manufacturing callings, it is a monstrous exception in the general aspect of society. The small aristocratic societies which are formed by some manufacturers in the midst of the immense democracy of our age, contain, like the great aristocratic societies of former ages, some men who are very opulent, and a multitude who are wretchedly poor. The poor have few means of escaping from their condition and becoming rich; but the rich are constantly becoming poor, or they give up business when they have realised a fortune. Thus the elements of which the class of the poor is composed are fixed; but the elements of which the class of the rich is composed are not so. To say the truth, though there are rich men, the class of rich men does not exist; for these rich individuals have no feelings or purposes in common, no mutual traditions or mutual hopes; there are therefore members, but no body.

Not only are the rich not compactly united amongst themselves, but there is no real bond between them and the poor. Their relative position is not a permanent one; they are constantly drawn together or separated by their interests. The workman is generally dependent on the master, but not on any particular master; these two men meet in the factory, but know not each other elsewhere; and whilst they come into contact on one point, they stand very wide apart on all others. The manufacturer asks nothing of the workman but his labour; the workman expects nothing from him but his wages. The one contracts no obligation to protect, nor the other to defend; and they are not permanently connected either by habit or by duty. The aristocracy created by business rarely settles in the midst of the manufacturing population which it directs: the object is not to govern that population, but to use it. An aristocracy thus constituted can have no great hold upon these whom it employs; and even if it succeed in retaining them at one moment, they escape the next: it knows not how to will, and it cannot act. The territorial aristocracy of former ages was either bound by law, or thought itself bound by usage, to come to the relief of its serving-men, and to succour their distresses. But the manufacturing aristocracy of our age first impoverishes and debases the men who serve it, and then abandons them to be supported by the charity of the public. This is a natural consequence of what has been said before. Between the workman and the master there are frequent relations, but no real partnership.

I am of opinion, upon the whole, that the manufacturing aristocracy which is growing up under our eyes, is one of the harshest which ever existed in the world; but at the same time it is one of the most confined and least dangerous. Nevertheless the friends of democracy should keep their eyes anxiously fixed in this direction; for if ever a permanent inequality of conditions and aristocracy again penetrate into the world, it may be predicted that this is the channel by which they will enter.

John Dos Passos (1896–1970)

The House of Morgan

I commit my soul into the hands of my savior, wrote John Pierpont Morgan in his will, *in full confidence that having redeemed it and washed it in His most precious blood, He will present it faultless before my heavenly father, and entreat my children to maintain and defend at all hazard and at any cost of personal sacrifice the blessed doctrine of complete atonement for sin through the blood of Jesus Christ once offered and through that alone.*
    and into the hands of the House of Morgan represented by his son,
    he committed,
    when he died in Rome in 1913,
    the control of the Morgan interests in New York, Paris and London, four national banks, three trust companies, three life insurance companies, ten railroad systems, three street railway companies, an express company, the International Mercantile Marine,
    power,
    on the cantilever principle, through interlocking directorates
    over eighteen other railroads, U.S. Steel, General Electric, American Tel and Tel, five major industries;
    the interwoven cables of the Morgan Stillman Baker combination held credit up like a suspension bridge, thirteen percent of the banking resources of the world.

    The first Morgan to make a pool was Joseph Morgan, a hotelkeeper in Hartford Connecticut who organized stagecoach lines and bought up Ætna Life Insurance stock in a time of panic caused by one of the big New York fires in the 1830's;
    his son Junius followed in his footsteps, first in the drygoods business, and then as partner to George Peabody, a Massachusetts banker who built up an enormous underwriting and mercantile business in London and became a friend of Queen Victoria;
    Junius married the daughter of John Pierpont, a Boston preacher, poet, eccentric, and abolitionist; and their eldest son,

John Pierpont Morgan
arrived in New York to make his fortune
after being trained in England, going to school at Vevey, proving himself a crack mathematician at the University of Göttingen,
a lanky morose young man of twenty,
just in time for the panic of '57.
(war and panics on the stock exchange, bankruptcies, warloans, good growing weather for the House of Morgan.)

When the guns started booming at Fort Sumter, young Morgan turned some money over reselling condemned muskets to the U.S. army and began to make himself felt in the gold room in downtown New York; there was more in trading in gold than in trading in muskets; so much for the Civil War.

During the Franco-Prussian war Junius Morgan floated a huge bond issue for the French government at Tours.

At the same time young Morgan was fighting Jay Cooke and the German-Jew bankers in Frankfort over the funding of the American war debt (he never did like the Germans or the Jews).

The panic of '75 ruined Jay Cooke and made J. Pierpont Morgan the boss croupier of Wall Street; he united with the Philadelphia Drexels and built the Drexel building where for thirty years he sat in his glassedin office, redfaced and insolent, writing at his desk, smoking great black cigars, or, if important issues were involved, playing solitaire in his inner office; he was famous for his few words, Yes or No, and for his way of suddenly blowing up in a visitor's face and for that special gesture of the arm that meant, *What do I get out of it?*

In '77 Junius Morgan retired; J. Pierpont got himself made a member of the board of directors of the New York Central railroad and launched the first *Corsair.* He liked yachting and to have pretty actresses call him Commodore.

He founded the Lying-in Hospital on Stuyvesant Square, and was fond of going into St. George's church and singing a hymn all alone in the afternoon quiet.

In the panic of '93
at no inconsiderable profit to himself
Morgan saved the U.S. Treasury; gold was draining out, the

country was ruined, the farmers were howling for a silver standard, Grover Cleveland and his cabinet were walking up and down in the blue room at the White House without being able to come to a decision, in Congress they were making speeches while the gold reserves melted in the Subtreasuries; poor people were starving; Coxey's army was marching to Washington; for a long time Grover Cleveland couldn't bring himself to call in the representative of the Wall Street moneymasters; Morgan sat in his suite at the Arlington smoking cigars and quietly playing solitaire until at last the president sent for him;

he had a plan all ready for stopping the gold hemorrhage.

After that what Morgan said went; when Carnegie sold out he built the Steel Trust.

J. Pierpont Morgan was a bullnecked irascible man with small black magpie's eyes and a growth on his nose; he let his partners work themselves to death over the detailed routine of banking, and sat in his back office smoking black cigars; when there was something to be decided he said Yes or No or just turned his back and went to his solitaire.

Every Christmas his librarian read him Dickens' A *Christmas Carol* from the original manuscript.

He was fond of canarybirds and pekinese dogs and liked to take pretty actresses yachting. Each *Corsair* was a finer vessel than the last.

When he dined with King Edward he sat at His Majesty's right; he ate with the Kaiser tête-à-tête; he liked talking to cardinals or the pope, and never missed a conference of Episcopal bishops;

Rome was his favorite city.

He liked choice cookery and old wines and pretty women and yachting, and going over his collections, now and then picking up a jewelled snuffbox and staring at it with his magpie's eyes.

He made a collection of the autographs of the rulers of France, owned glass cases full of Babylonian tablets, seals, signets, statuettes, busts,

Gallo-Roman bronzes,

Merovingian jewels, miniatures, watches, tapestries, porcelains, cuneiform inscriptions, paintings by all the old masters, Dutch, Italian, Flemish, Spanish,
   manuscripts of the gospels and the Apocalypse,
   a collection of the works of Jean-Jacques Rousseau,
   and the letters of Pliny the Younger.

His collectors bought anything that was expensive or rare or had the glint of empire on it, and he had it brought to him and stared hard at it with his magpie's eyes. Then it was put in a glass case.

The last year of his life he went up the Nile on a dahabiyeh and spent a long time staring at the great columns of the Temple of Karnak.

The panic of 1907 and the death of Harriman, his great opponent in railroad financing, in 1909, had left him the undisputed ruler of Wall Street, most powerful private citizen in the world;

an old man tired of the purple, suffering from gout, he had deigned to go to Washington to answer the questions of the Pujo Committee during the Money Trust Investigation: Yes, I did what seemed to me to be for the best interest of the country.

So admirably was his empire built that his death in 1913 hardly caused a ripple in the exchanges of the world: the purple descended to his son, J. P. Morgan,
   who had been trained at Groton and Harvard and by associating with the British ruling class
   to be a more constitutional monarch: J. P. *Morgan suggests* . . .

By 1917 the Allies had borrowed one billion, nine-hundred million dollars through the House of Morgan: we went overseas for democracy and the flag,
   and by the end of the Peace Conference the phrase J. P. *Morgan suggests* had compulsion over a power of seventyfour billion dollars.

J. P. Morgan is a silent man, not given to public utterances, but during the great steel strike, he wrote Gary: *Heartfelt congratulations on your stand for the open shop, with which I am, as you know, absolutely in accord. I believe American principles of liberty are deeply involved, and must win if we stand firm.*

   (Wars and Panics on the stock exchange,
   machinegunfire and arson,

bankruptcies, warloans,
starvation, lice, cholera and typhus:
good growing weather for the House of Morgan.)

Ellen Goodman (1941–   )

Just Singin' the Office Workers' Summer Blues

The peonies are long gone. The astilbe have turned brown. It is the daylilies that fill the garden now, great bunches of them, peach and yellow, allotted one day's life cycle apiece. I go out this morning and quickly pick off yesterday's blooms while my coffee is cooling.

On the way to my car, I spot a pink cosmos, a volunteer from last year's planting. I don't have time to stop. Soon there will be asters and autumn.

These days, I feel like a divorced parent allowed only visitation rights to my garden, to home life, to summer. One hour in the morning, two at night, every other weekend . . . if the weather is nice. I see generations of daylilies only in passing, check the tomatoes ripening as I come and go to work.

I think I am suffering from homesickness. It strikes a lot of us this time of year. Suddenly, the office has all the attraction of a summer school to which we are confined when our friends are outside playing. I want to be outside, playing. I want to skip school with Ferris Bueller and never get caught. I want a note from my mother.

Maybe this homesickness is some childish piece of imprinting behavior. We spend 12 years waiting for the last day of school. Even when we are parents we still wait to jump on the last bus—no more pencils, no more books, no more teacher's dirty looks. Instead, grown up, responsible, held together by bills and neckties, we keep commuting.

I think of a colleague who left his journalism job for college teaching. Once he listed the three things he liked best about his new work: June, July, August.

This is no plea to sympathize for the plight of office workers. I do inside work. Mine is not a coal mine or a sweatshop. There is no "heavy lifting" here, except for an occasional weighty idea.

But like most office workers, I spend days in an environment that has only one season, one ubiquitous weather report, all year round. It is artificially overcast, low-humidity, cooled to just the right temperature for the computer. Suitable for business suits.

Our climate is controlled. Our windows, if we have them, rarely open. The thermostat is in the distant hands of an engineer. There is absolutely no way for someone in a typical office to know whether it is August or February.

Nothing changes in this inside world. We are encouraged by a magic trick of technology to calculate days in identical 9-to-5 shifts. We are encouraged to think about weeks in terms of tasks instead of seasons.

There is a barrier as thick as thermal pane that separates us from the natural world, from the thought that a different order of time is passing.

It is remarkable how summer ever seeps through this window seal. But it does. Just when the days get longer, time seems shorter. For a few months the contrast between our work environment and natural environment is so stark that we can feel miscast in our own species, like an iguana in a jacket and shoes.

Is it greediness? Maybe Northerners just want more summer, want it to stay, stretched out like a blanket on a beach. No one in New England yearns for more February.

But I suspect that it is also the garden, the growing season, the rush of ripeness all around us. It's the natural world we visit mornings, evenings, weekends, that slips in a message about time. This word processor and this chilled beige office may mute all the workdays of our lives into one endless pattern. But the daylilies in the garden confront me with a perennial reminder of our own transience.

This is summer, then, the season for the most seditious thoughts. Playing hooky. Righting the imbalance of life. Doing nothing even remotely "productive." Asking the scariest question of all: How do you want to spend your time?

Pretty soon there will be asters and autumn.

VIEWPOINTS

J. Bronowski

The Drive for Power

Societies like the Lunar Society represent the sense of the makers of the Industrial Revolution (that very English sense) that they had a social responsibility. I call it an English sense, though in fact that is not quite fair; the Lunar Society was much influenced by Benjamin Franklin and by other Americans associated with it. What ran through it was a simple faith: the good life is *more* than material decency, but the good life must be *based* on material decency.

It took a hundred years before the ideals of the Lunar Society became reality in Victorian England. When it did come, the reality seemed commonplace, even comic, like a Victorian picture postcard. It is comic to think that cotton underwear and soap could work a transformation in the lives of the poor. Yet these simple things—coal in an iron range, glass in the windows, a choice of food—were a wonderful rise in the standard of life and health. By our standards, the industrial towns were slums, but to the people who had come from a cottage, a house in a terrace was a liberation from hunger, from dirt, and from disease; it offered a new wealth of choice. The bedroom with the text on the wall seems funny and pathetic to us, but for the working class wife it was the first experience of private decency. Probably the iron bedstead saved more women from childbed fever than the doctor's black bag, which was itself a medical innovation.

These benefits came from mass production in factories. And the factory system was ghastly; the schoolbooks are right about that. But it was ghastly in the old traditional way. Mines and workshops had been dank, crowded and tyrannical long before the Industrial Revolution. The factories simply carried on as village industry had always done, with a heartless contempt for those who worked in them.

Pollution from the factories was not new either. Again, it was the tradition of the mine and the workshop, which had always fouled their environment. We think of pollution as a modern blight, but it is not. It is another expression of the squalid indifference to health and decency that in past centuries had made the Plague a yearly visitation.

The new evil that made the factory ghastly was different: it was the domination of men by the pace of the machines. The workers for the first time were driven by an inhuman clockwork; the power first of water and then of steam. It seems insane to us (it *was* insane) that manufacturers should be intoxicated by the gush of power that spurted from the factory boiler without a stop. A new ethic was preached in which the cardinal sin was not cruelty or vice, but idleness. Even the Sunday schools warned children that

> *Satan* finds some Mischief still
> For idle Hands to do.

The change in the scale of time in the factories was ghastly and destructive. But the change in the scale of power opened the future. Matthew Boulton of the Lunar Society, for example, built a factory which was a showplace, because Boulton's kind of metalwork depended on the skill of craftsmen. Here James Watt came to build the sun-god of all power, the steam engine, because only here was he able to find the standards of accuracy needed to make the engine steam-tight.

In 1776 Matthew Boulton was very excited about his new partnership with James Watt to build the steam engine. When James Boswell, the biographer, came to see Boulton that year, he said to him grandly, "I sell here, sir, what all the world desires to have—power." It is a lovely phrase. But it is also true.

2
Organization as an Influence on Values

> Forgive the Europeans for their sins,
> Establish work, that values may go on.
> —KARL SHAPIRO

Earlier ages had little doubt about the meaning of the word values, for "values" referred to the body of standards passed down through the centuries by religious and governmental institutions. Even when people questioned the source of those standards, they did not question the values themselves. Since the Renaissance most people have agreed that material progress is desirable, hard work is essential, and we should help one another—in other words, certain attitudes are right and others are wrong.

Today, religious and governmental institutions still receive much credit and/or blame for our values, but many other organizations have come to determine or at least modify values. Often, commitment to an organization seems to take precedence over commitments to individuals, to families, and to traditional values. As modern organizations have increased in size and complexity, so has our dependence on them—but so also have our doubts about the values they represent. We live in a time when people tend to believe that all values are relative, an attitude that causes serious problems for many of us. For example, we recognize that modern organizations are responsible for our material wealth and for the progress we have made in many areas, but we debate the effects of such progress on our lives. We question whether or not we should avail ourselves of some of the technological advances open to us; are the human risks too high in relation to the material gains involved? Is the convenience of the privately owned automobile worth the drain on our natural resources? How could we cope with the economic disruption of using fewer cars and using them less often? How should we respond to the promise and danger of nuclear energy? Are we willing to make the sacrifices necessary to develop such alternative sources of energy as solar energy? Does bigness in our organizations, which seems necessary to deal with our complex problems, automatically call for the sacrifice of human dignity?

Some organizations may exert such powerful influences that we feel helpless before them; still, issues come up about which we are compelled to take stands. Should we—can we—do anything to help a worker who is no longer beneficial to the organization, whose work holds back the progress of a company? Do we ignore that worker as an individual? Such decisions are not easy to make, yet we shall all confront similar problems at one time or another.

Many of the writers represented here present grim pictures of the influence of organizations. They concentrate on the inability of individuals to commit themselves to values separate from those of their particular organization, as in "Life Without Principle." The limitations that result from an abdication of personal responsibility include a narrowness of vision that makes the people involved seem mere extensions of the organization, as in "Office Love." Elsewhere we find human beings who long ago stopped trying to form individual values, if indeed they ever tried to do so. Among works dealing with this loss of individuality are John Ciardi's "What Was Her Name?" where the speaker considers a dead colleague almost as if she were an office machine.

Occasionally, a writer presents a conflict between the values of an organization and those of a strong individual. In John Galsworthy's "Quality," we see an old craftsman trying to maintain his standards against the competition of the assembly line. In "I Am a Union Woman," people risk setting up their own organization in order to counter the power of an established organization.

In a sense, the writers are commenting not only on the organizations' effects on the values of individuals, but also on the values of the organizations; as people care less about human values, so too may organizations.

Sometimes writers do not write about organizations per se, but within their writing lies some concept very pertinent to organizations. In Carl Sandburg's "Limited," for example, a limited, short-run view takes precedence over a long-run view. This is a problem of many American businesses. Some common examples are businesses that emphasize quarterly reports to the detriment of strategic planning, or lack concern for environmental impact in pursuing short-run profit.

We need organizations, but we must learn how to live with them; otherwise, we will not be able to avoid the constriction of spirit that results from delegating our personal responsibilities to an organization. How do we define the limits of duty to an organization, to others, to ourselves? How do we establish values that will allow us to work with the organization as human beings rather than as mechanical extensions of the organization? Can we still accept traditional values? These are not new questions, but they take on a new dimension when modern organizations influence so much of our lives. And they are questions with which we must contend before we can discuss the effects of the organization on fulfillment.

POEMS

Carl Sandburg   (1878–1967)

The Hangman at Home

What does the hangman think about
When he goes home at night from work?
When he sits down with his wife and
Children for a cup of coffee and a
Plate of ham and eggs, do they ask
Him if it was a good day's work
And everything went well or do they
Stay off some topics and talk about
The weather, baseball, politics
And the comic strips in the papers
And the movies? Do they look at his
Hands when he reaches for the coffee
Or the ham and eggs? If the little
Ones say, Daddy, play horse, here's
A rope—does he answer like a joke:
I seen enough rope for today?
Or does his face light up like a
Bonfire of joy and does he say:
It's a good and dandy world we live
In. And if a white face moon looks
In through a window where a baby girl
Sleeps and the moon-gleams mix with
Baby ears and baby hair—the hangman—
How does he act then? It must be easy
For him. Anything is easy for a hangman,
I guess.

Aunt Molly Jackson (1880–1961)

I Am a Union Woman

I am a union woman,
As brave as I can be;
I do not like the bosses,
And the bosses don't like me.

   Refrain:

Join the NMU,
Come join the NMU

I was raised in old Kentucky,
In Kentucky borned and bred;
And when I joined the union
They called me a Rooshian Red.

When my husband asked the boss for a job
These is the words he said:
"Bill Jackson, I can't work you sir,
Your wife's a Rooshian Red."

This is the worst time on earth
That I have ever saw;
To get shot down by gun thugs
And framed up by the law.

If you want to join a union
As strong as one can be,
Join the dear old NMU
And come along with me.

We are many thousand strong
And I am glad to say,
We are getting stronger
And stronger every day.

The bosses ride fine horses
While we walk in the mud;
Their banner is a dollar sign
While ours is striped with blood.

e e cummings   (1894–1962)

pity this busy monster,manunkind

pity this busy monster,manunkind,

not. Progress is a comfortable disease:
your victim (death and life safely beyond)

plays with the bigness of his littleness
—electrons deify one razorblade
into a mountainrange;lenses extend

unwish through curving wherewhen till unwish
returns on its unself.
                        A world of made
is not a world of born—pity poor flesh

and trees,poor stars and stones,but never this
fine specimen of hypermagical
ultraomnipotence. We doctors know

a hopeless case if—listen:there's a hell
of a good universe next door;let's go

E. B. WHITE (1899–1985)

I Paint What I See
(A Ballad of Artistic Integrity)

"What do you paint, when you paint on a wall?"
   Said John D.'s grandson Nelson.
"Do you paint just anything there at all?
"Will there be any doves, or a tree in fall?
"Or a hunting scene, like an English hall?"

   "*I paint what I see,*" *said Rivera.*

"What are the colors you see when you paint?"
   Said John D.'s grandson Nelson.
"Do you use any red in the beard of a saint?
"If you do, is it terribly red, or faint?
"Do you use any blue? Is it Prussian?"

   "*I paint what I paint,*" *said Rivera.*

"Whose is that head that I see on my wall?"
   Said John D.'s grandson Nelson.
"Is it anyone's head whom we know, at all?
"A Rensselaer, or a Saltonstall?
"Is it Franklin D? Is it Mordaunt Hall?
"Or is it the head of a Russian?"

   "*I paint what I think,*" *said Rivera.*

"*I paint what I paint, I paint what I see,*
   "*I paint what I think,*" *said Rivera,*
"*And the thing that is dearest in life to me*
"*In a bourgeois hall is Integrity;*
   "*However . . .*
"*I'll take out a couple of people drinkin'*
"*And put in a picture of Abraham Lincoln;*
"*I could even give you McCormick's reaper*

62/POEMS

> "And still not make my art much cheaper.
> "But the head of Lenin has got to stay
> "Or my friends will give me the bird today,
>   "The bird, the bird, forever."

"It's not good taste in a man like me,"
  Said John D.'s grandson Nelson,
"To question an artist's integrity
"Or mention a practical thing like a fee,
"But I know what I like to a large degree,
  "Though art I hate to hamper;
"For twenty-one thousand conservative bucks
"You painted a radical. I say shucks,
  "I never could rent the offices—
  "The capitalistic offices.
"For this, as you know, is a public hall
"And people want doves, or a tree in fall,
"And though your art I dislike to hamper,
"I owe a *little* to God and Gramper,
  "And after all,
  "It's *my* wall . . ."

"*We'll see if it is,*" said Rivera.

Jacques Prévert   (1900–1977)

At the Florist's

A man enters a florist's
and chooses some flowers
the florist wraps up the flowers
the man puts his hand in his pocket
to find the money
the money to pay for the flowers

but at the same time he puts
all of a sudden
his hand on his heart
and he falls

At the same time that he falls
the money rolls on the floor
and then the flowers fall
at the same time as the man
at the same time as the money
and the florist stands there
with the money rolling
with the flowers spoiling
with the man dying
obviously all this is very sad
and she's got to do something
the florist
but she doesn't know quite where to start
she doesn't know
at which end to begin

There's so many things to do
with this man dying
with these flowers spoiling
and this money
this money that rolls
that doesn't stop rolling

Frank Marshall Davis (1905–)

Three Poems

Robert Whitmore

Having attained success in business
possessing three cars
one wife and two mistresses

a home and furniture
talked of by the town
and thrice ruler of the local Elks
Robert Whitmore
died of apoplexy
when a stranger from Georgia
mistook him
for a former Macon waiter.

Arthur Ridgewood, M.D.

He debated whether
as a poet
to have dreams and beans
or as a physician
have a long car and caviar.
Dividing his time between both
he died from a nervous breakdown
caused by worry
from rejection slips
and final notices from the Finance company.

Giles Johnson, Ph.D.

Giles Johnson
had four college degrees
knew the whyfore of this
the wherefore of that
could orate in Latin
or cuss in Greek
and, having learned such things
he died of starvation
because he wouldn't teach
and he couldn't porter.

Karl Shapiro (1913–   )

Boy-Man

England's lads are miniature men
To start with, grammar in their shiny hats,
And serious; in America who knows when
Manhood begins? Presidents grin and hug,
And while the suave King waves and gravely chats,
America wets on England's old green rug.

The boy-man roars. Worry alone will give
This one the verisimilitude of age.
Those white teeth are his own, for he must live
Longer, grow taller than the Texas race.
Fresh are his eyes, his darkening skin the gauge
of bloods that freely mix beneath his face.

He knows the application of the book
But not who wrote it; shuts it like a shot.
Rather than read, he thinks that he will look;
Rather than look, he thinks that he will talk;
Rather than talk, he thinks that he will not
Bother at all; would rather ride than walk.

His means of conversation is the joke,
Humor his language, underneath which lies
The undecoded dialect of the folk.
Abroad, he scorns the foreigner; what's old
Is worn, what's different bad, what's odd unwise.
He gives off heat and is enraged by cold.

Charming, becoming to the suits he wears,
The boy-man, younger than his eldest son,
Inherits the state; upon his silver hairs
Time, like a panama hat, sits at a tilt
And smiles. To him the world has just begun
And every city waiting to be built.

Mister, remove your shoulder from the wheel
And say this prayer, "Increase my vitamins,
Make my decisions of the finest steel,
Pour motor oil upon my troubled spawn,
Forgive the Europeans for their sins,
Establish work, that values may go on."

Office Love

Office love, love of money and fight, love of calculated sex. The offices reek with thin volcanic metal. Tears fall in typewriters like drops of solder. Brimstone of brassieres, low voices, the whirr of dead-serious play. From the tropical tree and the Rothko[1] in the Board Room to the ungrammatical broom closet fragrant with waxes, to the vast typing pool where coffee is being served by dainty waitresses maneuvering their hand trucks, music almost unnoticeable falls. The very telephones are hard and kissable, the electric water cooler sweetly sweats. Gold simmers to a boil in braceleted and sunburned cheeks. What ritual politeness nevertheless, what subtlety of clothing. And if glances meet, if shoulders graze, there's no harm done. Flowers, celebrations, pregnancy leave, how the little diamonds sparkle under the psychologically soft-colored ceilings. It's an elegant windowless world of soft pressures and efficiency joys, of civilized mishaps—mere runs in the stocking, papercuts.

Where the big boys sit the language is rougher. Phone calls to China and a private shower. No paper visible anywhere. Policy is decided by word of mouth like gangsters. There the power lies and is sexless.

---

1. Twentieth-century painter.

John Ciardi   (1916–1986)

What *Was* Her Name?

Someone must make out the cards
for the funeral of the filing clerk.
Poor bony rack with her buzzard's
jowled eyes bare as a dirk
and as sharp for dead fact, she
could have done it better than anyone
will do it for her. It will be,
to be sure, done.
And the flowers sent. And the office closed
for the half day it takes
for whatever we are supposed
to make of the difference it makes
to file the filing clerk
where we can forget her.

Someone will do the work
she used to do better.

Carl Sandburg   (1878–1967)

Limited

I am riding on a limited express, one of the crack trains of the
      nation.
Hurtling across the prairie into blue haze and dark air go fif-
      teen all-steel coaches holding a thousand people.
(All the coaches shall be scrap and rust and all the men and
      women laughing in the diners and sleepers shall pass to
      ashes).
I ask a man in the smoker where he is going and he answers:
      "Omaha."

Donald Hall (1928–)

Transcontinent

Where the cities end, the
dumps grow the oil-can shacks
from Portland, Maine,

to Seattle. Broken
cars rust in Troy, New York,
and Cleveland Heights.

On the train, the people
eat candy bars, and watch,
or fall asleep.

When they look outside and
see cars and shacks, they know
they're nearly there.

Carl Sandburg (1878–1967)

Theorem

There are prices and costs.
The price is what you are willing to pay.
The cost is what you put across as pay.
The circles of price and cost intersect
    in a kiss or a curse or a song.

Marge Piercy (1936–)

The Development

The bulldozers come, they rip
a hole in the sand along
the new blacktop road with a tony name
(Trotting Park, Pamet Hills)
and up goes another glass-walled-
split-level-livingroom-vast-as-a-
roller-rink-$100,000
summer home for a psychiatrist
and family.

Nine months vacation homes
stand empty except for mice
and spiders, an occasional
bird with a broken back twitching
on the deck under a gape of glass.

I live in such a development
way at the end of a winding
road where the marsh begins
to close in: two houses,
the one next door a local
fisherman lost to the bank
last winter, ours a box
half buried in the sand.
This land is rendered
too expensive
to live on. We feed
four people off it,
a kind of organic tall corn
ornery joke at road's end.
We planted for the birds cover
and berries, we compost, we set out
trees and at night

the raccoons come shambling.
Yet the foxes left us,
shrinking into the marsh.
I found their new den.
I don't show it
to anyone.
Forgive us, grey fox, our stealing
your home, our loving
this land carved into lots
over a shrinking watertable
where the long sea wind that blows
the sand whispers to developers
money, money, money.

Ogden Nash (1902–1971)

The Purist

I give you now Professor Twist,
A conscientious scientist.
Trustees exclaimed, "He never bungles!"
And sent him off to distant jungles.
Camped on a tropic riverside,
One day he missed his loving bride.
She had, the guide informed him later,
Been eaten by an alligator.
Professor Twist could not but smile.
"You mean," he said, "a crocodile."

JoAllen Bradham (1937–)

Systems

"We use eunuchs," he said.
At the adjoining table,
I ceased carving capon.
"Yes. We are pleased with eunuchs."

There, in the watering hole, planted and plush,
Indigenous to brunch of chichi quiche,
I hear again, "We use eunuchs."

My blood rises to Cleopatran sands,
Tanned arms bound in snake-headed amulets,
Lion-faced stones, Yeats' blank and pitiless stare,
Ibis and Cheops, drifteers near Gizeh,
Taut loin cloths—crimson, indigo, chrome.
As palms languish in the lush air,
Ghawazee sway languidly in the streets,
Where smug non-eunuchs smirk,
And women titter shamelessly at want.

They guard the bed, eunuchs do.
Old safe bed watchers, lolling with dormant pulse.
"Since we installed eunuchs. . . ."
For what in the world in East Tennessee
Can they install eunuchs?
And do they actively recruit,
Inserting columned ads in house organs:
"Wanted: Twenty eunuchs.
Salary commensurate with . . ."?

Pulling back, I look at the neighbor table.
"UNIX"[1] the red promo print thrusts out.
"Yes," he drawls in flat East Tennessee tongue,
"We use UNIX."!
Cleopatra shrugs,
Her bare shoulder beckons silver in the starlight
While Babylonia collapses spent and past.
"Less rigid than DOS, we feel."
Mincing, Mardian exits the program.

1. A trademark of AT&T.

Parrot as Per Tech Specs

Lore and legend,
Pirates' treasure;
Children's marvel,
Chaucer's jester;
Four-clawed cracker-asker.

Never again,
You gaudy raucous.
Now we know:

Pre-programmed
Finite model;
Encoded voice outputting
Interactive elastic
Feathered biped.

JOHN STONE (1936–)

The Truck

I was coming back from
wherever I'd been when
I saw the truck and
the sign on the back repeated
on the side to be certain
you knew it was no mistake

> PROGRESS CASKETS
>
> ARTHUR ILLINOIS

Now folks have different
thoughts it's true about
death but in general it's

not like any race for
example you ever ran
everyone wanting to come in

last and all   And I admit
a business has to have a good
name   No one knows better
than I the value of a good
name   A name is what sells
the product in the first

and in the final place
All this time the Interstate
was leading me into Atlanta
and I was following the sign
and the truck was heavier
climbing the hill than

going down which is as
it should be   What I really
wanted to see was the driver
up close maybe talk to him
find out his usual run
so I could keep off it

Not that I'm superstitious   It's just
the way I was raised   A casket
may be Progress up in Arthur
but it's thought of
down here
as a setback.

John Godfrey Saxe (1816–1887)

The News

The News, Indeed!—pray do you call it news
When shallow noddles publish shallow views?
Pray, is it news that turnips should be bred
As large and hollow as the owner's head?
News, that a clerk should rob his master's hoard,
Whose meagre salary scarcely pays his board?
News, that two knaves, their spurious friendship o'er,
Should tell the truths which they concealed before?
News, that a maniac, weary of his life,
Should end his sorrows with a rope or knife?
News, that a wife should violate the vows
That bind her, loveless, to a tyrant spouse?
News, that a daughter cheats paternal rule,
And weds a scoundrel to escape a fool?—
The news, indeed!—Such matters are as old
As sin and folly, rust and must and mould!

John Dickson (1916–   )

Delayed Decision

It's Friday and there's hardly any time—
the week is dying, and the temporary typist
trim in her posture, impeccable in her clack
displays her various dimensions.

Would she go with me and sit cool and correct
on mezzanines of exquisite cuisine,
smile me her smile designed for strangers,

raise her cup of Stilted Comment tea,
small finger arched in delicate refinement,
lips reserved for delightful repartee?

Or would she glare with eyes
like nails of a boarded-up expression?
Would she press habitual buttons activating
"Smile," "Look interested," or "Yawn"?
Perhaps be like the willow. Or the oak.
Or the tenacious land-crab
who won't release its hold 'til thunder roars.

Maybe we would walk with our umbrellas
through the dark arrhythmic streets
to rut in the wallow of her pillowed room,
its walls of high school aspiration
caked with cigarettes and loneliness,

maybe laugh for no reason,
talk without a thing to say
as I ponder fireplace embers or the moon
for ways to reveal to her such things
as beetle tracks or stars or shiny stones

as though she were blind . . .
as though she had no sense.

But it's already Friday afternoon.
Soon Monday will smother us like smog,
like shovelsful of clumping earth
and the star will be part of the sky again,
the tree part of the landscape
and she part of the typewriter,
part of the room.

Edna St. Vincent Millay (1892–1950)

Apostrophe to Man

(on reflecting that the world is ready to go to war again)[1]

Detestable race, continue to expunge yourself, die out.
Breed faster, crowd, encroach, sing hymns, build bombing
    airplanes;
Make speeches, unveil statues, issue bonds, parade;
Convert again into explosives the bewildered ammonia
    and the distracted cellulose;
Convert again into putrescent matter drawing flies
The hopeful bodies of the young; exhort,
Pray, pull long faces, be earnest, be all but overcome,
    be photographed;
Confer, perfect your formulae, commercialize
Bacteria harmful to human tissue,
Put death on the market;
Breed, crowd, encroach, expand, expunge yourself, die out,
Homo called *sapiens*.[2]

1. Written in the decade before World War II.
2. The scientific Latin name for the human species, meaning "intelligent man."

Anonymous

Art

The hen remarked to the mooley cow,
As she cackled her daily lay,
(That is, the hen cackled) "It's funny how
I'm good for an egg a day.
I'm a fool to do it, for what do I get?
My food and my lodging. My!
But the poodle gets that—he's the household pet,
And he never has laid a single egg yet—
Not even when eggs are high."

The mooley cow remarked to the hen,
As she masticated her cud,
(That is, the cow did) "Well, what then?
You quit, and your name is mud.
I'm good for eight gallons of milk each day,
And I'm given my stable and grub;
But the parrot gets that much, anyway,—
All she can gobble—and what does she pay?
Not a dribble of milk, the dub!"

But the hired man remarked to the pair,
"You get all that's coming to you.
The poodle does tricks, and the parrot can swear,
Which is better than you can do.
You're necessary, but what's the use
Of bewailing your daily part?
You're bourgeois—working's your only excuse;
You can't do nothing but just produce—
What them fellers does is ART!"

FICTION

O. Henry (1862–1910)

The Man Higher Up

Across our two dishes of spaghetti, in a corner of Provenzano's restaurant, Jeff Peters was explaining to me the three kinds of graft.

Every winter Jeff comes to New York to eat spaghetti, to watch the shipping in East River from the depths of his chinchilla overcoat, and to lay in a supply of Chicago-made clothing at one of the Fulton Street stores. During the other three seasons he may be found further west—his range is from Spokane to Tampa. In his profession he takes a pride which he supports and defends with a serious and unique philosophy of ethics. His profession is no new one. He is an incorporated, uncapitalized, unlimited asylum for the reception of the restless and unwise dollars of his fellowmen.

In the wilderness of stone in which Jeff seeks his annual lonely holiday he is glad to palaver of his many adventures, as a boy will whistle after sundown in a wood. Wherefore, I mark on my calendar the time of his coming, and open a question of privilege at Provenzano's concerning the little wine-stained table in the corner between the rakish rubber plant and the framed palazzo della something on the wall.

"There are two kinds of graft," said Jeff, "that ought to be wiped out by law. I mean Wall Street speculation and burglary."

"Nearly everybody will agree with you as to one of them," said I, with a laugh.

"Well, burglary ought to be wiped out, too," said Jeff; and I wondered if the laugh had been redundant.

"About three months ago," said Jeff, "it was my privilege to become familiar with a sample of each of the aforesaid branches of illegitimate art. I was *sine qua grata* with a member of the housebreakers' union and one of the John D. Napoleons of finance at the same time."

"Interesting combination," said I, with a yawn. "Did I tell you I bagged a duck and a ground squirrel at one shot last week over in the Ramapos?" I knew well how to draw Jeff's stories.

"Let me tell you first about these barnacles that clog the wheels of society by poisoning the springs of rectitude with their upas-like eye," said Jeff, with the pure gleam of the muckraker in his own.

"As I said, three months ago I got into bad company. There are two times in a man's life when he does this—when he's dead broke, and when he's rich.

"Now and then the most legitimate business runs out of luck. It was out in Arkansas I made the wrong turn at a cross-road, and drives into this town of Peavine by mistake. It seems I had already assaulted and disfigured Peavine the spring of the year before. I had sold $600 worth of young fruit trees there—plums, cherries, peaches and pears. The Peaviners were keeping an eye on the country road and hoping I might pass that way again. I drove down Main street as far as the Crystal Palace drugstore before I realized I had committed ambush upon myself and my white horse Bill.

"The Peaviners took me by surprise and Bill by the bridle and began a conversation that wasn't entirely disassociated with the subject of fruit trees. A committee of 'em ran some trace-chains through the armholes of my vest, and escorted me through their gardens and orchards.

"Their fruit trees hadn't lived up to their labels. Most of 'em had turned out to be persimmons and dogwoods, with a grove or two of blackjacks and poplars. The only one that showed any signs of bearing anything was a fine young cottonwood that had put forth a hornet's nest and half of an old corset-cover.

"The Peaviners protracted our fruitless stroll to the edge of town. They took my watch and money on account; and they kept Bill and the wagon as hostages. They said the first time one of them dogwood trees put forth an Amsden's June peach I might come back and get my things. Then they took off the trace-chains and jerked their thumbs in the direction of the Rocky Mountains;

and I struck a Lewis and Clark lope for the swollen rivers and impenetrable forests.

"When I regained intellectualness I found myself walking into an unidentified town on the A., T. & S. F. railroad. The Peaviners hadn't left anything in my pockets except a plug of chewing—they wasn't after my life—and that saved it. I bit off a chunk and sits down on a pile of ties by the track to recogitate my sensations of thought and perspicacity.

"And then along comes a fast freight which slows up a little at the town; and off of it drops a black bundle that rolls for twenty yards in a cloud of dust and then gets up and begins to spit soft coal and interjections. I see it is a young man broad across the face, dressed more for Pullmans than freights, and with a cheerful kind of smile in spite of it all that made Phœbe Snow's job look like a chimney-sweep's.

"'Fall off?' says I.

"'Nunk,' says he. 'Got off. Arrived at my destination. What town is this?'

"'Haven't looked it up on the map yet,' says I. 'I got in about five minutes before you did. How does it strike you?'

"'Hard,' says he, twisting one of his arms around. 'I believe that shoulder—no, it's all right.'

"He stoops over to brush the dust off his clothes, when out of his pocket drops a fine, nine-inch burglar's steel jimmy. He picks it up and looks at me sharp, and then grins and holds out his hand.

"'Brother,' says he, 'greetings. Didn't I see you in Southern Missouri last summer selling colored sand at half-a-dollar a teaspoonful to put into lamps to keep the oil from exploding?'

"'Oil,' says I, 'never explodes. It's the gas that forms that explodes.' But I shakes hands with him, anyway.

"'My name's Bill Bassett,' says he to me, 'and if you'll call it professional pride instead of conceit, I'll inform you that you have the pleasure of meeting the best burglar that ever set a gum-shoe on ground drained by the Mississippi River.'

"Well, me and this Bill Bassett sits on the ties and exchanges brags as artists in kindred lines will do. It seems he didn't have a cent, either, and we went into close caucus. He explained why an able burglar sometimes had to travel on freights by telling me that a servant girl had played him false in Little Rock, and he was making a quick getaway.

"'It's part of my business,' says Bill Bassett, 'to play up to the ruffles when I want to make a riffle as Raffles. 'Tis loves that make the bit go 'round. Show me a house with the swag in it and a pretty parlor-maid and you might as well call the silver melted down and sold, and me spilling truffles and that Château stuff on the napkin under my chin, while the police are calling it an inside job because the old lady's nephew teaches a Bible class. I first make an impression on the girl,' says Bill, 'and when she lets me inside I make an impression on the locks. But this one in Little Rock done me,' says he. 'She saw me taking a trolley ride with another girl, and when I came 'round on the night she was to leave the door open for me it was fast. And I had keys made for the doors upstairs. But, no sir. She had sure cut off my locks. She was a Delilah,' says Bill Bassett.

"It seems that Bill tried to break in anyhow with his jimmy, but the girl emitted a succession of bravura noises like the top-riders of a tally-ho, and Bill had to take all hurdles between there and the depot. As he had no baggage they tried hard to check his departure, but he made a train that was just pulling out.

"'Well,' says Bassett, when we had exchanged memoirs of our dead lives, 'I could eat. This town don't look like it was kept under a Yale lock. Suppose we commit some mild atrocity that will bring in temporary expense money. I don't suppose you've brought along any hair tonic or rolled gold watch-chains, or similar law-defying swindles that you could sell on the plaza to the pikers of the paretic populace, have you?'

"'No,' says I, 'I left an elegant line of Patagonian diamond earrings and rainy-day sunbursts in my valise at Peavine. But they're to stay there till some of them black-gum trees begin to glut the market with yellow clings and Japanese plums. I reckon we can't count on them unless we take Luther Burbank in for a partner.'

"'Very well,' says Bassett, 'we'll do the best we can. Maybe after dark I'll borrow a hairpin from some lady, and open the Farmers and Drovers Marine Bank with it.'

"While we were talking, up pulls a passenger train to the depot near by. A person in a high hat gets off on the wrong side of the train and comes tripping down the track towards us. He was a little, fat man with a big nose and rat's eyes, but dressed expensive, and carrying a hand-satchel careful, as if it had eggs or railroad bonds in it. He passes by us and keeps on down the track, not appearing to notice the town.

"'Come on,' says Bill Bassett to me, starting after him.

"'Where?' I asks.

"'Lordy!' says Bill, 'had you forgot you was in the desert? Didn't you see Colonel Manna drop down right before your eyes? Don't you hear the rustling of General Raven's wings? I'm surprised at you, Elijah.

"We overtook the stranger in the edge of some woods, and, as it was after sun-down and in a quiet place, nobody saw us stop him. Bill takes the silk hat off the man's head and brushes it with his sleeve and puts it back.

"'What does this mean, sir?' says the man.

"'When I wore one of these,' says Bill, 'and felt embarrassed, I always done that. Not having one now I had to use yours. I hardly know how to begin, sir, in explaining our business with you, but I guess we'll try your pockets first.'

"Bill Bassett felt in all of them, and looked disgusted.

"'Not even a watch,' he says. 'Ain't you ashamed of yourself, you whited sculpture? Going about dressed like a headwaiter, and financed like a Count! You haven't even got carfare. What did you do with your transfer?'

"The man speaks up and says he has no assets or valuables of any sort. But Bassett takes his hand-satchel and opens it. Out comes some collars and socks and a half a page of a newspaper clipped out. Bill reads the clipping careful, and holds out his hand to the help-up party.

"'Brother,' says he, 'greetings! Accept the apologies of friends. I am Bill Bassett, the burglar. Mr. Peters, you must make the acquaintance of Mr. Alfred E. Ricks. Shake hands. Mr. Peters,' says Bill, 'stands about halfway between me and you, Mr. Ricks, in the line of havoc and corruption. He always gives something for the money he gets. I'm glad to meet you, Mr. Ricks—you and Mr. Peters. This is the first time I ever attended a full gathering of the National Synod of Sharks—housebreaking, swindling, and financiering all represented. Please examine Mr. Rick's credentials, Mr. Peters.'

"The piece of newspaper that Bill Bassett handed me had a good picture of this Ricks on it. It was a Chicago paper, and it had obloquies of Ricks in every paragraph. By reading it over I harvested the intelligence that said alleged Ricks had laid off all that portion of the State of Florida that lies under water into town lots and sold 'em to alleged innocent investors from his magnificently furnished offices in Chicago. After he had taken in a hundred thousand or so dollars one of these fussy purchasers that are always making trouble (I've had 'em actually try gold watches I've sold 'em with acid) took a cheap excursion down to the land where it is always just before supper to look at his lot and see if it didn't need a new paling or two on the fence, and market a few lemons in time for the Christmas present trade. He hires a surveyor to find his lot for him. They run the line out and find the flourishing town of Paradise Hollow, so advertised, to be about 40 rods and 16 poles S., 27° E. of the middle of Lake Okeechobee. This man's lot was under thirty-six feet of water, and besides, had been preempted so long by the alligators and gars that his title looked fishy.

"Naturally, the man goes back to Chicago and makes it as hot for Alfred E. Ricks as the morning after a prediction of snow by the weather bureau. Ricks defied the allegation, but he couldn't deny the alligators. One morning the papers came out with a column about it, and Ricks come out by the fire-escape. It seems the alleged authorities had beat him the safe-deposit box where he kept his winnings, and Ricks has to westward ho! with only feetwear and a dozen 15½ English pokes in his shopping bag. He happened to have some mileage left in his book, and that took him as far as the town in the wilderness where he was spilled out on me and Bill Bassett as Elijah III with not a raven in sight for any of us.

"Then this Alfred E. Ricks lets out a squeak that he is hungry, too, and denies the hypothesis that he is good for the value, let alone the price of a meal. And so, there was the three of us, representing, if we had a mind to draw syllogisms and parabolas, labor and trade and capital. Now, when trade has no capital there isn't a dicker to be made. And when capital has no money there's a stagnation in steak and onions. That put it up to the man with the jimmy.

"'Brother bushrangers,' says Bill Bassett, 'never yet, in trouble, did I desert a pal. Hard-by, in yon wood, I seem to see unfurnished lodgings. Let us go there and wait till dark.'

"There was an old, deserted cabin in the grove, and we three took possession of it. After dark Bill Bassett tells us to wait, and goes out for half an hour. He comes back with an armful of bread and spareribs and pies.

"'Panhandled 'em at a farmhouse on Washita Avenue,' says he. 'Eat, drink and be leary.'

"The full moon was coming up bright, so we sat on the floor of the cabin and ate in the light of it. And this Bill Bassett begins to brag.

"'Sometimes,' says he, with his mouth full of country produce, 'I lose all patience with you people that think you are higher up in the profession than I am. Now, what could either of you have done in the present emergency to set us on our feet again? Could you do it, Ricksy?'

"'I must confess, Mr. Bassett,' says Ricks, speaking nearly inaudible out of a slice of pie, 'that at this immediate juncture I could not, perhaps, promote an enterprise to relieve the situation. Large operations, such as I direct, naturally require careful preparation in advance. I—'

"'I know, Ricksy,' breaks in Bill Bassett. 'You needn't finish. You need $500 to make the first payment on a blond typewriter, and four roomsful of quartered oak furniture. And you need $500 more for advertising contracts. And you need two weeks' time for the fish to begin to bite. Your line of relief would be about as useful in an emergency as advocating municipal ownership to cure a man suffocated by eighty-cent gas. And your graft ain't much swifter, Brother Peters,' he winds up.

"'Oh,' says I, 'I haven't seen you turn anything into gold with your wand yet, Mr. Good Fairy. 'Most anybody could rub the magic ring for a little leftover victuals.'

"'That was only getting the pumpkin ready,' says Bassett, braggy and cheerful. 'The coach and six'll drive up to the door before you know it, Miss Cinderella. Maybe you've got some scheme under your sleeve-holders that will give us a start.'

"'Son,' says I, 'I'm fifteen years older than you are, and young enough yet to take out an endowment policy. I've been broke before. We can see the lights of that town not half a mile away. I learned under Montague Silver, the greatest street man that ever spoke from a wagon. There are hundreds of men walking the streets this moment with grease spots on their clothes. Give me a gasoline lamp, a dry-goods box, and a two-dollar bar of white castile soap, cut into little—'

"'Where's your two dollars?' snickered Bill Bassett into my discourse. There was no use arguing with that burglar.

"'No,' he goes on; 'you're both babes-in-the-wood. Finance has closed the mahogany desk, and trade has put the shutters up. Both of you look to labor to start the wheels going. All right. You admit it. To-night I'll show you what Bill Bassett can do.'

"Bassett tells me and Ricks not to leave the cabin till he comes back, even if it's daylight, and then he struts off toward town, whistling gay.

"This Alfred E. Ricks pulls off his shoes and his coat, lays a silk handkerchief over his hat, and lays down on the floor.

"'I think I will endeavour to secure a little slumber,' he squeaks. 'The day has been fatiguing. Goodnight, my dear Mr. Peters.'

"'My regards to Morpheus,'[1] says I. 'I think I'll sit up a while.'

"About two o'clock, as near as I could guess by my watch in Peavine, home comes our laboring man and kicks up Ricks, and calls us to the streak of bright moonlight shining in the cabin door. Then he spreads out five packages of one thousand dollars each on the floor, and begins to cackle over the nestegg like a hen.

"'I'll tell you a few things about that town,' says he. 'It's named Rocky Springs, and they're building a Masonic Temple, and it looks like the Democratic candidate for mayor is going to get soaked by a Pop, and Judge Tucker's wife, who has been down with pleurisy, is some better. I had a talk with these lilliputian thesises before I got a siphon in the fountain of knowlege that I was after. And there's a bank there called the Lumberman's Fidelity and Plowman's Savings Institution. It closed for business

---

1. God of sleep in classical mythology.

yesterday with $23,000 cash on hand. It will open this morning with $18,000—all silver—that's the reason I didn't bring more. There you are, trade and capital. Now, will you be bad?'

"'My young friend,' says Alfred E. Ricks, holding up his hands, 'have you robbed this bank? Dear me, dear me!'

"'You couldn't call it that,' says Bassett. '"Robbing" sounds harsh. All I had to do was to find out what street it was on. That town is so quiet that I could stand on the corner and hear the tumblers clicking in that safe lock—"right to 45; left twice to 80; right to 60; left to 15"—as plain as the Yale captain giving orders in the football dialect. Now, boys,' says Bassett, 'this is an early rising town. They tell me the citizens are all up and stirring before daylight. I asked what for, and they said because breakfast was ready at that time. And what of merry Robin Hood? It must be Yoicks! and away with the tinkers' chorus. I'll stake you. How much do you want? Speak up, Capital.'

"'My dear young friend,' says this ground squirrel of a Ricks, standing on his hind legs and juggling nuts in his paws, 'I have friends in Denver who would assist me. If I had a hundred dollars I—'

"Bassett unpins a package of the currency and throws five twenties to Ricks.

"'Trade, how much?' he says to me.

"'Put your money up, Labor,' says I. 'I never yet drew upon honest toil for its hard-earned pittance. The dollars I get are surplus ones that are burning the pockets of damfools and greenhorns. When I stand on a street corner and sell a solid gold diamond ring to a yap for $3.00, I make just $2.60. And I know he's going to give it to a girl in return for all the benefits accruing from a $125.00 ring. His profits are $122.00. Which of us is the biggest fakir?'

"'And when you sell a poor woman a pinch of sand for fifty cents to keep her lamp from exploding,' says Bassett, 'what do you figure her gross earnings to be, with sand at forty cents a ton?'

"'Listen,' says I, 'I instruct her to keep her lamp clean and well filled. If she does that it can't burst. And with the sand in it she knows it can't, and she don't worry. It's a kind of Industrial Christian Science. She pays fifty cents, and gets both Rockefeller and Mrs. Eddy on the job. It ain't everybody that can let the gold-dust twins do their work.'

"Alfred E. Ricks all but licks the dust off of Bill Bassett's shoes.

"'My dear young friend,' says he, 'I will never forget your generosity. Heaven will reward you. But let me implore you to turn from your ways of violence and crime.'

"'Mousie,' says Bill, 'the hole in the wainscoting for yours. Your dogmas and inculcations sound to me like the last words of a bicycle pump. What has your high moral, elevator-service system of pillage brought you to? Penuriousness and want. Even Brother Peters, who insists upon contaminating the art of robbery with theories of commerce and trade, admitted he was on the lift. Both of you live by the gilded rule. Brother Peters,' says Bill, 'you'd better choose a slice of his embalmed currency. You're welcome.'

"I told Bill Bassett once more to put his money in his pocket. I never had the respect for burglary that some people have. I always gave something for the money I took even if it's only some little trifle for a souvenir to remind 'em not to get caught again.

"And then Alfred E. Ricks grovels at Bill's feet again, and bids us adieu. He says he will have a team at a farmhouse, and drive to the station below, and take the train for Denver. It salubrified the atmosphere when that lamentable boll-worm took his departure. He was a disgrace to every nonindustrial profession in the country. With all his big schemes and fine offices he had wound up unable even to get an honest meal except by the kindness of a strange and maybe unscrupulous burglar. I was glad to see him go, though I felt a little sorry for him, now that he was ruined forever. What could such a man do without a big capital to work with? Why, Alfred E. Ricks, as we left him, was as helpless as a turtle on its back. He couldn't have worked a scheme to beat a little girl out of a penny slate-pencil.

"When me and Bill Bassett was left alone I did a little sleight-of-mind turn in my head with a trade secret at the end of it. Thinks I, I'll show this Mr. Burglar Man the difference between business and labor. He had hurt some of my professional self-adulation by casting his Persians upon commerce and trade.

"'I won't take any of your money as a gift, Mr. Bassett,' says

I to him, 'but if you'll pay my expenses as a traveling companion until we get out of the danger zone of the immoral deficit you have caused in this town's finances to-night, I'll be obliged.'

"Bill Bassett agreed to that, and we hiked westward as soon as we could catch a safe train.

"When we got to a town in Arizona called Los Perros I suggested that we once more try our luck on terra-cotta. That was the home of Montague Silver, my old instructor, now retired from business. I knew Monty would stake me to web money if I could show him a fly buzzing 'round in the locality. Bill Bassett said all towns looked alike to him as he worked mainly in the dark. So we got off the train in Los Perros, a fine little town in the silver region.

"I had an elegant little sure thing in the way of a commercial slungshot that I intended to hit Basset behind the ear with. I wasn't going to take his money while he was asleep, but I was going to leave him with a lottery ticket that would represent in experience to him $4,755—I think that was the amount he had when he got off the train. But the first time I hinted to him about an investment, he turns on me and disencumbers himself of the following terms and expressions.

"'Brother Peters,' says he, 'it ain't a bad idea to go into an enterprise of some kind, as you suggest. I think I will. But if I do it will be such a cold proposition that nobody but Robert E. Peary and Charlie Fairbanks will be able to sit on the board of directors.'

"'I thought you might want to turn your money over,' says I.

"'I do,' says he, 'frequently. I can't sleep on one side all night. I'll tell you, Brother Peters,' says he, "I'm going to start a poker room. I don't seem to care for the humdrum in swindling, such as peddling egg-beaters and working off breakfast food on Barnum and Bailey for sawdust to strew in their circus rings. But the gambling business,' says he, 'from the profitable side of the table is a good compromise between swiping silver spoons and selling penwipers at a Waldorf-Astoria charity bazaar.'

"'Then,' says I, 'Mr. Bassett, you don't care to talk over my business proposition?'

"'Why,' says he, 'do you know, you can't get a Pasteur institute to start up within fifty miles of where I live. I bite so seldom.'

"So, Bassett rents a room over a saloon and looks around for some furniture and chromos. The same night I went to Monty Silver's house, and he let me have $200 on my prospects. Then I went to the only store in Los Perros that sold playing cards and bought every deck in the house. The next morning when the store opened I was there bringing all the cards back with me. I said that my partner that was going to back me in the game had changed his mind; and I wanted to sell the cards back again. The storekeeper took 'em at half price.

"Yes, I was seventy-five dollars loser up to that time. But while I had the cards that night I marked every one in every deck. That was labor. And then trade and commerce had their innings, and the bread I had cast upon the waters began to come back in the form of cottage pudding with wine sauce.

"Of course I was among the first to buy chips at Bill Bassett's game. He had bought the only cards there was to be had in town; and I knew the back of every one of them better than I know the back of my head when the barber shows me my haircut in the two mirrors.

"When the game closed I had the five thousand and a few odd dollars, and all Bill Bassett had was the wanderlust and a black cat he had bought for a mascot. Bill shook hands with me when I left.

"'Brother Peters,' says he, 'I have no business being in business. I was preordained to labor. When a No. 1 burglar tries to make a James out of his jimmy he perpetrates an improfundity. You have a well-oiled and efficacious system of luck at cards,' says he. 'Peace go with you.' And I never afterward sees Bill Bassett again."

"Well, Jeff," said I, when the Autolycan adventure seemed to have divulged the gist of his life, "I hope you took care of the money. That would be a respecta—that is a considerable working capital if you should choose some day to settle down to some sort of regular business."

"Me?" said Jeff, virtuously. "You can bet I've taken care of that five thousand."

He tapped his coat over the region of his chest exultantly.

"Gold mining stock," he explained, "every cent of it. Shares par value one dollar. Bound to go up 500 per cent within a year. Non-assessable. The Blue Gopher Mine. Just discovered a month ago. Better get in yourself if you've any spare dollars on hand."

"Sometimes," said I, "these mines are not—"

"Oh, this one's solid as an old goose," said Jeff. "Fifty thousand dollars worth of ore in sight, and 10 per cent monthly earnings guaranteed."

He drew a long envelope from his pocket and cast it on the table.

"Always carry it with me," said he. "So the burglar can't corrupt or the capitalist break in and water it."

I looked at the beautifully engraved certificate of stock.

"In Colorado, I see," said I. "And, by the way, Jeff, what was the name of the little man who went to Denver—the one you and Bill met at the station?"

"Alfred E. Ricks," said Jeff, "was the toad's designation."

"I see," said I, "the president of this mining company signs himself A. L. Fredericks. I was wondering—"

"Let me see that stock," said Jeff quickly, almost snatching it from me.

To mitigate, even though slightly, the embarrassment I summoned the waiter and ordered another bottle of the Barbera. I thought it was the least I could do.

John Galsworthy (1867–1933)

Quality

I knew him from the days of my extreme youth, because he made my father's boots; inhabiting with his elder brother two little shops let into one, in a small by-street—now no more, but then most fashionably placed in the West End.

That tenement had a certain quiet distinction; there was no sign upon its face that he made for any of the Royal Family— merely his own German name of Gessler Brothers; and in the window a few pairs of boots. I remember that it always troubled me to account for those unvarying boots in the window, for he made only what was ordered, reaching nothing down, and it seemed so inconceivable that what he made could ever have failed to fit. Had he bought them to put there? That, too, seemed inconceivable. He would never have tolerated in his house leather on which he had not worked himself. Besides, they were too beautiful—the pair of pumps, so inexpressibly slim, the patent leathers with cloth tops, making water come into one's mouth, the tall brown riding boots with marvellous sooty glow, as if, though new, they had been worn a hundred years. Those pairs could only have been made by one who saw before him the Soul of Boot—so truly were they prototypes incarnating the very spirit of all foot-gear. These thoughts, of course, came to me later, though even when I was promoted to him, at the age of perhaps fourteen, some inkling haunted me of the dignity of himself and brother. For to make boots—such boots as he made—seemed to me then, and still seems to me, mysterious and wonderful.

I remember well my shy remark, one day, while stretching out to him my youthful foot:

"Isn't it awfully hard to do, Mr. Gessler?"

And his answer, given with a sudden smile from out of the sardonic redness of his beard: "Id is an Ardt!"

Himself, he was a little as if made from leather, with his yellow crinkly face, and crinkly reddish hair and beard, and neat folds slanting down his cheeks to the corners of his mouth, and his guttural and one-toned voice; for leather is a sardonic substance, and stiff and slow of purpose. And that was the character of his face, save that his eyes, which were gray-blue, had in them the simple gravity of one secretly possessed by the Ideal. His elder brother was so very like him—though watery, paler in every way, with a great industry—that sometimes in early days I was not quite sure of him until the interview was over. Then I knew that it was he, if the words, "I will ask my brudder," had not been spoken; and, that, if they had, it was his elder brother.

When one grew old and wild and ran up bills, one somehow never ran them up with Gessler Brothers. It would not have seemed becoming to go in there and stretch out one's foot to that blue iron-spectacled glance, owing him for more than—say—two pairs, just the comfortable reassurance that one was still his client.

For it was not possible to go to him very often—his boots lasted terribly, having something beyond the temporary—some, as it were, essence of boot stitched into them.

One went in, not as into most shops, in the mood of: "Please serve me, and let me go!" but restfully, as one enters a church; and, sitting on the single wooden chair, waited—for there was never anybody there. Soon, over the top edge of that sort of well—rather dark, and smelling soothingly of leather—which formed the shop, there would be seen his face, or that of his elder brother, peering down. A guttural sound, and the tip-tap of bast slippers beating the narrow wooden stairs, and he would stand before one without coat, a little bent, in leather apron, with sleeves turned back, blinking—as if awakened from some dream of boots, or like an owl surprised in daylight and annoyed at this interruption.

And I would say: "How do you do, Mr. Gessler? Could you make me a pair of Russia leather boots?"

Without a word he would leave me, retiring whence he came, or into the other portion of the shop, and I could continue to rest in the wooden chair, inhaling the incense of his trade. Soon he would come back, holding in his thin, veined hand a piece of gold-brown leather. With eyes fixed on it, he would remark: "What a beaudiful biece!" When I, too, had admired it, he would speak again. "When do you wand dem?" And I would answer: "Oh! As soon as you conveniently can." And he would say: "Tomorrow fordnighd?" Or if he were his elder brother: "I will ask my brudder!"

Then I would murmur: "Thank you! Good-morning, Mr. Gessler." "Goot-morning!" he would reply, still looking at the leather in his hand. And as I moved to the door, I would hear the tip-tap of his bast slippers restoring him, up the stairs, to his dream of boots. But if it were some new kind of foot-gear that he had not yet made me, then indeed he would observe ceremony—divesting me of my boot and holding it long in his hand, looking at it with eyes at once critical and loving, as if recalling the glow with which he had created it, and rebuking the way in which one had disorganized this masterpiece. Then, placing my foot on a piece of paper, he would two or three times tickle the outer edges with a pencil and pass his nervous fingers over my toes, feeling himself into the heart of my requirements.

I cannot forget that day on which I had occasion to say to him: "Mr. Gessler, that last pair of town walking-boots creaked, you know."

He looked at me for a time without replying, as if expecting me to withdraw or qualify the statement, then said:

"Id shouldn'd 'ave greaked."

"It did, I'm afraid."

"You goddem wed before dey found demsleves?"

"I don't think so."

At that he lowered his eyes, as if hunting for memory of those boots, and I felt sorry I had mentioned this grave thing.

"Zend dem back!" he said; "I will look at dem."

A feeling of compassion for my creaking boots surged up in me, so well could I imagine the sorrowful long curiosity of regard which he would bend on them.

"Zome boods," he said slowly, "are bad from birdt. If I can do noding wid dem, I dake dem off your bill."

Once (once only) I went absent-mindedly into his shop in a pair of boots bought in an emergency at some large firm's. He took my order without showing me any leather, and I could feel his eyes penetrating the inferior integument of my foot. At last he said:

"Dose are nod by boods."

The tone was not one of anger, nor of sorrow, not even of contempt, but there was in it something quiet that froze the blood. He put his hand down and pressed a finger on the place where the left boot, endeavoring to be fashionable, was not quite comfortable.

"Id 'urds you dere," he said. "Dose big virms 'ave no self-respect. Drash!" And then, as if something had given way within him, he spoke long and bitterly. It was the only time I ever heard him discuss the conditions and hardships of his trade.

"Dey get id all," he said, "dey get id by adverdisement, nod by work. Dey dake it away from us, who lofe our boods. Id gomes to this—bresently I haf no work. Every year id gets less—you will see." And looking at his lined face I saw things I had never noticed before, bitter things and bitter struggle—and what a lot of gray hairs there seemed suddenly in his red beard!

As best I could, I explained the circumstances of the purchase of those ill-omened boots. But his face and voice made so deep impression that during the next few minutes I ordered many pairs. Nemesis fell! They lasted more terribly than ever. And I was not able conscientiously to go to him for nearly two years.

When at last I went I was surprised to find that outside one of the two little windows of his shop another name was painted, also that of a bootmaker—making, of course, for the Royal Family. The old familiar boots, no longer in dignified isolation, were huddled in the single window. Inside, the now contracted well of the one little shop was more scented and darker than ever. And it was longer than usual, too, before a face peered down, and the tip-tap of the bast slippers began. At last he stood before me, and, gazing through those rusty iron spectacles, said:

"Mr.——, isn'd it?"

"Ah! Mr. Gessler," I stammered, "but your boots are really *too* good, you know! See, these are quite decent still!" And I stretched out to him my foot. He looked at it.

"Yes," he said, "beople do nod wand good boods, id seems."

To get away from his reproachful eyes and voice I hastily remarked: "What have you done to your shop?"

He answered quietly: "Id was too exbensif. Do you wand some boods?"

I ordered three pairs, though I had only wanted two, and quickly left. I had, I do not know quite what feeling of being part, in his mind, of a conspiracy against him; or not perhaps so much against him as against his idea of boot. One does not, I suppose, care to feel like that; for it was again many months before my next visit to his shop, paid, I remember, with the feeling: "Oh! well, I can't leave the old boy—so here goes! Perhaps it'll be his elder brother!"

For his elder brother, I knew, had not character enough to reproach me, even dumbly.

And, to my relief, in the shop there did appear to be his elder brother, handling a piece of leather.

"Well, Mr. Gessler," I said, "how are you?"

He came close, and peered at me.

"I am breddy well," he said slowly; "but my elder brudder is dead."

And I saw that it was indeed himself—but how aged and wan! And never before had I heard him mention his brother. Much shocked, I murmured: "Oh! I am sorry!"

"Yes," he answered, "he was a good man, he made a good bood; but he is dead." And he touched the top of his head, where the hair had suddenly gone as thin as it had been on that of his poor brother, to indicate, I suppose, the cause of death. "He could nod ged over losing de oder shop. Do you wand any boods?" And he held up the leather in his hand: "Id's a beautiful biece."

I ordered several pairs. It was very long before they came—but they were better than ever. One simply could not wear them out. And soon after that I went abroad.

It was over a year before I was again in London. And the first shop I went to was my old friend's. I had left a man of sixty, I came back to one of seventy-five, pinched and worn and tremulous, who genuinely, this time, did not at first know me.

"Oh! Mr. Gessler," I said, sick at heart; "how splendid your boots are! See, I've been wearing this pair nearly all the time I've been abroad; and they're not half worn out, are they?"

He looked long at my boots—a pair of Russia leather, and his face seemed to regain steadiness. Putting his hand on my instep, he said:

"Do dey vid you here? I 'ad drouble wid dat bair, I remember."

I assured him that they had fitted beautifully.

"Do you wand any boods?" he said. "I can make dem quickly; id is a slack dime."

I answered: "Please, please! I want boots all round—every kind!"

"I will make a vresh model. Your food must be bigger." And with utter slowness, he traced round my foot, and felt my toes, only once looking up to say:

"Did I dell you my brudder was dead?"

To watch him was painful, so feeble had he grown; I was glad to get away.

I had given those boots up, when one evening they came. Opening the parcel, I set the four pairs in a row. Then one by one I tried them on. There was no doubt about it. In shape and fit, in finish and quality of leather, they were the best he had ever made me. And in the mouth of one of the Town walking-boots I found his bill. The amount was the same as usual, but it gave me quite a shock. He had never before sent it in till quarter day. I flew down-stairs, and wrote a cheque, and posted it at once with my own hand.

A week later, passing the little street, I thought I would go in and tell him how splendidly the new boots fitted. But when I came to where his shop had been, his name was gone. Still there, in the window, were the slim pumps, the patent leathers with cloth tops, the sooty riding boots.

I went in, very much disturbed. In the two little shops—again made into one—was a young man with an English face.

"Mr. Gessler in?" I said.

He gave me a strange, ingratiating look.

"No, sir," he said, "no. But we can attend to anything with pleasure. We've taken the shop over. You've seen our name, no doubt, next door. We make for some very good people."

"Yes, yes," I said; "but Mr. Gessler?"

"Oh!" he answered; "dead."

"Dead! But I only received these boots from him last Wednesday week."

"Ah!" he said; "a shockin' go. Poor old man starved 'imself."

"Good God!"

"Slow starvation, the doctor called it! You see he went to work in such a way! Would keep the shop on; wouldn't have a soul touch his boots except himself. When he got an order, it took him such a time. People won't wait. He lost everybody. And there he'd sit, goin' on and on—I will say that for him—not a man in London made a better boot! But look at the competition! He never advertised! Would 'ave the best leather, too, and do it all 'imself. Well, there it is. What could you expect with his ideas?"

"But starvation——!"

"That may be a bit flowery, as the sayin' is—but I know myself he was sittin' over his boots day and night, to the very last. You see I used to watch him. Never gave 'imself time to eat; never had a penny in the house. All went in rent and leather.

How he lived so long I don't know. He regular let his fire go out. He was a character. But he made good boots."

"Yes," I said, "he made good boots."

And I turned and went out quickly, for I did not want that youth to know that I could hardly see.

James Thurber (1894–1961)

The Catbird Seat

Mr. Martin bought the pack of Camels on Monday night in the most crowded cigar store on Broadway. It was theatre time and seven or eight men were buying cigarettes. The clerk didn't even glance at Mr. Martin, who put the pack in his overcoat pocket and went out. If any of the staff at F & S had seen him buy the cigarettes, they would have been astonished, for it was generally known that Mr. Martin did not smoke, and never had. No one saw him.

It was just a week to the day since Mr. Martin had decided to "rub out" Mrs. Ulgine Barrows. The term "rub out" pleased him because it suggested nothing more than the correction of an error—in this case an error of Mr. Fitweiler. Mr. Martin had spent each night of the past week working out his plan and examining it. As he walked home now he went over it again. For the hundredth time he resented the element of imprecision, the margin of guesswork that entered into the business. The project as he had worked it out was casual and bold, the risks were considerable. Something might go wrong anywhere along the line. And therein lay the cunning of his scheme. No one would ever see in it the cautious, painstaking hand of Erwin Martin, head of the filing department at F & S, of whom Mr. Fitweiler had once said, "Man is fallible but Martin isn't." No one would see his hand, that is, unless it were caught in the act.

Sitting in his apartment, drinking a glass of milk, Mr. Martin reviewed his case against Mrs. Ulgine Barrows, as he had every night for seven nights. He began at the beginning. Her quacking voice and braying laugh had first profaned the halls of F & S on March 7, 1941 (Mr. Martin had a head for dates). Old Roberts, the personnel chief, had introduced her as the newly appointed special adviser to the president of the firm, Mr. Fitweiler. The woman had appalled Mr. Martin instantly, but he hadn't shown it. He had given her his dry hand, a look of studious concentration, and a faint smile. "Well," she had said, looking at the papers on his desk, "are you lifting the oxcart out of the ditch?" As Mr. Martin recalled that moment, over his milk, he squirmed slightly. He must keep his mind on her crimes as a special adviser, not on her peccadillos as a personality. This he found difficult to do, in spite of entering an objection and sustaining it. The faults of the woman as a woman kept chattering on in his mind like an unruly witness. She had, for almost two years now, baited him. In the halls, in the elevator, even in his own office, into which she romped now and then like a circus horse, she was constantly shouting these silly questions at him. "Are you lifting the oxcart out of the ditch? Are you tearing up the pea patch? Are you hollering down the rain barrel? Are you scraping around the bottom of the pickle barrel? Are you sitting in the catbird seat?"

It was Joey Hart, one of Mr. Martin's two assistants, who had explained what the gibberish meant. "She must be a Dodger fan," he had said. "Red Barber announces the Dodger games over the radio and he uses those expressions—picked 'em up down South." Joey had gone on to explain one or two. "Tearing up the pea patch" meant going on a rampage; "sitting in the catbird seat" meant sitting pretty, like a batter with three balls and no strikes on him. Mr. Martin dismissed all this with an effort. It had been annoying, it had driven him near to distraction, but he was too solid a man to be moved to murder by anything so childish. It was fortunate, he reflected as he passed on to the important charges against Mrs. Barrows, that he had stood up under it so well. He had maintained always an outward appearance of polite tolerance. "Why, I even believe you like the woman," Miss Paird, his other assistant, had once said to him. He had simply smiled.

A gavel rapped in Mr. Martin's mind and the case proper was resumed. Mrs. Ulgine Barrows stood charged with willful, blatant, and persistent attempts to destroy the efficiency and system of F & S. It was competent, material, and relevant to review her advent and rise to power. Mr. Martin had got the story from Miss Paird, who seemed always able to find things out. According to her, Mrs. Barrows had met Mr. Fitweiler at a party, where she had rescued him from the embraces of a powerfully built drunken man who had mistaken the president of F & S for a famous retired Middle Western football coach. She had led him to a sofa and somehow worked upon him a monstrous magic. The aging gentleman had jumped to the conclusion there and then that this was a woman of singular attainments, equipped to bring out the best in him and in the firm. A week later he had introduced her into F & S as his special adviser. On that day confusion got its foot in the door. After Miss Tyson, Mr. Brundage, and Mr. Bartlett had been fired and Mr. Munson had taken his hat and stalked out, mailing in his resignation later, old Roberts had been emboldened to speak to Mr. Fitweiler. He mentioned that Mr. Munson's department had been "a little disrupted" and hadn't they perhaps better resume the old system there? Mr. Fitweiler had said certainly not. He had the greatest faith in Mrs. Barrows' ideas. "They require a little seasoning, a little seasoning, is all," he had added. Mr. Roberts had given it up. Mr. Martin reviewed in detail all the changes wrought by Mrs. Barrows. She had begun chipping at the cornices of the firm's edifice and now she was swinging at the foundation stones with a pickaxe.

Mr. Martin came now, in his summing up, to the afternoon of Monday, November 2, 1942—just one week ago. On that day, at 3 P.M., Mrs. Barrows had bounced into his office. "Boo!" she had yelled. "Are you scraping around the bottom of the pickle barrel?" Mr. Martin had looked at her from under his green eyeshade, saying nothing. She had begun to wander about the office, taking it in with her great, popping eyes. "Do you really need *all* these filing cabinets?" she had demanded suddenly. Mr. Martin's heart had jumped. "Each of these files," he had said, keeping his voice even, "plays an indispensable part in the system of F & S." She had brayed at him, "Well, don't tear up the pea patch!" and gone to the door. From there she had bawled, "But you sure have got a lot of fine scrap in here!" Mr. Martin could no longer doubt that the finger was on his beloved department. Her pickaxe was on the upswing, poised for the first blow. It had not come yet; he had received no blue memo from the enchanted Mr. Fitweiler bearing nonsensical instructions deriving from the obscene woman. But there was no doubt in Mr. Martin's mind that one would be forthcoming. He must act quickly. Already a precious week had gone by. Mr. Martin stood up in his living room, still holding his milk glass. "Gentlemen of the jury," he said to himself, "I demand the death penalty for this horrible person."

The next day Mr. Martin followed his routine, as usual. He polished his glasses more often and once sharpened an already sharp pencil, but not even Miss Paird noticed. Only once did he catch sight of his victim; she swept past him in the hall with a patronizing "Hi!" At five-thirty he walked home, as usual, and had a glass of milk, as usual. He had never drunk anything stronger in his life—unless you could count ginger ale. The late Sam Schlosser, the S of F & S, had praised Mr. Martin at a staff meeting several years before for his temperate habits. "Our most efficient worker neither drinks nor smokes," he had said. "The results speak for themselves." Mr. Fitweiler had sat by, nodding approval.

Mr. Martin was still thinking about the red-letter day as he walked over to the Schrafft's on Fifth Avenue near Forty-Sixth Street. He got there, as he always did, at eight o'clock. He finished his dinner and the financial page of the *Sun* at a quarter to nine, as he always did. It was his custom after dinner to take a walk. This time he walked down Fifth Avenue at a casual pace. His gloved hands felt moist and warm, his forehead cold. He transferred the Camels from his overcoat to a jacket pocket. He wondered, as he did so, if they did not represent an unnecessary note of strain. Mrs. Barrows smoked only Luckies. It was his idea to puff a few puffs on a Camel (after the rubbing-out), stub it out in the ashtray holding her lipstick-stained Luckies, and thus drag a small red herring across the trail. Perhaps it was not a good idea. It would take time. He might even choke, too loudly.

Mr. Martin had never seen the house on West Twelfth Street where Mrs. Barrows lived, but he had a clear enough picture of it. Fortunately, she had bragged to everybody about her ducky first-floor apartment in the perfectly darling three-story red-brick. There would be no doorman or other attendants; just the tenants of the second and third floors. As he walked along, Mr. Martin realized that he would get there before nine-thirty. He had considered walking north on Fifth Avenue from Schrafft's to a point from which it would take him until ten o'clock to reach the house. At that hour people were less likely to be coming in or going out. But the procedure would have made an awkward loop in the straight thread of his casualness, and he had abandoned it. It was impossible to figure when people would be entering or leaving the house, anyway. There was a great risk at any hour. If he ran into anybody, he would simply have to place the rubbing-out of Ulgine Barrows in the inactive file forever. The same thing would hold true if there were someone in her apartment. In that case he would just say that he had been passing by, recognized her charming house, and thought to drop in.

It was eighteen minutes after nine when Mr. Martin turned into Twelfth Street. A man passed him, and a man and a woman, talking. There was no one within fifty paces when he came to the house, halfway down the block. He was up the steps and in the small vestibule in no time, pressing the bell under the card that said "Mrs. Ulgine Barrows." When the clicking in the lock started, he jumped forward against the door. He got inside fast, closing the door behind him. A bulb in a lantern hung from the hall ceiling on a chain seemed to give a monstrously bright light. There was nobody on the stair, which went up ahead of him along the left wall. A door opened down the hall in the wall on the right. He went toward it swiftly, on tiptoe.

"Well, for God's sake, look who's here!" bawled Mrs. Barrows, and her braying laugh rang out like the report of a shotgun. He rushed past her like a football tackle, bumping her. "Hey, quit shoving!" she said, closing the door behind them. They were in her living room, which seemed to Mr. Martin to be lighted by a hundred lamps. "What's after you?" she said. "You're as jumpy as a goat." He found he was unable to speak. His heart was wheezing in his throat. "I—yes," he finally brought out. She was jabbering and laughing as she started to help him off with his coat. "No, no," he said. "I'll put it here." He took it off and put it on a chair near the door. "Your hat and gloves, too," she said. "You're in a lady's house." He put his hat on top of the coat. Mrs. Barrows seemed larger than he had thought. He kept his gloves on. "I was passing by," he said. "I recognized—is there anyone here?" She laughed louder than ever. "No," she said, "we're all alone. You're as white as a sheet, you funny man. Whatever *has* come over you? I'll mix you a toddy." She started toward a door across the room. "Scotch-and-soda be all right? But say, you don't drink, do you?" She turned and gave him her amused look. Mr. Martin pulled himself together. "Scotch-and-soda will be all right," he heard himself say. He could hear her laughing in the kitchen.

Mr. Martin looked quickly around the living room for the weapon. He had counted on finding one there. There were andirons and a poker and something in a corner that looked like an Indian club. None of them would do. It couldn't be that way. He began to pace around. He came to a desk. On it lay a metal paper knife with an ornate handle. Would it be sharp enough? He reached for it and knocked over a small brass jar. Stamps spilled out of it and it fell to the floor with a clatter. "Hey," Mrs. Barrows yelled from the kitchen, "are you tearing up the pea patch?" Mr. Martin gave a strange laugh. Picking up the knife, he tried its point against his left wrist. It was blunt, it wouldn't do.

When Mrs. Barrows reappeared, carrying two highballs, Mr. Martin, standing there with his gloves on, became acutely conscious of the fantasy he had wrought. Cigarettes in his pocket, a drink prepared for him—it was all too grossly improbable. It was more than that; it was impossible. Somewhere in the back of his mind a vague idea stirred, sprouted. "For heaven's sake, take off those gloves," said Mrs. Barrows. "I always wear them in the house," said Mr. Martin. The idea began to bloom, strange and wonderful. She put the glasses on a coffee table in front of a sofa and sat on the sofa. "Come over here, you odd little man," she said. Mr. Martin went over and sat beside her. It was difficult getting a cigarette out of the pack of Camels, but he managed it. She held a match for him, laughing. "Well," she said, handing him his drink, "this is perfectly marvelous. You with a drink and a cigarette."

Mr. Martin puffed, not too awkwardly, and took a gulp of the highball. "I drink and smoke all the time," he said. He clinked his glass against hers. "Here's nuts to that old windbag, Fitweiler," he said, and gulped again. The stuff tasted awful, but he made no grimace. "Really, Mr. Martin," she said, her voice and posture changing, "you are insulting our employer." Mrs. Barrows was now all special adviser to the president. "I am preparing a bomb," said Mr. Martin, "which will blow the old goat higher than hell." He had only a little of the drink, which was not strong. It couldn't be that. "Do you take dope or something?" Mrs. Barrows asked coldly. "Heroin," said Mr. Martin. "I'll be coked to the gills when I bump that old buzzard off." "Mr. Martin!" she shouted, getting to her feet. "That will be all of that. You must go at once." Mr. Martin took another swallow of his drink. He tapped his cigarette out in the ashtray and put the pack of Camels on the coffee table. Then he got up. She stood glaring at him. He walked over and put on his hat and coat. "Not a word about this," he said, and laid an index finger against his lips. All Mrs. Barrows could bring out was "Really!" Mr. Martin put his hand on the doorknob. "I'm sitting in the catbird seat," he said. He stuck his tongue out at her and left. Nobody saw him go.

Mr. Martin got to his apartment, walking, well before eleven. No one saw him go in. He had two glasses of milk after brushing his teeth, and he felt elated. It wasn't tipsiness, because he hadn't been tipsy. Anyway, the walk had worn off all effects of the whiskey. He got in bed and read a magazine for a while. He was asleep before midnight.

Mr. Martin got to the office at eight-thirty the next morning, as usual. At a quarter to nine, Ulgine Barrows, who had never before arrived at work before ten, swept into his office. "I'm reporting to Mr. Fitweiler now!" she shouted. "If he turns you over to the police, it's no more than you deserve!" Mr. Martin gave her a look of shocked surprise. "I beg your pardon?" he said. Mrs. Barrows snorted and bounced out of the room, leaving Miss Paird and Joey Hart staring after her. "What's the matter with that old devil now?" asked Miss Paird. "I have no idea," said Mr. Martin, resuming his work. The other two looked at him and then at each other. Miss Paird got up and went out. She walked slowly past the closed door of Mr. Fitweiler's office. Mrs. Barrows was yelling inside, but she was not braying. Miss Paird could not hear what the woman was saying. She went back to her desk.

Forty-five minutes later, Mrs. Barrows left the president's office and went into her own, shutting the door. It wasn't until half an hour later that Mr. Fitweiler sent for Mr. Martin. The head of the filing department, neat, quiet, attentive, stood in front of the old man's desk. Mr. Fitweiler was pale and nervous. He took his glasses off and twiddled them. He made a small, bruffing sound in his throat. "Martin," he said, "you have been with us more than twenty years." "Twenty-two, sir," said Mr. Martin. "In that time," pursued the president, "your work and your—uh—manner have been exemplary." "I trust so, sir," said Mr. Martin. "I have understood, Martin," said Mr. Fitweiler, "that you have never taken a drink or smoked." "That is correct, sir," said Mr. Martin. "Ah, yes." Mr. Fitweiler polished his glasses. "You may describe what you did after leaving the office yesterday, Martin," he said. Mr. Martin allowed less than a second for his bewildered pause. "Certainly, sir," he said. "I walked home. Then I went to Schrafft's for dinner. Afterward I walked home again. I went to bed early, sir, and read a magazine for a while. I was asleep before eleven." "Ah, yes," said Mr. Fitweiler again. He was silent for a moment, searching for the proper words to say to the head of the filing department. "Mrs. Barrows," he said finally, "Mrs. Barrows has worked hard, Martin, very hard. It grieves me to report that she has suffered a severe breakdown. It has taken the form of a persecution complex accompanied by distressing hallucinations." "I am very sorry, sir," said Mr. Martin. "Mrs. Barrows is under the delusion," continued Mr. Fitweiler, "that you visited her last evening and behaved yourself in an—uh—unseemly manner." He raised his hand to silence Mr. Martin's little pained outcry. "It is the nature of these psychological diseases," Mr.

Fitweiler said, "to fix upon the least likely and most innocent party as the—uh—source of persecution. These matters are not for the lay mind to grasp, Martin. I've just had my psychiatrist, Doctor Fitch, on the phone. He would not, of course, commit himself, but he made enough generalizations to substantiate my suspicions. I suggested to Mrs. Barrows, when she had completed her—uh—story to me this morning, that she visit Doctor Fitch, for I suspected a condition at once. She flew, I regret to say, into a rage, and demanded—uh—requested that I call you on the carpet. You may not know, Martin, but Mrs. Barrows had planned a reorganization of your department—subject to my approval, of course, subject to my approval. This brought you, rather than anyone else, to her mind—but again that is a phenomenon for Doctor Fitch and not for us. So, Martin, I am afraid Mrs. Barrows' usefulness here is at an end." "I am dreadfully sorry, sir," said Mr. Martin.

It was at this point that the door to the office blew open with the suddenness of a gas-main explosion and Mrs. Barrows catapulted through it. "Is the little rat denying it?" she screamed. "He can't get away with that!" Mr. Martin got up and moved discreetly to a point beside Mr. Fitweiler's chair. "You drank and smoked at my apartment," she bawled at Mr. Martin, "and you know it! You called Mr. Fitweiler an old windbag and said you were going to blow him up when you got coked to the gills on your heroin!" She stopped yelling to catch her breath and a new glint came into her popping eyes. "If you weren't such a drab, ordinary little man," she said. "I'd think you'd planned it all. Sticking your tongue out, saying you were sitting in the catbird seat, because you thought no one would believe me when I told it! My God, it's really too perfect!" She brayed loudly and hysterically, and the fury was on her again. She glared at Mr. Fitweiler. "Can't you see how he has tricked up, you old fool? Can't you see his little game?" But Mr. Fitweiler had been surreptitiously pressing all the buttons under the top of his desk and employees of F & S began pouring into the room. "Stockton," said Mr. Fitweiler, "you and Fishbein will take Mrs. Barrows to her home. Mrs. Powell, you will go with them." Stockton, who had played a little football in high school, blocked Mrs. Barrows as she made for Mr. Martin. It took him and Fishbein together to force her out of the door into the hall, crowded with stenographers and office boys. She was still screaming imprecations at Mr. Martin, tangled and contradictory imprecations. The hubbub finally died down the corridor.

"I regret that this has happened," said Mr. Fitweiler. "I shall ask you to dismiss it from your mind, Martin." "Yes, sir," said Mr. Martin, anticipating his chief's "That will be all" by moving to the door. "I will dismiss it." He went out and shut the door, and his step was light and quick in the hall. When he entered his department he had slowed down to his customary gait, and he walked quietly across the room to the W20 file, wearing a look of studious concentration.

ESSAYS

Montesquieu (1689–1755)

Letters 105 and 106

Letter 105   Rhedi to Usbek, at Paris[1]

You wrote at some length, in one of your letters, about the development of the arts, science and technology in the West. You will think me a barbarian, but I do not know whether the utility that we derive from them compensates mankind for the abuse that is constantly made of them.

I have heard it said that the invention of explosives alone had deprived every nation in Europe of its freedom. Kings, unable any long to entrust the protection of fortified towns to the townspeople, since they would have surrendered at the first cannonball, had a pretext for maintaining large numbers of regular troops, which they used subsequently to oppress their subjects.

You are aware that since the invention of gunpowder no fort is impregnable: which means, Usbek, that there is no asylum on earth against injustice and violence.

I am always afraid that they will eventually succeed in discovering some secret which will provide a quicker way of making men die, and exterminate whole countries and nations.

You have read the historians; you should look at them carefully. Almost every kingdom was established only because the arts and sciences were unknown, and destroyed only because they were cultivated to excess. We have an example familiar to us in the ancient Persian empire.

I have not been in Europe long, but I have heard intelligent people speak of the damage done by chemistry. It seems to be

---

1. Rhedi and Usbek are two Persians traveling for the first time in Europe. The letters they exchange contain comments and observations on European culture.

a fourth scourge of mankind, which harms and destroys men piecemeal, but continually, while war, plague and famine destroy them wholesale, but at intervals.

In what way has the invention of the compass, and the discovery of so many peoples, been useful, except in that they have conveyed to us not so much their wealth, but their diseases? Gold and silver had been accepted, by general agreement, as a means of paying for all goods and as a guarantee of their value, for the reason that these metals are rare and unfit for any other use: why then was it necessary for them to become commoner, and, in order to indicate the value of merchandise, for there to be two or three signs instead of one? It was simply more cumbersome.

But this invention was absolutely pernicious in another respect to the countries which were discovered. Whole nations were destroyed, and men who escaped death were reduced to such abject slavery that we Muslims shudder to think of it.

Happy is the ignorance of the children of Mohammed! It is a quality which, by its attractive ingenuousness, so dear to our holy Prophet, always reminds me of the simplicity characteristic of olden times, and the serenity which reigned in the hearts of our first fathers!

From Venice, the 5th of the moon of Ramadan, 1717

Letter 106   Usbek to Rhedi, at Venice

Either you do not believe in what you are saying, or else what you do is better than what you say. You leave your country in order to educate yourself, and you despise every type of education; in order to become cultivated, you go to a country where the arts are encouraged, and you consider them pernicious.

May I say, Rhedi, that I am more in agreement with you than you are yourself.

Have you ever thought about the state of barbarism and misery into which we should be plunged if knowledge and culture were to be lost—there is no need to imagine it, you could see for yourself: there are still tribes in the world among whom a reasonably well-educated ape could live and be respected; he would be on roughly the same level as the others; his ideas would not be considered peculiar, or his character strange; he would get by like anyone else, and indeed would stand out because of his gentle nature.

You say that founders of empires have almost all been ignorant of the arts of mankind. I will not deny that there have been barbarian races which, like rushing torrents, have managed to spread across the earth and overrun the best-organized kingdoms with their armies; but you must not forget that they have either learnt technical and artistic skills, or else have made the conquered peoples cultivate them; otherwise, their power would have vanished like the sound of thunder and storms.

You say that you are afraid of the discovery of some method of destruction that is crueller than those which are used now. No; if such a fateful invention came to be discovered, it would soon be banned by international law; by the unanimous consent of evey country the discovery would be buried. It is not in the interest of rulers to make conquests by such means: they ought to look for subjects, not territory.

You protest at the invention of gunpowder and shells; you find it surprising that there are no longer any impregnable strongholds; that is to say, you find it surprising that wars are over more quickly today than they used to be in the past.

You must have noticed in reading history that since the invention of gunpowder battles are much less bloody than they were, because there is hardly any hand-to-hand fighting.

And even if a particular instance were found in which some human skill was harmful, should it be rejected on that account? Do you think, Rhedi, that the religion brought down from Heaven by our holy Prophet is pernicious because one day it will be used to confound the faithless Christians?

You believe that knowledge and culture make nations soft, and therefore cause empires to fall, and you refer to the destruction of the ancient Persian empire as being due to its effeteness; but this example is far from being conclusive, since the Greeks, who conquered the Persians so many times, and subjugated them, cultivated the arts much more assiduously than they did.

When people say that the arts of civilization make men effeminate, they cannot at any rate be referring to the men who practise them; for they are never idle, and of all the vices idleness is the one which does most to diminish a man's courage.

The question therefore concerns only those who benefit from their skills. But since in a developed country those who enjoy the products of one skill are obliged to practise another if they are not to be reduced to poverty and disgrace, it follows that idleness and effeminacy are incompatible with the arts of civilization.

Paris, which is perhaps the most sensuous town in the world, is where pleasures are most subtly cultivated, but it is perhaps also the place where one leads the hardest life. For one man to live in luxury, a hundred others must work without respite. A woman gets it into her head that she must wear a particular outfit on some occasion, and at once it becomes impossible for fifty craftsmen to get any sleep or have leisure to eat and drink; she gives her commands and is obeyed more promptly than our monarch, since self-interest is the greatest monarch on earth.

This enthusiasm for work, this passion for getting rich, is transmitted from class to class, from workmen up to great nobles. Nobody likes to be poorer than somebody whom he recently saw just below him. In Paris you can see a man with enough to live on till Judgment Day working all the time, and running the risk of shortening his life, in order, he says, to get enough to live on.

This attitude is spreading through the nation: the scene is one of universal industry and ingenuity. Where then is the effeminate nation which you talk about so much?

Let us assume, Rhedi, that there was a kingdom in which no skills were allowed except those essential to agriculture, which in themselves are very numerous, and that all those serving only to produce fancy goods and luxuries were banned. I maintain that this state would be one of the most wretched on earth.

Even if the inhabitants had enough resolution to do without all the things that their requirements call for, the population would decrease all the time, and the nation would become so weak that any other power, however small, would be able to conquer it.

It would be easy for me to go into great detail and show you that the incomes of private individuals would be reduced almost to nothing, and that the same thing would therefore happen to the prince's. Economic relationships between citizens would virtually cease; there would be an end of the mutual exchange of money and progressive transference of earnings which derives from the dependence of one trade on others. Each individual citizen would live on his land, taking from it exactly what he needed, and no more, so as not to die of hunger. But since in some cases that would correspond to less than a twentieth of the national income, the number of inhabitants would necessarily decrease in the same ratio, and only a twentieth would remain.

It is important to remember how much income can be earned by professional skill. Capital provides its owner with an annual income amounting to a twentieth of its value, but with a pound's worth of paints an artist can produce a picture which will earn him fifty. The same can be said of jewellers, wool and silk workers, and every type of craftsman.

From all this, Rhedi, it must be concluded that, for a king to remain powerful, his subjects must live luxuriously. He must take as much care to provide them with every sort of superfluity as to provide them with the necessities of life.

From Paris, the 14th of the moon of Shawall, 1717

Henry David Thoreau (1817–1862)

Life Without Principle

At a lyceum, not long since, I felt that the lecturer had chosen a theme too foreign to himself, and so failed to interest me as much as he might have done. He described things not in or near to his heart, but toward his extremities and superficies. There was, in this sense, no truly central or centralizing thought in the lecture. I would have had him deal with his privatest experience, as the poet does. The greatest compliment that was ever paid me was when one asked me what

I *thought*, and attended to my answer. I am surprised, as well as delighted, when this happens, it is such a rare use he would make of me, as if he were acquainted with the tool. Commonly, if men want anything of me, it is only to know how many acres I make of their land,—since I am a surveyor,—or, at most, what trivial news I have burdened myself with. They never will go to law for my meat; they prefer the shell. A man once came a considerable distance to ask me to lecture on Slavery; but on conversing with him, I found that he and his clique expected seven eighths of the lecture to be theirs, and only one eighth mine; so I declined. I take it for granted, when I am invited to lecture anywhere,—for I have a little experience in that business,—that there is a desire to hear what I *think* on some subject, though I may be the greatest fool in the country,—and not that I should say pleasant things merely, or such as the audience will assent to; and I resolve, accordingly, that I will give them a strong dose of myself. They have sent for me, and engaged to pay for me, and I am determined that they shall have me, though I bore them beyond all precedent.

So now I would say something similar to you, my readers. Since *you* are my readers, and I have not been much of a traveller, I will not talk about people a thousand miles off but come as near home as I can. As the time is short, I will leave out all the flattery, and retain all the criticism.

Let us consider the way in which we spend our lives.

This world is a place of business. What an infinite bustle! I am awaked almost every night by the panting of the locomotive. It interrupts my dreams. There is no sabbath. It would be glorious to see mankind at leisure for once. It is nothing but work, work, work. I cannot easily buy a blankbook to write thoughts in; they are commonly ruled for dollars and cents. An Irishman, seeing me making a minute in the fields, took it for granted that I was calculating my wages. If a man was tossed out of a window when an infant, and so made a cripple for life, or scared out of his wits by the Indians, it is regretted chiefly because he was thus incapacitated for—business! I think that there is nothing, not even crime, more opposed to poetry, to philosophy, ay, to life itself, than this incessant business.

There is a coarse and boisterous money-making fellow in the outskirts of our town, who is going to build a bank-wall under the hill along the edge of his meadow. The powers have put this into his head to keep him out of mischief, and he wishes me to spend three weeks digging there with him. The result will be that he will perhaps get some more money to hoard, and leave for his heirs to spend foolishly. If I do this, most will commend me as an industrious and hard-working man; but if I choose to devote myself to certain labors which yield more real profit, though but little money, they may be inclined to look on me as an idler. Nevertheless, as I do not need the police of meaningless labor to regulate me, and do not see anything absolutely praiseworthy in this fellow's undertaking any more than in many an enterprise of our own or foreign governments, however amusing it may be to him or them, I prefer to finish my education at a different school.

If a man walk in the woods for love of them half of each day, he is in danger of being regarded as a loafer; if he spends his whole day as a speculator, shearing off those woods and making earth bald before her time, he is esteemed an industrious and enterprising citizen. As if a town had no interest in its forests but to cut them down!

Most men would feel insulted if it were proposed to employ them in throwing stones over a wall, and then in throwing them back, merely that they might earn their wages. But many are no more worthily employed now. For instance: just after sunrise one summer morning I noticed one of my neighbors walking beside his team, which was slowly drawing a heavy hewn stone swung under the axle, surrounded by an atmosphere of industry—his day's work begun, his brow commenced to sweat, a reproach to all sluggards and idlers—pausing abreast the shoulders of his oxen, and half turning round with a flourish of his merciful whip, while they gained their length on him. And I thought, Such is the labor which the American Congress exists to protect,—honest, manly toil,—honest as the day is long,—that makes his bread taste sweet, and keeps society sweet,—which, all men respect and have consecrated; one of the sacred band, doing the needful, but irksome drudgery. Indeed, I felt a slight reproach, because

I observed this from the window, and was not abroad and stirring about a similar business. The day went by, and at evening I passed the yard of another neighbor, who keeps many servants, and spends much money foolishly, while he adds nothing to the common stock, and there I saw the stone of the morning lying beside a whimsical structure intended to adorn this Lord Timothy Dexter's premises, and the dignity forthwith departed from the teamster's labor, in my eyes. In my opinion, the sun was made to light worthier toil than this. I may add that his employer has since run off, in debt to a good part of the town, and, after passing through Chancery, has settled somewhere else, there to become once more a patron of the arts.

The ways by which you may get money almost without exception lead downward. To have done anything by which you earned money *merely* is to have been truly idle or worse. If the laborer gets no more than the wages which his employer pays him, he is cheated, he cheats himself. If you would get money as a writer or a lecturer, you must be popular, which is to go down perpendicularly. Those services which the community will most readily pay for it is most disagreeable to render. You are paid for being something less than a man. The State does not commonly reward a genius any more wisely. Even the poet-laureate would rather not have to celebrate the accidents of royalty. He must be bribed with a pipe of wine; and perhaps another poet is called away from his muse to gauge that very pipe. As for my own business, even that kind of surveying which I could do with most satisfaction my employers do not want. They would prefer that I should do my work coarsely and not too well, ay, not well enough. When I observe that there are different ways of surveying, my employer commonly asks which will give him the most land, not which is most correct. I once invented a rule for measuring cordwood, and tried to introduce it in Boston; but the measurer there told me that the sellers did not wish to have their wood measured correctly,—that he was already too accurate for them, and therefore they commonly got their wood measured in Charlestown before crossing the bridge.

The aim of the laborer should be, not to get his living, to get "a good job," but to perform well a certain work; and even in a pecuniary sense, it would be economy for a town to pay its laborers so well that they would not feel that they were working for low ends, as for a livelihood merely, but for scientific, or even moral ends. Do not hire a man who does your work for money, but him who does it for love of it.

It is remarkable that there are few men so well employed, so much to their minds, but that a little money or fame would commonly buy them off from their present pursuit. I see advertisements for *active* young men, as if activity were the whole of a young man's capital. Yet I have been surprised when one has with confidence proposed to me, a grown man, to embark in some enterprise of his, as if I had absolutely nothing to do, my life having been a complete failure hitherto. What a doubtful compliment this to pay me! As if he had met me halfway across the ocean beating up against the wind, but bound nowhere, and proposed to me to go along with him! If I did, what do you think the underwriters would say? No, no! I am not without employment at this stage of the voyage. To tell the truth, I saw an advertisement for ablebodied seamen, when I was a boy, sauntering in my native port, and as soon as I became of age I embarked.

The community has no bribe that will tempt a wise man. You may raise money enough to tunnel a mountain, but you cannot raise money enough to hire a man who is minding *his own* business. An efficient and valuable man does what he can, whether the community pay him for it or not. The inefficient offer their inefficiency to the highest bidder, and are forever expecting to be put into office. One would suppose that they were rarely disappointed.

Perhaps I am more than usually jealous with respect to my freedom. I feel that my connection with and obligation to society are still very slight and transient. Those slight labors which afford me a livelihood, and by which it is allowed that I am to some extent serviceable to my contemporaries, are as yet commonly a pleasure to me, and I am not often reminded that they are a necessity. So far I am successful. But I foresee, that, if my wants should be much increased, the labor required to supply them would become a drudgery. If I should sell both my forenoons and afternoons to society, as most appear to do, I am sure that, for me, there would be nothing left worth living for.

I trust that I shall never thus sell my birthright for a mess of pottage. I wish to suggest that a man may be very industrious, and yet not spend his time well. There is no more fatal blunderer than he who consumes the greater part of his life getting his living. All great enterprises are self-supporting. The poet, for instance, must sustain his body by his poetry, as a steam planing-mill feeds its boilers with the shavings it makes. You must get your living by loving. But as it is said of the merchants that ninety-seven in a hundred fail, so the life of men generally, tried by this standard, is a failure, and bankruptcy may be surely prophesied.

Merely to come into the world the heir of a fortune is not to be born, but to be stillborn, rather. To be supported by the charity of friends, or a government-pension,—provided you continue to breathe,—by whatever fine synonyms you describe these relations, is to go into the almshouse. On Sundays the poor debtor goes to church to take an account of stock, and finds, of course, that his outgoes have been greater than his income. In the Catholic Church, especially, they go into chancery, make a clean confession, give up all, and think to start again. Thus men will lie on their backs, talking about the fall of man, and never make an effort to get up.

As for the comparative demand which men make on life, it is an important difference between the two, that the one is satisfied with a level success, that his marks can all be hit by point-blank shots, but the other, however low and unsuccessful his life may be, constantly elevates his aim, though at a very slight angle to the horizon. I should much rather be the last man,—though, as the Orientals say, "Greatness doth not approach him who is forever looking down; and all those who are looking high are growing poor."

It is remarkable that there is little or nothing to be remembered written on the subject of getting a living; how to make getting a living not merely honest and honorable, but altogether inviting and glorious; for if *getting* a living is not so, then living is not. One would think, from looking at literature, that this question had never disturbed a solitary individual's musings. Is it that men are too much disgusted with their experience to speak of it? The lesson of value which money teaches, which the Author of the Universe has taken so much pains to teach us, we are inclined to skip altogether. As for the means of living, it is wonderful how indifferent men of all classes are about it, even reformers, so called,—whether they inherit, or earn, or steal it. I think that Society has done nothing for us in this respect, or at least has undone what she has done. Cold and hunger seem more friendly to my nature than those methods which men have adopted and advise to ward them off.

The title *wise* is, for the most part, falsely applied. How can one be a wise man, if he does not know any better how to live than other men?—if he is only more cunning and intellectually subtle? Does Wisdom work in a treadmill? or does she teach how to succeed *by her example*? Is there any such thing as wisdom not applied to life? Is she merely the miller who grinds the finest logic? It is pertinent to ask if Plato got his *living* in a better way or more successfully than his contemporaries,—or did he succumb to the difficulties of life like other men? Did he seem to prevail over some of them merely by indifference, or by assuming grand airs? or find it easier to live, because his aunt remembered him in her will? The ways in which most men get their living, that is, live, are mere makeshifts, and a shirking of the real business of life,—chiefly because they do not know, but partly because they do not mean, any better.

The rush to California, for instance, and the attitude, not merely of merchants, but of philosophers and prophets, so called, in relation to it, reflect the greatest disgrace on mankind. That so many are ready to live by luck, and so get the means of commanding the labor of others less lucky, without contributing any value to society! And that is called enterprise! I know of no more startling development of the immorality of trade, and all the common modes of getting a living. The philosophy and poetry and religion of such a mankind are not worth the dust of a puff-ball. The hog that gets his living by rooting, stirring up the soil so, would be ashamed of such company. If I could command the wealth of all the worlds by lifting my finger, I would not pay *such* a price for it. . . .

To speak impartially, the best men that I know are not serene, a world in themselves. For the most part, they dwell in forms, and flatter and study effect only more finely than the rest. We select granite for the underpinning of our houses and barns; we build fences of stone; but we do not ourselves rest on an underpinning of granitic truth, the lowest primitive rock. Our sills are rotten. What stuff is the man made of who is not coexistent in our thought with the purest and subtilest truth? I often accuse my finest acquaintances of an immense frivolity; for, while there are manners and compliments we do not meet, we do not teach one another the lessons of honesty and sincerity that the brutes do, or of steadiness and solidity that the rocks do. The fault is commonly mutual, however; for we do not habitually demand any more of each other.

That excitement about Kossuth,[1] consider how characteristic, but superficial, it was!—only another kind of politics or dancing. Men were making speeches to him all over the country, but each expressed only the thought, or the want of thought, of the multitude. No man stood on truth. They were merely banded together, as usual one leaning on another, and all together on nothing; as the Hindoos made the world rest on an elephant, the elephant on a tortoise, and the tortoise on a serpent, and had nothing to put under the serpent. For all fruit of that stir we have the Kossuth hat.

Just so hollow and ineffectual, for the most part, is our ordinary conversation. Surface meets surface. When our life ceases to be inward and private, conversation degenerates into mere gossip. We rarely meet a man who can tell us any news which he has not read in a newspaper, or been told by his neighbor; and, for the most part, the only difference between us and our fellow is that he has seen the newspaper, or been out to tea, and we have not. In proportion as our inward life fails, we go more constantly and desperately to the post-office. You may depend on it, that the poor fellow who walks away with the greatest number of letters, proud of his extensive correspondence, has not heard from himself this long while.

---

1. A Hungarian patriot who visited the United States.

I do not know but it is too much to read one newspaper a week. I have tried it recently, and for so long it seems to me that I have not dwelt in my native region. The sun, the clouds, the snow, the trees say not so much to me. You cannot serve two masters. It requires more than a day's devotion to know and to possess the wealth of a day.

We may well be ashamed to tell what things we have read or heard in our day. I do not know why my news should be so trivial,—considering what one's dreams and expectations are, why the developments should be so paltry. The news we hear, for the most part, is not news to our genius. It is the stalest repetition. You are often tempted to ask why such stress is laid on a particular experience which you have had,—that, after twenty-five years, you should meet Hobbins, Registrar of Deeds, again on the sidewalk. Have you not budged an inch, then? Such is the daily news. Its facts appear to float in the atmosphere, insignificant as the sporules of fungi and impinge on some neglected *thallus*, or surface of our minds, which affords a basis for them, and hence a parasitic growth. We should wash ourselves clean of such news. Of what consequence, though our planet explode, if there is no character involved in the explosion? In health we have not the least curiosity about such events. We do not live for idle amusement. I would not run round a corner to see the world blow up.

All summer, and far into the autumn, perchance, you unconsciously went by the newspapers and the news, and now you find it was because the morning and the evening were full of news to you. Your walks were full of incidents. You attended, not to the affairs of Europe, but to your own affairs in Massachusetts fields. If you chance to live and move and have your being in that thin stratum in which the events that make the news transpire,—thinner than the paper on which it is printed,—then these things will fill the world for you; but if you soar above or dive below that plane, you cannot remember nor be reminded of them. Really to see the sun rise or go down every day, so to relate ourselves to a universal fact, would preserve us sane forever. Nations! What are nations? Tartars, and Huns, and Chinamen! Like insects, they swarm. The historian strives in vain to make them memorable. It is for want of a man that there are so many men. It is individuals that populate the world. Any man thinking may say with the Spirit of Lodin,—

> I look down from my height on nations,
> And they become ashes before me;—
> Calm is my dwelling in the clouds;
> Pleasant are the great fields of my rest.

Pray, let us live without being drawn by dogs, Esquimaux-fashion, tearing over hill and dale, and biting each other's ears.

Not without a slight shudder at the danger, I often perceive how near I had come to admitting into my mind the details of some trivial affair,—the news of the street; and I am astonished to observe how willing men are to lumber their minds with such rubbish,—to permit idle rumors and incidents of the most insignificant kind to intrude on ground which should be sacred to thought. Shall the mind be a public arena, where the affairs of the street and the gossip of the tea-table chiefly are discussed? Or shall it be a quarter of heaven itself,—an hypaethral temple, consecrated to the service of the gods? I find it so difficult to dispose of the few facts which to me are significant, that I hesitate to burden my attention with those which are insignificant, which only a divine mind could illustrate. Such is, for the most part, the news in newspapers and conversation. It is important to preserve the mind's chastity in this respect. Think of admitting the details of a single case of the criminal court into our thoughts, to stalk profanely through their very *sanctum sanctorum* for an hour, ay, for many hours! to make a very bar-room of the mind's inmost apartment, as if for so long the dust of the street had occupied us,—the very street itself, with all its travel, its bustle, and filth, had passed through our thoughts' shrine! Would it not be an intellectual and moral suicide? When I have been compelled to sit spectator and auditor in a courtroom for some hours, and have seen my neighbors,-who were not compelled, stealing in from time to time, and tiptoeing about with washed hands and faces, it has appeared to my mind's eye, that, when they took off their hats, their ears suddenly expanded into vast hoppers for sound, between which even their narrow heads were crowded. Like the vanes of windmills, they caught the broad but shallow stream of sound, which, after a few titillating gyrations in their coggy brains, passed out the other side. I wondered if, when they got home, they were as careful to wash their ears as before their hands and faces. It has seemed to me, at such a time, that the auditors and the witnesses, the jury and the counsel, the judge and the criminal at the bar,—if I may presume him guilty before he is convicted,—were all equally criminal, and a thunderbolt might be expected to descend and consume them all together.

By all kinds of traps and sign-boards, threatening the extreme penalty of the divine law, exclude such trespassers from the only ground which can be sacred to you. It is so hard to forget what it is worse than useless to remember! If I am to be a thoroughfare, I prefer that it be of the mountainbrooks, the Parnassian streams, and not the town-sewers. There is inspiration, that gossip which comes to the ear of the attentive mind from the courts of heaven. There is the profane and stale revelation of the bar-room and the police court. The same ear is fitted to receive both communications. Only the character of the hearer determines to which it shall be open, and to which closed. I believe that the mind can be permanently profaned by the habit of attending to trivial things, so that all our thoughts shall be tinged with triviality. Our very intellect shall be macadamized, as it were,—its foundation broken into fragments for the wheels of travel to roll over; and if you would know what will make the most durable pavement, surpassing rolled stones, spruce blocks, and asphaltum, you have only to look into some of our minds which have been subjected to this treatment so long.

If we have thus desecrated ourselves,—as who has not?—the remedy will be by wariness and devotion to reconsecrate ourselves, and make once more a fane of the mind. We should treat our minds, that is, ourselves, as innocent and ingenuous children, whose guardians we are, and be careful what objects and what subjects we thrust on their attention. Read not the Times. Read the Eternities. Conventionalities are at length as bad as impurities. Even the facts of science may dust the mind by their dryness, unless they are in a sense effaced each morning, or rather rendered fertile by the dews of fresh and living truth. Knowledge does not come to us by details, but in flashes of light from heaven.

Yes, every thought that passes through the mind helps to wear and tear it, and to deepen the ruts, which, as in the streets of Pompeii, evince how much it has been used. How many things there are concerning which we might well deliberate whether we had better know them,—had better let their peddling-carts be driven, even at the slowest trot or walk, over that bridge of glorious span by which we trust to pass at last from the farthest brink of time to the nearest shore of eternity! Have we no culture, no refinement,—but skill only to live coarsely and serve the Devil?—to acquire a little worldly wealth, or fame, or liberty, and make a false show with it, as if we were all husk and shell, with no tender and living kernel to us? Shall our institutions be like those chestnut-burs which contain abortive nuts, perfect only to prick the fingers. . . .

What is called politics is comparatively something so superficial and inhuman that, practically, I have never fairly recognized that it concerns me at all. The newspapers, I perceive, devote some of their columns specially to politics or government without charge; and this, one would say, is all that saves it; but as I love literature and to some extent the truth also, I never read those columns at any rate. I do not wish to blunt my sense of right so much. I have not got to answer for having read a single President's Message. A strange age of the world this, when empires, kingdoms, and republics come a-begging to a private man's door, and utter their complaints at his elbow! I cannot take up a newspaper but I find that some wretched government or other, hard pushed, and on its last legs, is interceding with me, the reader, to vote for it, more importunate than an Italian beggar; and if I have a mind to look at its certificate, made, perchance, by some benevolent merchant's clerk, or the skipper that brought it over, for it cannot speak a word of English itself, I shall probably read of the eruption of some Vesuvius, or the overflowing of some Po, true or forged, which brought it into this condition. I do not hesitate, in such a case, to suggest work, or the almshouse; or why not keep its castle in silence, as I do commonly? The poor President, what with preserving his popularity and doing his duty, is completely bewildered. The newspapers are the ruling power. Any other government is reduced to a few marines at Fort Independence. If a man neglects to read the Daily Times, government will go down on its knees to him, for this is the only treason in these days.

Those things which now most engage the attention of men, as politics and the daily routine, are, it is true, vital functions of human society, but should be unconsciously performed, like the corresponding functions of the physical body. They are *infra-human*, a kind of vegetation. I sometimes awake to a half-consciousness of them going on about me, as a man may become conscious of some of the processes of digestion in a morbid state, and so have the dyspepsia, as it is called. It is as if a thinker submitted himself to be rasped by the great gizzard of creation. Politics is, as it were, the gizzard of society, full of grit and gravel, and the two political parties are its two opposite halves,—sometimes split into quarters, it may be, which grind on each other. Not only individuals, but states, have thus a confirmed dyspepsia, which expresses itself, you can imagine by what sort of eloquence. Thus our life is not altogether a forgetting, but also, alas! to a great extent, a remembering, of that which we should never have been conscious of, certainly not in our waking hours. Why should we not meet, not always as dyspeptics, to tell our bad dreams, but sometimes as *eu*peptics, to congratulate each other on the ever-glorious morning? I do not make an exorbitant demand, surely.

Ellen Goodman (1941–)

The Business Illusion of Managing Emotions

More than 50 years ago, when Sigmund Freud was asked the prescription for a healthy life, he came up with two simple ingredients: work and love. But what the doctor had in mind was an integrated personality, not an integrated work force.

The corporate executives of today may also believe wholeheartedly in love and work, but they appear to be wary of love

AT work. Since Mary Cunningham and Bill Agee became a case study in how not to mix business and pleasure, a torrid interest has grown around the subject of love between executives.

Now the *Harvard Business Review*, which caters to the classiest of corporate leaders, has come out with some advice on dealing with dalliance at the top. In [a recent] issue, Senior Editor Eliza Collins concludes, after studying the business dynamics of four affairs, that "Love between managers is dangerous because it challenges—and can break down—the organizational structure."

The new coalition, the love coalition, makes everybody anxious, she says. It threatens to exclude others, makes subordinates worry about the judgment and the fairness of bosses who are blinded by love.

Having analyzed this, Collins makes some fairly bold recommendations. The senior executive should intervene in the executive love affair because "of the high degree of stress in the corporation."

"If the company sees rats in the basement they've got to get them out," said Collins in an interview. "It does have a responsibility to run an environment in which people can work."

Short of hiring a pied piper then, the best interest of business is apparently to separate love or at least one lover from work. Collins suggests that the senior executive persuade "the person least essential to the company" to leave. She advises this reluctantly, because the less important person is still "in almost all cases a woman."

Much of Collins' description of how a love affair can disrupt the office environment is astute. But her generalizations and recommendations are somewhere between offensive and dangerous.

For openers, a piece like this in the prestigious *Review* feeds into the wave of literature on how women are confronting the corporate world with all "their" messy little problems. The *Wall Street Journal*, for example, has been running an apparently endless series on the woes of young executive mothers. Apparently there are no young executive fathers.

Now the new women are mucking up the structure, by bringing love relationships into the board room, instead of keeping them where they belong, say, in the steno pool. The notion is that executives are so freaked out by their love that they cease functioning rationally at work. Love comes in and business-school training goes out.

But there are others, like Anne Jardim, a dean of the Simmons Graduate School of Management, who remain unconvinced of Collins' basic premise. For every bungled relationship, Jardim can count another "in which the people involved handled it with discretion, became scrupulously fair and survived."

More to the point, she says it is probably unnecessary and insulting to call in "Big Daddy" to separate adult executive lovers.

Rosabeth Kanter, professor of sociology and management at Yale University, suggests that senior executives handle love affairs the way they handle alcohol. Do nothing until there is an issue in job performance. Perhaps, she suggests, there should be a checklist for problem lovers that asks: How is this showing up at work?

The reality is that there are all sorts of special relationships between executives, all sorts of political and personal alliances in the corporate power structure that are untinged by sex. Kanter is not convinced that sexual love between executives is either widespread or disruptive enough for the sort of radical advice Collins has offered.

"People can behave in absolutely adolescent ways," says Kanter of executive lovers, "But it doesn't last that long in that stage. If we can indulge people when they are going through divorce or alcoholism, then we can indulge them with love."

What is most unsettling about the new advice on executives in love is that, once again, the business world is being fed the illusion that they can and, indeed, should manage emotions by removing them from the workplace. The prime candidate for emotional excision is, as always, love: first, family love and, now, sexual love.

In this case, the solution Collins recommends would effectively remove even the "carrier" of love in this society: women. We go back again to the notion that a healthy business personality is different from a healthy human personality. The message? If you want to get ahead in business, keep love off the books.

VIEWPOINTS

Russell Kirk

The Inhumane Businessman

American businessmen are inhumane. I do not mean that they are inhuman; they are all too human. I do not mean that they are insufficiently humanitarian. I mean that American businessmen, like most other Americans, are deficient in the disciplines that nurture the spirit. They are largely ignorant of the humanities, which, in a word, comprise that body of great literature that records the wisdom of the ages, and in recording it instructs us in the nature of man. The humanist believes in the validity of such wisdom.

Let us be quite clear about the difference between humanism and humanitarianism. In common usage, humanitarianism has simply come to mean generosity or charity; but strictly defined, as a system of thought, humanitarianism is a belief that mankind can be improved through the application of utilitarian principles, without divine aid; this is the idea that Rousseau pursued ecstatically and Stalin ruthlessly, while they overlooked the human law. Now there are a great many benevolent humanitarians among us who are neither ecstatic nor ruthless. The American businessman by and large is a benevolent humanitarian. In fact, probably no class of businessmen in all history has been so openhanded and so full of social conscience. So I do not mean to say that the American businessman is selfish when I say that he is not humane. But he misunderstands the limited virtues and even the profound hazards of humanitarianism so long as he neglects, as he does, the wisdom of humanism.

"The Triumph of Technology"

Humanism is a discipline that traces its origins back to the Hebrew prophets and the Greek philosophers, and has existed ever since to *humanize* men. Cicero and Seneca and Marcus Aurelius were at once the Roman exemplars and the Roman preceptors of this humanizing process, for which our term is "a liberal education." The humanists believed that through the study of great lives and great thoughts the minds of earnest men could be molded nobly. The process was both intellectual and ethical. This humane discipline, passed along in the literature of Christian theology, classic philosophy, poetry, history, biography, dominated the thinking of the whole of the Western world—until very late in the nineteenth century. Humanism persists today, but with influence greatly weakened.

The leaders of society in medieval Europe, the landed proprietors and the clergy, were trained in these humane disciplines. And later, the burghers of the Low Countries, the bankers of Lombardy and Tuscany, the manufacturers of England, aspired to know and to patronize humane letters and arts. The founders of the American Republic were practical and bold men; but they also were humane men, influenced by the classic tradition. The model for the American Republic was the Roman Republic, modified by the English political experience; the models for American leadership were Plutarch's heroes.

But with the successive industrial revolutions of the nineteenth and twentieth centuries, with what Friedrich Juenger calls "the triumph of technology," this veneration of humane learning began to disappear—especially among businessmen in America. Applied science, "positivism," seemed to be the keys to complete power. Powerful voices were raised then in disparagement of the humanities and in praise of "efficiency," "pragmatism," "progress." The School of Business Administration pushed the Schools of Theology and Classical Studies into a dim corner. People asked impatiently: Why waste years in school over Cicero?

A people can live upon their moral and intellectual capital for a long time. Yet eventually, unless the capital is replenished, they arrive at cultural bankruptcy. The intellectual and political and industrial leaders of the older generation die, and their places are not filled. The humanitarian cannot substitute for the humane man. The result of such bankruptcy is a society of meaninglessness, or a social revolution that brings up radical and unscrupulous talents to turn society inside out.

The young men who are to govern our industry and, to a considerable extent, our public polity, are in the condition of Aristotle's slaves, actually disqualified by the necessity of unremitting labor from taking part in public affairs. When they are in their sixties, they may have time for reflection and public service. But there are disadvantages to society in being led by emancipated slaves.

It is not easy to humanize oneself at the age of sixty. And not many businessmen do; the disciplines of humane studies, easily acquired in childhood, are thoroughly tedious in old age. Furthermore, the mortality rate among retired businessmen is notoriously high, perhaps in part because they lack the consolations of philosophy and the relaxation of purely intellectual pursuits.

The pity is that most of our businessmen are unaware of the fact that they are missing anything; they fail to appreciate how much of their intellectual power is wasted in getting and spending. Getting and spending are in themselves generally commendable activities; as Dr. Johnson said, "A man is seldom more innocently occupied than when he is engaged in making money." But that production and promotion should have become the whole of life for so many of the best minds in our country is unjust to the businessman, who deserves a better reward.

Underprivileged Businessmen

He is the underprivileged man. In an age of abundant production, when the problems of mass leisure are becoming more pressing than the problems of mass production, business executives are working harder and more single-mindedly than ever before. Nobody talks seriously about the four-day week for the executive. I am not proposing that the executive knock off in the middle of the week and take an adult-education course. But the original schooling of young men who will go into business ought to cultivate those tastes and provide those disciplines that enable the pleasures of a humane consciousness to make their way naturally and gracefully into even the busiest adult career. Businessmen would probably live longer as a result, and they certainly would live better.

Businessmen who were trained in law do stand out, on occasion, from their inhumane colleagues. Although our law schools have a good many deficiencies, anyone who goes to a reputable law school will have to know some Latin, a good deal of history, and even a smattering of philosophy. The best lawyers, busy as they are, can sometimes be found reading. Many of them read poetry, theology, the classics, philosophy, history.

Banking, too, still has its well-read men, though most of them seem to belong to the generation that is passing. The way things are going, we shall not have many well-read bankers around for long. For in banking as well as manufacturing or selling, the executive now is the least-leisured man in the world.

Much of the so-called business training at secondary, college, and even graduate-school levels is obsolete and burdensome. I doubt whether our technical and commercial and specialized curriculums really accomplish much except to shoulder aside those humane disciplines that equip a man for the private life of the mind and generally prepare him to do any kind of intelligent work.

"Business courses" at the secondary-school level are almost wholly useless, except for teaching young men how to typewrite and keep simple books. Business courses in college—except so far as they are courses in law or political economy in disguise—are worse than useless, for they fill up those short four years that are the best time to get some grasp of general principles of human nature and rational thinking. A graduate school of business administration may be a different matter, if the graduate students have already spent four years in genuinely humane studies. Yet many of the courses taught in graduate schools of business are trying to reduce to abstraction what can be got only by experience. And a large number of the students at graduate schools of business have had no proper preparation at all in humane studies. They can graduate from the business school innocent of ethical principle or decent tastes.

The Inhumane Teachers

The inhumane dean and the inhumane professor must share some responsibility for the inhumane businessman. Now and then I lunch with an investment broker who knows his Shakespeare and Dryden and Addison. (Graduate schools of business were not the fad when he was young, so he spent his time making money at an early age, and his spare time reading good books, mostly at random.) He likes to talk to professors occasionally, so that he can find out what professors are like nowadays. Generally he finds them overspecialized and overdogmatic. At a dinner not long ago he sat next to a professor of education, a genus my friend had not inspected before.

"Do you think," said the investment broker to the professor of education, "that young people are better educated now than they were in 1900?"

The professor of education did indeed think so: ever so much better educated; integrated with the group; adjusted to the environment. "I had wondered about it," the investment broker said, "because when I bring young men into my office, I generally find that they cannot write decent letters, or understand an alphabetical filing system." It is carrying on-the-job training rather far to expect a business to teach its employees the alphabet.

Imagination Rules Business

But the importance of humane disciplines to the functioning of industry and commerce transcends the simple skills of literacy. For even if the humanities are chiefly important to a man's soul and the higher purposes of life, it ought to be noted they are good for profits, too. One of the ends of a liberal education is to fit a person for whatever lot may happen to be his; and some of the accomplishments of the humane discipline, though that system developed in an age considerably different from ours, are remarkably important to the management of the modern economy.

A person truly educated in the humane tradition should have an orderly and disciplined mind—so far as any system of training can bring order into private personality. He has been taught the relationship between cause and effect. He should understand that predictable consequences follow from particular actions. He has in his mind a fund of precedent. He is acquainted with system. He has been taught a respect for just authority, and that the ego must be kept in check. The complexities of modern business require precisely those habits of thought that a liberal education has been trying to inculcate in young men these several centuries.

The sheer variety of the ideas that the liberal-arts man has explored can be counted upon to give him a resourcefulness generally superior to that of the man who has had only a technical training. Larger possiblities occur to the liberal intellect. Technique, as such, breeds only refinements of existing technique. Imagination rules the world, Napoleon said. Business imagination is not the highest form of imagination; but it certainly rules business in a competitive economy.

It could be argued that a degree in the humanities is even some added guarantee of integrity. The end of the old humanistic schooling, as I mentioned, is ethical: a man seeks virtue through philosophy. There are dishonest intellectuals, just as there are dishonest fools. It is a Latin poet who tells us that a man may perceive the good path and the evil, and yet chose the evil almost against his will, and certainly against his reason; there are no absolute sureties against a fall from virtue. But after reading the philosophers and the prophets and the poets, a man at least must be ashamed of misconduct, for he knows surely what misconduct is.

Liberal education cannot substitute for native shrewdness and knowledge of the ways of the world, but it can supplement and elevate such worldly wisdom. The humane man is able to appreciate human hopes and motives. He has some idea of the complexity and subtlety of the human heart. If he has learned his lessons, he is not likely to think of his own prejudices as universal aspirations, or put a utopian faith in his associates. He probably has taken on a healthy pessimism about the possiblities of human nature. He should know fairly well what may be expected of a man.

He is better prepared to deal with "personnel relations" than the young zealot fresh from courses in Freudian or behavioristic psychology, who immoderately applies the speculations of the clinician to situations and personalities that may require nothing more than a sprinkling of good humor.

B.S. in Packaging

Yet the doors of business and industry are too often closed to the liberal-arts graduate. In part, this is the result of an attitude manifested by certain businessmen who think of all education as "training" for a special vocation, and therefore expect to employ "trained" people for narrow specialties. And in part, it is the fault of educational administrators who pander to "the needs of industry" by setting up wondrously technical or even manual curriculums—and expect subsidies and gifts from business by way of reward. One state university now offers a "four-year curriculum in packaging, leading to the degree of bachelor of science in packaging." (The same university offers two courses, with full credit, in fly casting.) "There is nothing to which we will not stoop," says the president of a famous state university, "if the public seems to demand it."

The businessman with any concern for the future of business or the Republic would be well advised to set his face against these absurdities rather than encourage them.

The Businessman in Politics

We hear a good deal about businessmen in politics, and some of it to the effect that politics is something they have no business being in. Edmund Burke, though he always was supported by the greater part of the industrial and commercial interests of

England, did not trust businessmen as statesmen; on one occasion he said that men of commerce were not at all fit to judge of the high concerns of state. The late Robert Taft more than once expressed his annoyance at the notion that the U.S. needed "a businessman's government." Businessmen, he said, should take care of business, and politicians should take care of politics.

Nevertheless, the businessman does matter in American politics, and he has an important role to play, whether he likes it or not. Many businessmen definitely do not like it; they are busy, and they know when they are out of their element. We hear a lot about the political power of U.S. business, but the country suffers far more from the political indifference of the businessman than from his alleged political influence.

The businessman has to be concerned with our public polity. Whoever possesses money and influence must play a large role in politics, or else he will not keep money and influence long.

And it is in politics that the businessman without humane disciplines is most conspicuously at a disadvantage. If ignorant of history and political theory and the record of human nature, he may fall victim to the sentimental humanitarian, or worse still, to the zealot of social collectivism. Vaguely eager to be approved by the Advanced Social Thinker, disturbed by denunciations from radical and liberal publications, the inhumane businessman may become a party to his own undoing.

The radical man of action is aware of this weakness of the businessman. More than a generation ago, G. Lowes Dickinson, a British man of letters who happened to be an ardent Socialist, informed his friends that they could count upon the conquest of businessmen without a struggle; it would simply entail, said Dickinson, a "slow, half-conscious detachment of all of them who have intelligence and moral force from the interest and active support of their class." The Robber Barons did some damage in their day; but the possibilities of damage to our social structure by confused and sentimental humanitarians may be even greater.[1]

1. A number of our great private charitable foundations are committed not to collectivism, as their adversaries often cry, but to a vague, well-intentioned humanitarianism, looking toward the perfection of society and human nature. Almost any sum of money can be got for almost any "social research project," or plan for material amelioration. But the men running our foundations, taken as a body, seem quite indifferent to the ethical and intellectual premises of the humane tradition.

If the businessmen don't assume some political leadership, leaders of a disagreeable and violent sort will make themselves felt in the land. Burke described Jacobinism, the fierce radicalism of France, as "the revolt of the enterprising talents of a country against its property." Jacobinism lies latent in any generation or country. But the possessors of property must be fortified by the councils of humane disciplines. It will do no good for them to flail around in the political arena simply repeating slogans about "the American way of life," or "the American standard of living."

The Accidental Leaders

If only by accident, the American businessman has come to be the chief guardian of our civil and cultural inheritance. It is not altogether convenient to have greatness thrust upon one. Yet the American businessman owes it to himself, his economic system, and his country to shoulder such responsibilities. I do not expect that any considerable proportion of the business community will set out overnight to read Plato through. We can hope that some of our businessmen will begin to pay some heed to the springs of imagination and reason, and open their minds to our intellectual heritage. Professor Wilhelm Röpke, the Swiss economist and social philosopher, recently suggested that nowhere is the gulf between the man of property and the man of intellect wider than in the U.S. This is a perilous condition.

3
Organization as Fulfillment

> Only where love and need are one,
> And the work is play for mortal stakes,
> Is the deed ever really done.
> —ROBERT FROST

Over the past six centuries a major shift has occurred in the Western outlook on the world and on the individual's role in it. The preoccupation of people at one time centered on their preparation for the next world, often accompanied by a ready acceptance of hardship in this life. Starting with the Renaissance, however, people gradually turned their attention to the conditions of life in this world, and as the selections in this chapter illustrate, they have yet to refocus their interest and energies. Along with their greater involvement in the things of this life, people began to assume more responsibility for their well-being. That is to say, they placed their trust not only in God, but they also ventured to trust their own capabilities to improve their lot. This shifting perspective on life reached a high point in the eighteenth century with its faith in the limitless powers of reason to achieve the moral and material improvement of humankind.

In fact, this tremendous trust expressed by the people in their abilities to achieve self-improvement, on the material as well as the moral level, was distilled into one powerful concept—"progress." This is the idea that fired the people's imagination and won their allegiance. Many believed then, as they do now, that progress would bring happiness to humankind. And what is happiness if not the fulfillment of a person's various needs and wishes? Some of the more obvious needs that demand satisfaction on a day-to-day basis range from the purely material and emotional to the more elusive intellectual and spiritual. To whom or where do people turn for fulfillment? Some answers come quickly to mind: one's job may offer material fulfillment and possibly also intellectual satisfaction; one's family and friends more or less answer emotional and perhaps intellectual needs; one's religion cares for the spiritual side. At first glance, the quest for fulfillment appears to be rather easily satisfied—yet this basic question of fulfillment has been raised by the literary artist again and again over the centuries.

In the selections in this chapter the problem of fulfillment focuses on the individual, his or her job, and the impact of progress. The technical and material aspects of progress are the ones most frequently alluded to here. In general, what does "progress" mean to us? Do all segments of society hold the same view of progress? Do we still believe wholeheartedly in material progress as a universal answer to the shortcomings of the human condition? Do the poems "The Report" and "Chicago" express similar attitudes toward progress? What about one of the most personal and concrete byproducts of progress: the job? What is its relationship to the search for fulfillment?

Fulfillment in the world of organization is approached here in many different ways and illuminated from various angles. For instance, various kinds of fulfillment—ranging from the material to the spiritual—are sought by many in their work alone. Robert Frost's "Two Tramps in Mud Time" clearly touches on the concept of work motivation "where love and need are one." Moreover, several writers are enthusiastic about the benefits that science, organization, industry, and business—in short, that progress—has bestowed on us. For example, Voltaire defends with zest and humor the luxuries made possible by progress. And in "Chicago" Carl Sandburg illustrates not only the pain but also the accomplishments of organizational and technological know-how. On the other hand, some writers consider the proclaimed fulfillment of human needs by work clearly illusory. The "Lone Striker," for instance, chooses to turn his back on the factory and finds peace and satisfaction in nature. Others experience, often subconsciously, the pain of the spiritual void, the utter lack of fulfillment in their life within the organization; "Secretary," both "Richard Cory" poems, and "The Report" are illustrations of this emptiness.

In this complex world, is some assurance of stability really possible at the individual level, according to Julie Porosky's "For Granted" and Rod McKuen's "Plan"? Does science make us and our institutions safe?

Are we placing too much emphasis on the individual? Have we blown personal needs and wishes out of all proportion and lost sight of the human community as a whole? And seen from the point of view of the organization, a position rarely dealt with in literature, what is it able to offer in terms of fulfillment? Is work capable of satisfying the extensive gamut of human needs; in fact, were such claims ever made about work? Is one side making demands that the other was never meant to answer? Or is organization shirking its responsibility? Are we overloading the circuit—that is, are we making too many demands on work? Are we asking the "organizational family" to take the place of the "real" family? Is work to be the sole source of friends and intellectual stimulation? As we have withdrawn from religion, are we making a religion of work and making organizations our churches and temples?

POEMS

Voltaire (1694–1778)

The Worldling

Others may with regret complain
That 'tis not fair Astrea's[1] reign,
That the famed golden age is o'er
That Saturn, Rhea[2] rule no more:
Or, to speak in another style,
That Eden's groves no longer smile.
For my part, I thank Nature sage,
That she has placed me in this age:
Religionists may rail in vain;
I own, I like this age profane;
I love the pleasures of a court;
I love the arts of every sort;
Magnificence, fine buildings, strike me;
In this, each man of sense is like me.
I have, I own, a worldly mind,
That's pleased abundance here to find;
Abundance, mother of all arts,
Which with new wants new joys imparts
The treasures of the earth and main,
With all the creatures they contain:
These, luxury and pleasures raise;
This iron age brings happy days.
Needful superfluous things appear;
They have joined together either sphere.
See how that fleet, with canvas wings,
From Texel, Bordeaux, London brings,

1. Goddess of Justice during the mythological Golden Age.
2. Saturn and Rhea brought the Golden Age to humankind.

By happy commerce to our shores,
All Indus, and all Ganges stores;
Whilst France, that pierced the Turkish lines,
Sultans make drunk with rich French wines.
Just at the time of Nature's birth,
Dark ignorance o'erspread the earth;
None then in wealth surpassed the rest,
For naught the human race possessed.
Of clothes, their bodies then were bare,
They nothing had, and could not share:
Then too they sober were and sage,
Martialo lived not in that age.
Eve, first formed by the hand divine,
Never so much as tasted wine.
Do you our ancestors admire,
Because they wore no rich attire?
Ease was like wealth to them unknown,
Was't virtue? ignorance alone.
Would any fool, had he a bed,
On the bare ground have laid his head?
My fruit-eating first father, say,
In Eden how rolled time away?
Did you work for the human race,
And clasp dame Eve with close embrace!
Own that your nails you could not pare,
And that you wore disordered hair,
That you were swarthy in complexion,
And that your amorous affection
Had very little better in't
Than downright animal instinct.
Both weary of the marriage yoke
You supped each night beneath an oak
On millet, water, and on mast,
And having finished your repast,
On the ground you were forced to lie,
Exposed to the inclement sky:
Such in the state of simple nature
Is man, a helpless, wretched creature.
Would you know in this cursed age,

Against which zealots so much rage,
To what men blessed with taste attend
In cities, how their time they spend?
The arts that charm the human mind
All at his house a welcome find;
In building it, the architect
No grace passed over with neglect.
To adorn the rooms, at once combine
Poussin,[3] Correggio[4] the divine,
Their works on every panel placed
Are in rich golden frames incased.
His statues show Bouchardon's[5] skill,
Plate of Germain, his sideboards fill.
The Gobelin tapestry, whose dye
Can with the painter's pencil vie,
With gayest coloring appear
As ornaments on every pier.
From the superb salon are seen
Gardens with Cyprian myrtle green.
I see the sporting waters rise
By jets d'eau[6] almost to the skies.
But see the master's self approach
And mount into his gilded coach,
A house in motion, to the eyes
It seems as through the streets it flies.
I see him through transparent glasses
Loll at his ease as on he passes.
Two pliant and elastic springs
Carry him like a pair of wings.
At Bath, his polished skin inhales
Perfumes, sweet as Arabian gales.
Camargot[7] at the approach of night
Julia, Gossin[8] by turns invite.

3. French painter of the seventeenth century.
4. Italian painter of the sixteenth century.
5. French sculptor of the eighteenth century.
6. Jets of water.
7. Well-known dancer.
8. Gossin—famous actress.

Love kind and bounteous on him pours
Of choicest favors plenteous showers.
To the opera house he must repair,
Dance, song and music charm him there.
The painter's art to strike the sight,
Does there with that blest art unite;
The yet more soft, persuasive skill,
Which can the soul with pleasure thrill.
He may to damn an opera go,
And yet perforce admire Rameau.[9]
The cheerful supper next invites
To luxury's less refined delights.
How exquisite those sauces flavor!
Of those ragouts I like the savor.
The man who can in cookery shine,
May well be deemed a man divine.
Chloris and Ægle[10] at each course
Serve me with wine, whose mighty force
Makes the cork from the bottle fly
Like lightning darting from the sky.
Bounce! to the ceiling it ascends,
And laughter the apartment rends.
In this froth, just observers see
The emblem of French vivacity.
The following day new joys inspires,
It brings new pleasures and desires.
Mentor, Telemachus descant
Upon frugality, and vaunt
Your Ithaca and your Salentum
To ancient Greeks, since they content them:
Since Greeks in abstinence could find
Ample supplies of every kind.
The work, though not replete with fire,
I for its elegance admire:
But I'll be whipped Salentum through
If thither I my bliss pursue.

9. French composer of the eighteenth century.
10. Chloris and Aegle, minor goddesses of classical mythology.

Garden of Eden, much renowned,
Since there the devil and fruit were found,
Huetius, Calmet,[11] learned and bold,
Inquired where Eden lay of old:
I am not so critically nice,
Paris to me's a paradise.

11. Huetius and Calmet, Bible scholars.

William Wordsworth (1770–1850)

Composed Upon Westminster Bridge, September 3, 1802

Earth has not anything to show more fair:
Dull would he be of soul who could pass by
A sight so touching in its majesty:
This City now doth, like a garment, wear
The beauty of the morning; silent, bare,
Ships, towers, domes, theatres, and temples lie
Open unto the fields, and to the sky;
All bright and glittering in the smokeless air.
Never did sun more beautifully steep
In his first splendour, valley, rock, or hill;
Ne'er saw I, never felt, a calm so deep!
The river glideth at his own sweet will:
Dear God! the very houses seem asleep;
And all that mighty heart is lying still!

Anonymous

Hard Times Cotton Mill Girls

I've worked in a cotton mill all of my life
And I ain't got nothing but a Barlow knife,
It's hard times cotton mill girls,
It's hard times everywhere.

   Chorus:

It's hard times cotton mill girls,
It's hard times cotton mill girls,
It's hard times cotton mill girls,
It's hard times everywhere.

In nineteen and fifteen we heard it said,
Go to the country and get ahead.
It's hard times cotton mill girls,
It's hard times everywhere.

Us girls work twelve hours a day
For fourteen cents of measly pay.
It's hard times cotton mill girls,
It's hard times everywhere.

When I die don't bury me at all,
Just pickle my bones in alcohol,
Hang me up on the spinning room wall,
It's hard times everywhere.

(Chorus)

Ilya Ivanovich Sadofief (1889–1965)

In the Factory

Only today I have felt, only today I have comprehended,
Here, in the factory, the daily, noisy festive carnival.

Daily, at an appointed hour, the steam sings out inviting.
The guests are gaily clad, there are peals and roars, dancing and singing.
The peals and cadence of ringing uproar—the speech of sounds without words.
The shapely rhythmical dance of sheaves—joyful and drunken.

In the dance there is the dream of youth, eternal motion, and freedom.
In the sounds is the world's secret, in the sounds are the words of wisdom.
In the songs are vigor, inspiration, burning faith, challenge, and anger.
Oh, how sweet it is to hear this tune so passionately ardent.

Men in overalls understand these words and cries. . . .
Men in overalls are like titans, stern and proud, and quiet.

In their silence there is a hidden wisdom, a strength, a creating force;
And in their movements—power of steel, sternness, will, might.

To understand the iron tongue, to hear the mystery of the revelation;
To learn from the machines and lathes the boisterous force—how to destroy,
And how to create incessantly something brand new and different;
To be in the factory daily, to be there, is ecstasy!

Claude McKay (1890–1948)

The Tired Worker

O whisper, O my soul! The afternoon
Is waning into evening, whisper soft!
Peace, O my rebel heart! for soon the moon
From out its misty veil will swing aloft!
Be patient, weary body, soon the night
Will wrap thee gently in her sable sheet,
And with a leaden sigh thou wilt invite
To rest thy tired hands and aching feet.
The wretched day was theirs, the night is mine;
Come tender sleep, and fold me to thy breast.
But what steals out the gray clouds red like wine?
Oh dawn! O dreaded dawn! O let me rest.
Weary my veins, my brain, my life! Have pity!
No! Once again the harsh, the ugly city.

Leslie M. Collins (1914–   )

Stevedore

The enigmatic moon has at long last died.
Even as the ancient Cathedral Saint Louis
Peals her lazy call
To a sleepy solemn worship,
Night's mysterious shadows reveal their secrets
And rise into nothingness
As honest day unfurls her bright banners.

The stevedore,
Sleep spilled on his black face,
Braves the morning's rising fog,
The saturating chill.

As the sun burns itself out in summer brilliance,
Though his heart he sweated out
In water glistening from gargantuan shoulders,
He finds strength in his voice,
Singing of Moses down in Egyptland,
Of yesterday's untrue love.

By evening
The sun-scorched stevedore has packed strange cargoes
On alien ships
Whose destinations stir no romantic desires.

All day
A little of his soul is put to sea.
And now that the heaven's sun-burnt gold
Has quickened to deepest lapis-lazuli,
He turns an unkempt head

Homeward
To a dreamless slumber.

Robert Frost (1874–1963)

A Lone Striker

The swinging mill bell changed its rate
To tolling like the count of fate,
And though at that the tardy ran,
One failed to make the closing gate.
There was a law of God or man
That on the one who came too late
The gate for half an hour be locked,
His time be lost, his pittance docked.
He stood rebuked and unemployed.
The straining mill began to shake.
The mill, though many-many-eyed,
Had eyes inscrutably opaque;

So that he couldn't look inside
To see if some forlorn machine
Was standing idle for his sake.
(He couldn't hope its heart would break.)

And yet he thought he saw the scene:
The air was full of dust of wool.
A thousand yarns were under pull,
But pull so slow, with such a twist,
All day from spool to lesser spool,
It seldom overtaxed their strength;
They safely grew in slender length.
And if one broke by any chance,
The spinner saw it at a glance.
The spinner still was there to spin.
That's where the human still came in.
Her deft hand showed with finger rings
Among the harplike spread of strings.
She caught the pieces end to end
And, with a touch that never missed,
Not so much tied as made them blend.
Man's ingenuity was good.
He saw it plainly where he stood,
Yet found it easy to resist.

He knew another place, a wood,
And in it, tall as trees, were cliffs;
And if he stood on one of these,
'Twould be among the tops of trees
Their upper branches round him wreathing,
Their breathing mingled with his breathing.
If—if he stood! Enough of ifs!
He knew a path that wanted walking;
He knew a spring that wanted drinking;
A thought that wanted further thinking;
A love that wanted re-renewing.
Nor was this just a way of talking
To save him the expense of doing.
With him it boded action, deed.

The factory was very fine;
He wished it all the modern speed.
Yet, after all, 'twas not divine,
That is to say, 'twas not a church.
He never would assume that he'd
Be any institution's need.
But he said then and still would say,
If there should ever come a day
When industry seemed like to die
Because he left it in the lurch,
Or even merely seemed to pine
For want of his approval, why,
Come get him—they knew where to search.

Two Tramps in Mud Time

Out of the mud two strangers came
And caught me splitting wood in the yard.
And one of them put me off my aim
By hailing cheerily "Hit them hard!"
I knew pretty well why he dropped behind
And let the other go on a way.
I knew pretty well what he had in mind:
He wanted to take my job for pay.

Good blocks of oak it was I split,
As large around as the chopping block;
And every piece I squarely hit
Fell splinterless as a cloven rock.
The blows that a life of self-control
Spares to strike for the common good,
That day, giving a loose to my soul,
I spent on the unimportant wood.

The sun was warm but the wind was chill.
You know how it is with an April day
When the sun is out and the wind is still,

You're one month on in the middle of May.
But if you so much as dare to speak,
A cloud comes over the sunlit arch,
A wind comes off a frozen peak,
And you're two months back in the middle of March.

A bluebird comes tenderly up to alight
And turns to the wind to unruffle a plume,
His song so pitched as not to excite
A single flower as yet to bloom.
It is snowing a flake: and he half knew
Winter was only playing possum.
Except in color he isn't blue,
But he wouldn't advise a thing to blossom.

The water for which we may have to look
In summertime with a witching wand,
In every wheelrut's now a brook,
In every print of a hoof a pond.
Be glad of water, but don't forget
The lurking frost in the earth beneath
That will steal forth after the sun is set
And show on the water its crystal teeth.

The time when most I loved my task
These two must make me love it more
By coming with what they came to ask.
You'd think I never had felt before
The weight of an ax-head poised aloft,
The grip on earth of outspread feet,
The life of muscles rocking soft
And smooth and moist in vernal heat.

Out of the woods two hulking tramps
(From sleeping God knows where last night,
But not long since in the lumber camps).
They thought all chopping was theirs of right.
Men of the woods and lumberjacks,

They judged me by their appropriate tool.
Except as a fellow handled an ax
They had no way of knowing a fool.

Nothing on either side was said.
They knew they had but to stay their stay
And all their logic would fill my head:
As that I had no right to play
With what was another man's work for gain.
My right might be love but theirs was need.
And where the two exist in twain
Theirs was the better right—agreed.

But yield who will to their separation,
My object in living is to unite
My avocation and my vocation
As my two eyes make one in sight.
Only where love and need are one,
And the work is play for mortal stakes,
Is the deed ever really done
For Heaven and the future's sakes.

Carl Sandburg (1878–1967)

Happiness

I asked professors who teach the meaning of life to tell me
    what is happiness.
And I went to famous executives who boss the work of thousands
    of men.
They all shook their heads and gave me a smile as though I
    was trying to fool with them.
And then one Sunday afternoon I wandered out along the
    Desplaines river
And I saw a crowd of Hungarians under the trees with their
    women and children and a keg of beer and an accordion.

Edwin Arlington Robinson
(1869–1935)

Richard Cory

Whenever Richard Cory went down town,
    We people on the pavement looked at him:
He was a gentleman from sole to crown,
    Clean favored, and imperially slim.

And he was always quietly arrayed,
    And he was always human when he talked;
But still he fluttered pulses when he said,
    "Good-morning," and he glittered when he walked.

And he was rich—yes, richer than a king,
    And admirably schooled in every grace:
In fine, we thought that he was everything
    To make us wish that we were in his place.

So on we worked, and waited for the light,
    And went without the meat, and cursed the bread;
And Richard Cory, one calm summer night,
    Went home and put a bullet through his head.

Paul Simon   (1941–   )

Richard Cory

1. They say that Richard Cory owns one-half of this old town
With political connections to spread his wealth around.
Born into society, A banker's only child;
He had everything a man could want:
Power, grace, style.

Refrain:

But I work in his factory
And I curse the life I'm livin',
And I curse my poverty.
And I wish that I could be,
O, I wish that I could be
O, I wish that I could be
Richard Cory.

II. The papers print his picture almost everywhere he goes—
Richard Cory at the opera, Richard Cory at a show,
And the rumor of his parties and the orgies on his yacht;
He surely must be happy with everything he's got.

Refrain:

III. He really gave to charity; he had the common touch.
And they were grateful for his patronage,
And they thanked him very much.
So the mind was filled with wonder
When the evening headlines read:
"Richard Cory went home last night
And put a bullet through his head."

(Refrain)

Carl Sandburg   (1878–1967)

Fish Crier

I know a Jew fish crier down on Maxwell Street with a voice
    like a north wind blowing over corn stubble in January.
He dangles herring before prospective customers evincing a joy
    identical with that of Pavlova dancing.

His face is that of a man terribly glad to be selling fish,
> terribly glad that God made fish, and customers to whom he
> may call his wares from a pushcart.

Chicago

> Hog Butcher for the World,
> Tool Maker, Stacker of Wheat,
> Player with Railroads and the Nation's Freight Handler;
> Stormy, husky, brawling,
> City of the Big Shoulders:

They tell me you are wicked and I believe them, for I have
> seen your painted women under the gas lamps luring the
> farm boys.
And they tell me you are crooked and I answer: Yes, it is true
> I have seen the gunman kill and go free to kill again.
And they tell me you are brutal and my reply is: On the faces
> of women and children I have seen the marks of wanton
> hunger.
And having answered so I turn once more to those who sneer
> at this my city, and I give them back the sneer and say to
> them:
Come and show me another city with lifted head singing so
> proud to be alive and coarse and strong and cunning.
Flinging magnetic curses amid the toil of piling job on job,
> here is a tall bold slugger set vivid against the little soft
> cities;
Fierce as a dog with tongue lapping for action, cunning as a
> savage pitted against the wilderness,
> Bareheaded,
> Shoveling,
> Wrecking,
> Planning,
> Building, breaking, rebuilding,

Under the smoke, dust all over his mouth, laughing with white
   teeth,
Under the terrible burden of destiny laughing as a young man
   laughs,
Laughing even as an ignorant fighter laughs who has never lost
   a battle,
Bragging and laughing that under his wrist is the pulse, and
   under his ribs the heart of the people,
Laughing!
Laughing the stormy, husky, brawling laughter of Youth, half-
   naked, sweating, proud to be Hog Butcher, Tool Maker,
   Stacker of Wheat, Player with Railroads and Freight
   Handler to the Nation.

David Wagoner (1926–)

A Valedictory to Standard Oil of Indiana

In the darkness east of Chicago, the sky burns over the plumbers'
   nightmares
Red and blue, and my hometown lies there loaded with gasoline.
Registers ring like gas pumps, pumps like pinballs, pinballs like
   broken alarm clocks,
And it's time for morning, but nothing's going to work.
From cat-cracker to candle shop, from greaseworks along the
   pipeline,
Over storage tanks like kings on a checkerboard ready to jump
   the county,
The word goes out: With refined regrets,
We suggest you sleep all day in your houses shaped like lunch
   buckets
And don't show up at the automated gates.
Something else will tap the gauges without yawning
And check the valves at the feet of the cooling-towers without
   complaining.

VALEDICTORY TO STANDARD OIL OF INDIANA

Standard Oil is canning my high-school classmates
And the ones who fell out of junior high or slipped in the grades.
What should they do, gassed up in their Tempests and Comets,
    raring to go
Somewhere, with their wives scowling in front and kids stuffed in
    the back,
Past drive-ins jammed like car lots, trying to find the beaches
But blocked by freights for hours, stopped dead in their tracks
Where the rails, as thick as thieves along the lake front,
Lower their crossing gates to shut the frontier? What can they
    think about
As they stare at the sides of boxcars for a sign,
And Lake Michigan drains slowly into Lake Huron,
The mills level the Dunes, and the eels go sailing through the
    trout
And mosquitoes inherit the evening while toads no bigger than
    horseflies
Hop crazily after them over the lawns and sidewalks, and the
    rainbows fall
Flat in the oil they came from? There are two towns now,
One dark, one going to be dark, divided by cyclone fences;
One pampered and cared for like pillboxes and cathedrals,
The other vanishing overnight in the dumps and swamps like
    a struck sideshow.
As the Laureate of the Class of '44—which doesn't know it has
    one—
I offer this poem, not from hustings or barricades
Or the rickety stage where George Rogers Clark stood glued to
    the wall,
But from another way out, like Barnum's "This Way to the
    Egress,"
Which moved the suckers when they'd seen enough. Get
    out of town.

Randall Jarrell   (1914–1965)

The Woman at the Washington Zoo

The saris go by me from the embassies.

Cloth from the moon. Cloth from another planet.
They look back at the leopard like the leopard.

And I. . . .
          this print of mine, that has kept its color
Alive through so many cleanings; this dull null
Navy I wear to work, and wear from work, and so
To my bed, so to my grave, with no
Complaints, no comment: neither from my chief,
The Deputy Chief Assistant, nor his chief—
Only I complain. . . . this serviceable
Body that no sunlight dyes, no hand suffuses
But, dome-shadowed, withering among columns,
Wavy beneath fountains—small, far-off, shining
In the eyes of animals, these beings trapped
As I am trapped but not, themselves, the trap,
Aging, but without knowledge of their age,
Kept safe here, knowing not of death, for death—
Oh, bars of my own body, open, open!

The world goes by my cage and never sees me.
And there come not to me, as come to these,
The wild beasts, sparrows pecking the llamas' grain,
Pigeons settling on the bears' bread, buzzards
Tearing the meat the flies have clouded. . . .
                                Vulture,
When you come for the white rat that the foxes left,
Take off the red helmet of your head, the black
Wings that have shadowed me, and step to me as man:
The wild brother at whose feet the white wolves fawn,

To whose hand of power the great lioness
Stalks, purring. . . .
                        You know what I was,
You see what I am: change me, change me!

TED HUGHES (1930–)

Secretary

If I should touch her she would shriek and weeping
Crawl off to nurse the terrible wound: all
Day like a starling under the bellies of bulls
She hurries among men, ducking, peeping,

Off in a whirl at the first move of a horn.
At dusk she scuttles down the gauntlet of lust
Like a clockwork mouse. Safe home at last
She mends socks with holes, shirts that are torn

For father and brother, and a delicate supper cooks:
Goes to bed early, shuts out with the light
Her thirty years, and lies with buttocks tight,
Hiding her lovely eyes until day break.

ROD McKUEN (1933–)

Plan

My cousin Max is being married
        on a quiz show.
He is getting a Westinghouse refrigerator
        a Singer sewing machine

        a set of furniture from Sears and Roebuck
                   an ant farm
              a General Electric toaster
and a girl.

It is not enough.
He expects babies and happiness
good times and money
and a government that wars on war.

My cousin Max expects too much.

JON SWAN (1929–   )

The Report

I

When I wake up again, when I wake up
Ready for small talk and a coffee cup,
Hearing the noise of time and break of dawn
In distinct alarms and a common yawn,
I wonder how those days will pass that do,
Though seldom exactly as I want them to;
And rise again and drink and eat, and go
Down the hall, down the elevator and, so,
Out. Buildings stand out, a pigeon-gray,
And a gray street climbs the hill to Broadway.
I climb it. I slip into the people
And, like a lot of them, pick the hole
At Ninety-sixth Street to walk into.
And down, leaving the sky behind, we go—
Swallowed up without a bite
By a mouth without an appetite.

II

I come up seeing the same pigeons and different people
Or the same people and different pigeons that I left uptown.
They seem inescapable, grumpy or affable,
Brown, gray, plump, gray or brown.
The same things still seen on the same level.
We are not used to change.

In my office building there are four ranks of elevators.
Lobby captains, the idle brass of automation, stand
Ready for the nothing that usually occurs,
Looking alert, lost, grand,
As if I were a guest, they the waiters.
At what strange banquet, pray?

There are others. We go up in a scattered, speechless cluster,
Swung up in the humming air. The machine is impatient,
Closing its rubber-lipped doors anxiously after
Each of us has left—sent,
Delivered to our proper floor,
To open our own black door.

I open my own black door, walk in feeling rather dapper,
Feeling at home almost, master in that cubicle,
Free enough to sit and finish the morning paper,
And wheel my swivel
To the window where the flat skyscraper
Is half of what I see.

Two-thirds of the other half is equally fat and tall.
Hundreds of windows and a continual repetition
Of straight lines and the buildings are interchangeable.
The miscalculation
Of the sky stands out, blue, against that wall—
The park, a gap of green.

Tell me whether, when you, when you look out on such a scene,
The windows all the same and each repeating the same hard gaze
That yours repeats to them, you too feel there must be one
Behind which stares a face
And sits a body in all ways like your own,
That turns now as you turn.

I turn to work, to do what others in my building do.
I hear—through walls that are thin, dun, easily removable—
Others at work, as perhaps I am intended to.
Perhaps it makes us feel
As one—this listening, being listened to—
Although we rarely meet.

We see each other in a corridor. The smiles come.
Ride up together to another floor. What is there to say?
We live together, minor, in a gigantic home.
We criticize. We stay.
It is a world within a world for some.
For most, security.

And yet on evenings when I stay till ten, almost alone,
Saunter the halls and pay the automat that, hit, spits coffee
In a cup—there's a high-pitched, keen, whistling overtone
As elevators, empty,
Their affable, bland music playing on,
Rise in their shafts and fall,

Ecstatically mechanical, as if, if that place
Had a spirit, it rode there singing in the emptiness.
I listen, drink, and then return to my office,
Where, by night, I feel less
Single than during the days, when faces
Have voices and the rooms hum.

III

I shall not stay forever. I will go,
Someday, when I can afford to go,

Will leave that stiff, repetitive view
That still suggests there is another who,
With a similar, patient irony,
With the same wishes and glasses, looks at me
As I look out my window, as I wait
For him to move before it grows too late
To move, and walk, decisive, down the hall
To push the button and wait to fall,
And so continue, travelling in air,
Suspended, but moving downward in there,
Stepping out when the quick doors yawn
That close the minute we are gone—
Like a mouth without an appetite.
And, after the subway, walk up to the night.

JULIE POROSKY (1945–   )

For Granted

They've decided a volcano extinct,
and Idaho safe from hurricanes.
You read about it in the newspaper
at your front door three hundred

and sixty-nine days, and you
can stop counting and instead
count on it, like the mailman,
the dandelions, your indigestion,
and the sun keeping its distance
from our ancient revolving.

You think you know where
your next day is coming from,
and your time runs clockwise.
But listen—

Somebody is always getting lost
from somebody else, steps in front
of the car you are driving
and changes your life.

Hold your heart in the night,
believe that.

Naomi H. Barnard (1925–)

Retirement

He lay the years by in a fattening heap,
his buildings rose up steep
over the hills of need. Filled
past the surfeit of his appetite
he stilled his coil
of grasping reach
to look upon his properties
and smile with satisfaction,
and pleasured sigh.
But time had passed him
and his soul was dead
from fat. He only lived to die.

Marge Piercy (1936–)

What's That Smell in the Kitchen?

All over America women are burning dinners.
It's lambchops in Peoria; it's haddock
in Providence; it's steak in Chicago
tofu delight in Big Sur; red
rice and beans in Dallas.
All over America women are burning

food they're supposed to bring with calico
smile on platters glittering like wax.
Anger sputters in her brainpan, confined
but spewing out missiles of hot fat.
Carbonized despair presses like a clinker
from a barbecue against the back of her eyes.
If she wants to grill anything, it's
her husband spitted over a slow fire.
If she wants to serve him anything
it's a dead rat with a bomb in its belly
ticking like the heart of an insomniac.
Her life is cooked and digested,
nothing but leftovers in Tupperware.
Look, she says, once I was roast duck
on your platter with parsley but now I am Spam.
Burning dinner is not incompetence but war.

JAY PARINI (1948–   )

Town Life
For Ann Beattie

It strikes me as the best of every world
this morning as I leave the house at nine
and walk uptown, past shuttered houses
I have learned by heart down to the angle
of each sloping roof, the kinds of siding
and their various degrees of disrepair.
I've memorized the shrubbery and lawns,
all so reflective of their owners' minds,
the blend of trees, some planted by the town
in 1920, others here by chance,
the drift of wind, or someone's purpose.
Today September-blooming mountain laurels
burn with flowers to fill the gaps where long-
necked elms once made a tunnel of their leaves.
I know this sidewalk as a blind man knows

his way around his rooms: the tilting flagstones
and the gravel drives, macadam stretches
that will heave with frost by mid-December.
All my joints adjust to ups and downs
as I proceed, half drunk on air, on night-
rinsed grasses and the gilt-edged leaves
that riffle in the slightest wind with that
low rustling tinny note of early fall,
the note of loss that makes me savor
what befalls each step: the wedge of geese
that arrows overhead between slate roofs,
the exoskeletons of huge black ants
that file like soldiers through the Kiber Pass
to certain failure in the winter's grip,
the squirrels rippling in grey blurs up trees
with preservations in their iron jaws.
There's so much going on I'll never know
but happily assume has its own pattern;
I have mine, which fits into the town's
slow ritual so well no doubt you'll wonder
if some parts of me were not lopped off
to make this fitting. Wouldn't I prefer
to wake at dawn in country heaven, with acres
of raw land around my house, with crops to tend,
with cows dewlapping through the shallow swales?
Some friends saw wood to save their souls
while I burn oil; they hike into the hills
for rustic solace as I walk these streets.
I've other friends who live in cities and believe
in motion multiplied by time, the swirl
of faces, calendars with no blank spaces left.
Their lives are vertical, like glass and steel,
and full of light at any time of day.
I don't begrudge them what they've found to work.
I'm all for anything that makes you feel
the gravity afoot, the tug of light
particulars, the sway of chosen hours,
though I love town life for its Lazy Susan
of well-timed events, the tower that chimes,

the surge of traffic at appointed moments,
life in slow concentric circles that acknowledge
morning, noon, and night, imperious seasons
that enforce their rules, make us accede
to larger motions than we make ourselves.
I love the neighborliness of little towns,
the expectations that are so well met:
the waitress at the diner where I drink
my de-caf coffee, one old cop who never
says hello, too charged with duty to descend
to pleasantries on county time, the dozen
keepers of the dozen shops who fill my life
with necessary objects, foods, and service.
Their worlds depend upon my morning walk,
my needs and whims. And so we live in
symbiotic swirl around the center
of the village green: its white gazebo
like a hub of sorts, the centrifugal
aim of all our motion, though it's really
useless as a building goes, except for
concerts by the local bands on summer nights.
That white gazebo is the town's real heart:
a minor symbol of nostalgic longing
for our fictive past amid the hubbub
of our daily work in buildings shaped
to useful ends: the Greco-Roman banks
with much more cash than any of us needs
to make one life, the small post office
that can ship our mail to Bognor Regis
or Addis Abbaba without any hitch.
It seems that we can eat our cake and have it,
though all wisdom votes against that fact.
I use the royal "we" perhaps too glibly,
since I'll never stand for public office
or consent to join the Rotary or Masons.
(My love of town life doesn't go that far.)
But—on my oath—I'll fill these streets
with all the shambling presence I can muster
for enough good years to say I've been here

and have met them well on equal terms.
I'll be one spoke in this bright wheel
that spins through decades at its chosen speed,
that passing airplanes notice like a dime
in heavy grass—a glint of silver—
something they would probably pick up
if only it were not so far away.

Dorie LaRue (1948–   )

I'll Go to Crazy Ruby's

You say a check has bounced?
And books are due tomorrow?
Nevermind. I'll go to the river
where Crazy Ruby lives, and the wild fern
and the tame rabbit, twenty boneless cats
in various reposes, amid antimacassars;
a baby quail's grave, and the fat flap
of bream against the water's drift,
a weedy garlic patch, the oily well,
and untouched wisteria, and martins
living in gourds from last year's crop;
where kudzu's finally loved,
and privet grows tall as trees,
and a half-coyote can dare to trust.

You say no job opening? No matter.
I'll go where there are green tomatoes
on the windowsill, where salt licks
are not hard to find, nor deer
emboldened by the season. Oh, I'll go
to Crazy Ruby's and feed chickens
through the window, eat chili
from a broken bowl.

P. K. PAGE (1916–   )

Typists

They without message, having read
the running words on their machines,
know every letter as a stamp
cutting the stencils of their ears.
Deep in their hands, like pianists,
all longing gropes and moves, is trapped
behind the tensile gloves of skin.

Or blind, sit with their faces locked
away from work. Their varied eyes
are stiff as everlasting flowers.
While fingers on a different plane
perform the automatic act
as questions grope along the dark
and twisting corridors of brain.

Crowded together typists touch
softly as ducks and seem to sense
each others' anguish with the swift
sympathy of the deaf and dumb.

FICTION

Nathaniel Hawthorne (1804–1864)

Wakefield

In some old magazine or newspaper I recollect a story, told as truth, of a man—let us call him Wakefield—who absented himself for a long time from his wife. The fact, thus abstractedly stated, is not very uncommon, nor—without a proper distinction of circumstances—to be condemned either as naughty or nonsensical. Howbeit, this, though far from the most aggravated, is perhaps the strangest, instance on record, of marital delinquency; and, moreover, as remarkable a freak as may be found in the whole list of human oddities. The wedded couple lived in London. The man, under pretence of going a journey, took lodgings in the next street to his own house, and there, unheard of by his wife or friends, and without the shadow of a reason for such self-banishment, dwelt upwards of twenty years. During that period, he beheld his home every day, and frequently the forlorn Mrs. Wakefield. And after so great a gap in his matrimonial felicity—when his death was reckoned certain, his estate settled, his name dismissed from memory, and his wife, long, long ago, resigned to her autumnal widowhood—he entered the door one evening, quietly, as from a day's absence, and became a loving spouse till death.

This outline is all that I remember. But the incident, though of the purest originality, unexampled, and probably never to be repeated, is one, I think, which appeals to the generous sympathies of mankind. We know, each for himself, that none of us would perpetrate such a folly, yet feel as if some other might. To my own contemplations, at least, it has often recurred, always exciting wonder, but with a sense that the story must be true, and a conception of its hero's character. Whenever any subject so forcibly affects the mind, time is well spent in thinking of it. If the reader choose, let him do his own meditation; or if he prefer to ramble with me through the twenty years of Wakefield's vagary, I bid him welcome; trusting that there will be a pervading spirit and a moral, even should we fail to find them, done up neatly, and condensed into the final sentence. Thought has always its efficacy, and every striking incident its moral.

What sort of a man was Wakefield? We are free to shape out our own idea, and call it by his name. He was now in the meridian of life; his martrimonial affections, never violent, were sobered into a calm, habitual sentiment; of all husbands, he was likely to be the most constant, because a certain sluggishness would keep his heart at rest, wherever it might be placed. He was intellectual, but not actively so; his mind occupied itself in long and lazy musings, that ended to no purpose, or had not vigor to attain it; his thoughts were seldom so energetic as to seize hold of words. Imagination, in the proper meaning of the term, made no part of Wakefield's gifts. With a cold but not depraved nor wandering heart, and a mind never feverish with riotous thoughts, nor perplexed with originality, who could have anticipated that our friend would entitle himself to a foremost place among the doers of eccentric deeds? Had his acquaintances been asked, who was the man in London the surest to perform nothing to-day which should be remembered on the morrow, they would have thought of Wakefield. Only the wife of his bosom might have hesitated. She, without having analyzed his character, was partly aware of a quiet selfishness, that had rusted into his inactive mind; of a peculiar sort of vanity, the most uneasy attribute about him; of a disposition to craft, which had seldom produced more positive effects than the keeping of petty secrets, hardly worth revealing; and, lastly, of what she called a little strangeness, sometimes, in the good man. This latter quality is indefinable, and perhaps nonexistent.

Let us now imagine Wakefield bidding adieu to his wife. It is the dusk of an October evening. His equipment is a drab great-coat, a hat covered with an oilcloth, top-boots, an umbrella in one hand and a small portmanteau in the other. He has informed Mrs. Wakefield that he is to take the night coach into the country. She would fain inquire the length of his journey, its object, and the probable time of his return; but, indulgent to his harmless love of mystery, interrogates him only by a look. He tells her not to expect him positively by the return coach, nor to be alarmed should he tarry three or four days; but, at all events, to look for him at supper on Friday evening. Wakefield himself, be it considered, has no suspicion of what is before him. He holds out his hand, she gives her own, and meets his parting kiss in the matter-of-course way of a ten years' matrimony; and forth goes the middle-aged Mr. Wakefield, almost resolved to perplex his good lady by a whole week's absence. After the door has closed behind him, she perceives it thrust partly open, and a vision of her husband's face, through the aperture, smiling on her, and gone in a moment. For the time, this little incident is dismissed without a thought. But, long afterwards, when she has been more years a widow than a wife, that smile recurs, and flickers across all her reminiscences of Wakefield's visage. In her many musings, she surrounds the original smile with a multitude of fantasies, which make it strange and awful: as, for instance, if she imagines him in a coffin, that parting look is frozen on his pale features; or, if she dreams of him in heaven, still his blessed spirit wears a quiet and crafty smile. Yet, for its sake, when all others have given him up for dead, she sometimes doubts whether she is a widow.

But our business is with the husband. We must hurry after him along the street, ere he lose his individuality, and melt into the great mass of London life. It would be vain searching for him there. Let us follow close at his heels, therefore, until, after several superfluous turns and doublings, we find him comfortably established by the fireside of a small apartment, previously bespoken. He is in the next street to his own, and at his journey's end. He can scarcely trust his good fortune, in having got thither unperceived—recollecting that, at one time, he was delayed by the throng, in the very focus of a lighted lantern; and, again, there were footsteps that seemed to tread behind his own, distinct from the multitudinous tramp around him; and, anon, he heard a voice shouting afar, and fancied that it called his name. Doubtless, a dozen busybodies had been watching him, and told his wife the whole affair. Poor Wakefield! Little knowest thou thine own insignificance in this great world! No mortal eye but mine has traced thee. Go quietly to thy bed, foolish man; and, on the morrow, if thou wilt be wise, get thee home to good Mrs. Wakefield, and tell her the truth. Remove not thyself, even for a little week, from thy place in her chaste bosom. Were she, for a single moment, to deem thee dead, or lost, or lastingly divided from her, thou wouldst be woefully conscious of a change in thy true wife forever after. It is perilous to make a chasm in human affections; not that they gape so long and wide—but so quickly close again!

Almost repenting of his frolic, or whatever it may be termed, Wakefield lies down betimes, and starting from his first nap, spreads forth his arms into the wide and solitary waste of the unaccustomed bed. "No,"—thinks he, gathering the bedclothes about him,— "I will not sleep alone another night."

In the morning he rises earlier than usual, and sets himself to consider what he really means to do. Such are his loose and rambling modes of thought that he has taken this very singular step with the consciousness of a purpose, indeed, but without being able to define it sufficiently for his own contemplation. The vagueness of the project, and the convulsive effort with which he plunges into the execution of it, are equally characteristic of a feeble-minded man. Wakefield sifts his ideas, however, as minutely as he may, and finds himself curious to know the progress of matters at home—how his exemplary wife will endure her widowhood of a week; and, briefly, how the little sphere of creatures and circumstances, in which he was a central object, will be affected by his removal. A morbid vanity, therefore, lies nearest the bottom of the affair. But, how is he to attain his ends? Not, certainly, by keeping close in this comfortable lodging, where, though he slept and awoke in the next street to his home, he is as effectually abroad as if the stage-coach had been whirling him away all night. Yet, should he reappear, the whole project is knocked in the head. His poor brains being hopelessly puzzled with this dilemma, he at length ventures out, partly resolving to cross the head of the street, and send one hasty glance towards his forsaken domicile. Habit—for he is a man of habits—takes him by the hand, and guides him, wholly unaware, to his own door, where, just at the critical moment, he is aroused by the scraping of his foot upon the step. Wakefield! whither are you going?

At that instant his fate was turning on the pivot. Little dreaming of the doom to which his first backward step devotes him, he hurries away, breathless with agitation hitherto unfelt, and hardly dares turn his head at the distant corner. Can it be that nobody caught sight of him? Will not the whole household—the decent Mrs. Wakefield, the smart maid servant, and the dirty little footboy—raise a hue and cry, through London streets, in pursuit of their fugitive lord and master? Wonderful escape! He gathers courage to pause and look homeward, but is perplexed with a sense of change about the familiar edifice, such as affects us all, when, after a separation of months or years, we again see some hill or lake, or work of art, with which we were friends of old. In ordinary cases, this indescribable impression is caused by the comparison and contrast between our imperfect reminiscences and the reality. In Wakefield, the magic of a single night has wrought a similar transformation, because, in that brief period, a great moral change has been effected. But this is a secret from himself. Before leaving the spot, he catches a far and momentary glimpse of his wife, passing athwart the front window, with her face turned towards the head of the street. The crafty nincompoop takes to his heels, scared with the idea that, among a thousand such atoms of mortality, her eye must have detected him. Right glad is his heart, though his brain be somewhat dizzy, when he finds himself by the coal fire of his lodgings.

So much for the commencement of this long whim-wham. After the initial conception, and the stirring up of the man's sluggish temperament to put it in practice, the whole matter evolves itself in a natural train. We may suppose him, as the result of deep deliberation, buying a new wig, of reddish hair, and selecting sundry garments, in a fashion unlike his customary suit of brown, from a Jew's old-clothes bag. It is accomplished. Wakefield is another man. The new system being now established, a retrograde movement to the old would be almost as difficult as the step that placed him in his unparalleled position. Furthermore, he is rendered obstinate by a sulkiness occasionally incident to his temper, and brought on at present by the inadequate sensation which he conceives to have been produced in the bosom of Mrs. Wakefield. He will not go back until she be frightened half to death. Well; twice or thrice has she passed before his sight, each time with a heavier step, a paler cheek, and more anxious brow; and in the third week of his non-appearance he detects a portent of evil entering the house, in the guise of an apothecary. Next day the knocker is muffled. Towards nightfall comes the chariot of a physician, and deposits its big-wigged and solemn burden at Wakefield's door, whence, after a quarter of an hour's visit, he emerges, perchance the herald of a funeral. Dear woman! Will she die? By this time, Wakefield is excited to something like energy of feeling, but still lingers away from his wife's bedside, pleading with his conscience that she must not be disturbed at such a juncture. If aught else restrains him, he does not know it. In the course of a few weeks she gradually recovers; the crisis is over; her heart is sad, perhaps, but quiet; and, let him return soon or late, it will never be feverish for him again. Such ideas glimmer through the mist of Wakefield's mind, and render him indistinctly conscious that an almost impassable gulf divides his hired apartment from his former home. "It is but in the next street!" he sometimes says. Fool! it is in another world. Hitherto, he has put off his return from one particular day to another; henceforward, he leaves the precise time undetermined. Not tomorrow—probably next week—pretty soon. Poor man! The dead have nearly as much chance of revisiting their earthly homes as the self-banished Wakefield.

Would that I had a folio to write, instead of an article of a dozen pages! Then might I exemplify how an influence beyond our control lays its strong hand on every deed which we do, and weaves its consequences into an iron tissue of necessity. Wakefield is spell-bound. We must leave him, for ten years or so, to haunt around his house, without once crossing the threshold, and to be faithful to his wife, with all the affection of which his heart is capable, while he is slowly fading out of hers. Long since, it must be remarked, he had lost the perception of singularity in his conduct.

Now for a scene! Amid the throng of a London street we distinguish a man, now waxing elderly, with few characteristics to attract careless observers, yet bearing, in his whole aspect, the handwriting of no common fate, for such as have the skill to read it. He is meagre; his low and narrow forehead is deeply wrinkled; his eyes, small and lustreless, sometimes wander apprehensively about him, but oftener seem to look inward. He bends his head, and moves with an indescribable obliquity of gait, as if unwilling to display his full front to the world. Watch him long enough to see what we have described, and you will allow that circumstances—which often produce remarkable men from nature's ordinary handiwork—have produced one such here. Next, leaving him to sidle along the footwalk, cast your eyes in the opposite direction, where a portly female, considerably in the wane of life, with a prayer-book in her hand, is proceeding to yonder church. She has the placid mien of settled widowhood. Her regrets have either died away, or have become so essential to her heart, that they would be poorly exchanged for joy. Just as the lean man and well-conditioned woman are passing, a slight obstruction occurs, and brings these two figures directly in contact. Their hands touch; the pressure of the crowd forces her bosom against his shoulder; they stand, face to face, staring into each other's eyes. After a ten years' separation, thus Wakefield meets his wife!

The throng eddies away, and carries them asunder. The sober widow, resuming her former pace, proceeds to church, but pauses in the portal, and throws a perplexed glance along the street. She passes in, however, opening her prayer-book as she goes. And the man! with so wild a face that busy and selfish London stands to gaze after him, he hurries to his lodgings, bolts the door, and throws himself upon the bed. The latent feelings of years break out; his feeble mind acquires a brief energy from their strength; all the miserable strangeness of his life is revealed to him at a glance: and he cries out, passionately, "Wakefield! Wakefield! You are mad!"

Perhaps he was so. The singularity of his situation must have so moulded him to himself, that, considered in regard to his fellow-creatures and the business of life, he could not be said to possess his right mind. He had contrived, or rather he had happened, to dissever himself from the world—to vanish—to give up his place and privileges with living men, without being admitted among the dead. The life of a hermit is nowise parallel to his. He was in the bustle of the city, as of old; but the crowd swept by and saw him not; he was, we may figuratively say, always beside his wife and at his hearth, yet must never feel the warmth of the one nor the affection of the other. It was Wakefield's unprecedented fate to retain his original share of human sympathies, and to be still involved in human interests, while he had lost his reciprocal influence on them. It would be a most curious speculation to trace out the effect of such circumstances on his heart and intellect, separately, and in unison. Yet, changed as he was, he would seldom be conscious of it, but deem himself the same man as ever; glimpses of the truth, indeed, would come, but only for the moment; and still he would keep saying, "I shall soon go back!"—nor reflect that he had been saying so for twenty years.

I conceive, also, that these twenty years would appear, in the retrospect, scarcely longer than the week to which Wakefield had at first limited his absence. He would look on the affair as no more than an interlude in the main business of his life. When, after a little while more, he should deem it time to reenter his parlor, his wife would clap her hands for joy, on beholding the middle-aged Mr. Wakefield. Alas, what a mistake! Would Time but await the close of our favorite follies, we should be young men, all of us, and till Doomsday.

One evening, in the twentieth year since he vanished, Wakefield is taking his customary walk towards the dwelling which he still calls his own. It is a gusty night of autumn, with frequent showers that patter down upon the pavement, and are gone before a man can put up his umbrella. Pausing near the house, Wakefield discerns, through the parlor windows of the second floor, the red glow and the glimmer and fitful flash of a comfortable fire. On the ceiling appears a grotesque shadow of good Mrs. Wakefield. The cap, the nose and chin, and the broad waist, form an admirable caricature, which dances, moreover, with the up-flickering and down-sinking blaze, almost too merrily for the shade of an elderly widow. At this instant a shower chances to fall, and is driven, by the unmannerly gust, full into Wakefield's face and bosom. He is quite penetrated with its autumnal chill. Shall he stand, wet and shivering here, when his own hearth has a good fire to warm him, and his own wife will run to fetch the gray coat and small-clothes, which, doubtless, she has kept carefully in the closet of their bed chamber? No! Wakefield is no such fool. He ascends the steps—heavily!—for twenty years have stiffened his legs since he came down—but he knows it not. Stay, Wakefield! Would you go to the sole home that is left you? Then step into your grave! The door opens. As he passes in, we have a parting glimpse of his visage, and recognize the crafty smile, which was the precursor of the little joke that he has ever since been playing off at his wife's expense. How unmercifully has he quizzed the poor woman! Well, a good night's rest to Wakefield!

This happy event—supposing it to be such—could only have occurred at an unpremeditated moment. We will not follow our friend across the threshold. He has left us much food for thought, a portion of which shall lend its wisdom to a moral, and be shaped into a figure. Amid the seeming confusion of our mysterious world, individuals are so nicely adjusted to a system, and systems to one another and to a whole, that, by stepping aside for a moment, a man exposes himself to a fearful risk of losing his place forever. Like Wakefield, he may become, as it were, the Outcast of the Universe.

HERMAN MELVILLE (1819–1891)

Bartleby, the Scrivener

A Story of Wall Street

I am a rather elderly man. The nature of my avocations for the last thirty years has brought me into more than ordinary contact with what would seem an interesting and somewhat singular set of men, of whom as yet nothing that I know of has ever been written:—I mean the law-copyists or scriveners. I have known very many of them, professionally and privately, and if I pleased, could relate divers histories, at which good-natured gentlemen might smile, and sentimental souls might weep. But I waive the biographies of all other scriveners for a few passages in the life of Bartleby, who was a scrivener the strangest I ever saw or heard of. While of other law-copyists I might write the complete life, of Bartleby nothing of that sort can be done. I believe that no materials exist for a full and satisfactory biography of this man. It is an irreparable loss to literature. Bartleby was one of those beings of whom nothing is ascertainable, except from the original sources, and in his case those are very small. What my own astonished eyes saw of Bartleby, *that* is all I know of him, except, indeed, one vague report which will appear in the sequel.

Ere introducing the scrivener, as he first appeared to me, it is fit I make some mention of myself, my *employées*, my business, my chambers, and general surroundings; because some such description is indispensable to an adequate understanding of the chief character about to be presented.

Imprimis:[1] I am a man who, from his youth upwards, has been filled with a profound conviction that the easiest way of life is the best. Hence, though I belong to a profession proverbially energetic and nervous, even to turbulence, at times, yet nothing of that sort have I ever suffered to invade my peace. I am one of those unambitious lawyers who never addresses a jury, or in any way draws down public applause; but in the cool tranquillity of a snug retreat, do a snug business among rich men's bonds and mortgages and title-deeds. All who know me, consider me an eminently *safe* man. The late John Jacob Astor,[2] a personage little given to poetic enthusiasm, had no hesitation in pronouncing my first grand point to be prudence; my next, method. I do not speak it in vanity, but simply record the fact, that I was not unemployed in my profession by the late John Jacob Astor; a name which, I admit, I love to repeat, for it hath a rounded and orbicular sound to it, and rings like unto bullion. I will freely add that I was not insensible to the late John Jacob Astor's good opinion.

Some time prior to the period at which this little history begins, my avocations had been largely increased. The good old office, now extinct in the State of New York, of a Master in Chancery,

---

1. In the first place.
2. John Jacob Astor (1763–1848), New York fur trader, capitalist, and philanthropist.

had been conferred upon me. It was not a very arduous office, but very pleasantly remunerative. I seldom lose my temper; much more seldom indulge in dangerous indignation at wrongs and outrages; but I must be permitted to be rash here and declare, that I consider the sudden and violent abrogation of the office of Master in Chancery, by the new Constitution, as a—premature act; inasmuch as I had counted upon a life-lease of the profits, whereas I only received those of a few short years. But this is by the way.

My chambers were up stairs at No.——Wall Street. At one end they looked upon the white wall of the interior of a spacious skylight shaft, penetrating the building from top to bottom. This view might have been considered rather tame than otherwise, deficient in what landscape painters call "life." But if so, the view from the other end of my chambers offered, at least, a contrast, if nothing more. In that direction my windows commanded an unobstructed view of a lofty brick wall, black by age and everlasting shade, which wall required no spyglass to bring out its lurking beauties, but for the benefit of all near-sighted spectators, was pushed up to within ten feet of my window panes. Owing to the great height of the surrounding buildings, and my chambers being on the second floor, the interval between this wall and mine not a little resembled a huge square cistern.

At the period just preceding the advent of Bartleby, I had two persons as copyists in my employment, and a promising lad as an office-boy. First, Turkey; second, Nippers; third, Ginger Nut. These may seem names the like of which are not usually found in the Directory. In truth they were nicknames, mutually conferred upon each other by my three clerks, and were deemed expressive of their respective persons or characters. Turkey was a short, pursy Englishman of about my own age, that is, somewhere not far from sixty. In the morning, one might say, his face was of a fine florid hue, but after twelve o'clock, meridian—his dinner hour—it blazed like a grate full of Christmas coals; and continued blazing—but, as it were, with a gradual wane till 6 o'clock, P.M. or thereabouts, after which I saw no more of the proprietor of the face, which gaining its meridian with the sun, seemed to set with it, to rise, culminate, and decline the following day, with the like regularity and undiminished glory. There are many singular coincidences I have known in the course of my life, not the least among which was the fact, that exactly when Turkey displayed his fullest beams from his red and radiant countenance, just then, too, at the critical moment, began the daily period when I considered his business capacities as seriously disturbed for the remainder of the twenty-four hours. Not that he was absolutely idle, or averse to business then; far from it. The difficulty was, he was apt to be altogether too energetic. There was a strange, inflamed, flurried, flighty recklessness of activity about him. He would be incautious in dipping his pen into his inkstand. All his blots upon my documents were dropped there after twelve o'clock, meridian. Indeed, not only would he be reckless and sadly given to making blots in the afternoon, but some days he went further, and was rather noisy. At such times, too, his face flamed with augmented blazonry, as if cannel coal had been heaped on anthracite. He made an unpleasant racket with his chair; spilled his sand-box; in mending his pens, impatiently split them all to pieces, and threw them on the floor in a sudden passion; stood up and leaned over his table, boxing his papers about in a most indecorous manner, very sad to behold in an elderly man like him. Nevertheless, as he was in many ways a most valuable person to me, and all the time before twelve o'clock, meridian, was the quickest, steadiest creature too, accomplishing a great deal of work in a style not easy to be matched—for these reasons, I was willing to overlook his eccentricities, though indeed, occasionally, I remonstrated with him. I did this very gently, however, because, though the civilest, nay, the blandest and most reverential of men in the morning, yet in the afternoon he was disposed, upon provocation, to be slightly rash with his tongue, in fact, insolent. Now, valuing his morning services as I did, and resolved not to lose them; yet, at the same time made uncomfortable by his inflamed ways after twelve o'clock; and being a man of peace, unwilling by my admonitions to call forth unseemly retorts from him; I took upon me, one Saturday noon (he was always worse on Saturdays), to hint to him, very kindly, that perhaps now that he was growing old, it might be well to abridge his labors; in short, he need not come to my chambers after twelve o'clock, but, dinner over, had best go home to his lodgings and rest himself till tea-time. But no; he insisted upon his afternoon devotions. His countenance became intolerably fervid, as he oratorically assured me—gesticulating with a long ruler at the other end of the room—that if his services in the morning were useful, how indispensable, then, in the afternoon?

"With submission, sir," said Turkey on this occasion, "I consider myself your right-hand man. In the morning I but marshal and deploy my columns; but in the afternoon I put myself at their head, and gallantly charge the foe, thus!"—and he made a violent thrust with the ruler.

"But the blots, Turkey," intimated I.

"True,—but, with submission, sir, behold these hairs! I am getting old. Surely, sir, a blot or two to a warm afternoon is not to be severely urged against gray hairs. Old age—even if it blot the page—is honorable. With submission, sir, we *both* are getting old."

This appeal to my fellow-feeling was hardly to be resisted. At all events, I saw that go he would not. So I made up my mind to let him stay, resolving, nevertheless, to see to it, that during the afternoon he had to do with my less important papers.

Nippers, the second on my list, was a whiskered, sallow, and, upon the whole, rather piratical-looking young man of about five and twenty. I always deemed him the victim of two evil powers—ambition and indigestion. The ambition was evinced by a certain impatience of the duties of a mere copyist, an unwarrantable usurpation of strictly professional affairs, such as the original drawing up of legal documents. The indigestion seemed betokened in an occasional nervous testiness and grinning irritability, causing the teeth to audibly grind together over mistakes committed in copying; unnecessary maledictions, hissed, rather than spoken, in the heat of business; and especially by a continual discontent with the height of the table where he worked. Though of a very ingenious mechanical turn, Nippers could never get this table to suit him. He put chips under it, blocks of various sorts, bits of pasteboard, and at last went so far as to attempt an exquisite adjustment by final pieces of folded blotting-paper. But no invention would answer. If, for the sake of easing his back, he brought the table lid at a sharp angle well up towards his chin, and wrote there like a man using the steep roof of a Dutch house for his desk:—then he declared that it stopped the circulation in his arms. If now he lowered the table to his waistbands, and stooped over it in writing, then there was a sore aching in his back. In short, the truth of the matter was, Nippers knew not what he wanted. Or, if he wanted any thing, it was to be rid of a scrivener's table altogether. Among the manifestations of his diseased ambition was a fondness he had for receiving visits from certain ambiguous-looking fellows in seedy coats, whom he called his clients. Indeed I was aware that not only was he, at times, considerable of a ward-politician, but he occasionally did a little business at the Justices' courts, and was not unknown on the steps of the Tombs.[3] I have good reason to believe, however, that one individual who called upon him at my chambers, and who, with a grand air, he insisted was his client, was no other than a dun,[4] and the alleged title-deed, a bill. But with all his failings, and the annoyances he caused me, Nippers, like his compatriot Turkey, was a very useful man to me; wrote a neat, swift hand; and, when he chose, was not deficient in a gentlemanly sort of deportment. Added to this, he always dressed in a gentlemanly sort of way: and so, incidentally, reflected credit upon my chambers. Whereas with respect to Turkey, I had much ado to keep him from being a reproach to me. His clothes were apt to look oily and smell of eating-houses. He wore his pantaloons very loose and baggy in summer. His coats were execrable; his hat not to be handled. But while the hat was a thing of indifference to me, inasmuch as his natural civility and deference, as a dependent Englishman, always led him to doff it the moment he entered the room, yet his coat was another matter. Concerning his coats, I reasoned with him; but with no effect. The truth was, I suppose, that a man with so small an income, could not afford to sport such a lustrous face and a lustrous coat at one and the same time. As Nippers once observed, Turkey's money went chiefly for red ink. One winter day I presented Turkey with a highly-respectable looking coat of my own, a padded gray coat, of a most comfortable warmth, and which buttoned straight up from the knee to the neck. I thought Turkey would appreciate the favor, and abate his rashness and obstreperousness of after-

3. New York City prison.
4. Bill collector.

noons. But no, I verily believe that buttoning himself up in so downy and blanket-like a coat had a pernicious effect upon him; upon the same principle that too much oats are bad for horses. In fact, precisely as a rash, restive horse is said to feel his oats, so Turkey felt his coat. It made him insolent. He was a man whom prosperity harmed.

Though concerning the self-indulgent habits of Turkey I had my own private surmises, yet touching Nippers I was well persuaded that whatever might be his faults in other respects, he was, at least, a temperate young man. But indeed, nature herself seemed to have been his vintner,[5] and at his birth charged him so thoroughly with an irritable, brandy-like disposition, that all subsequent potations were needless. When I consider how, amid the stillness of my chambers, Nippers would sometimes impatiently rise from his seat, and stooping over his table, spread his arms wide apart, seize the whole desk, and move it, and jerk it, with a grim, grinding motion on the floor, as if the table were a perverse voluntary agent, intent on thwarting and vexing him; I plainly perceive that for Nippers, brandy and water were altogether superfluous.

It was fortunate for me that, owing to its peculiar cause—indigestion—the irritability and consequent nervousness of Nippers, were mainly observable in the morning, while in the afternoon he was comparatively mild. So that Turkey's paroxysms only coming on about twelve o'clock, I never had to do with their eccentricities at one time. Their fits relieved each other like guards. When Nippers' was on, Turkey's was off; and *vice versa*. This was a good natural arrangement under the circumstances.

Ginger Nut, the third on my list, was a lad some twelve years old. His father was a carman, ambitious of seeing his son on the bench instead of a cart, before he died. So he sent him to my office as student at law, errand boy, and cleaner and sweeper, at the rate of one dollar a week. He had a little desk to himself, but he did not use it much. Upon inspection, the drawer exhibited a great array of the shells of various sorts of nuts. Indeed, to this quick-witted youth the whole noble science of the law was contained in a nutshell. Not the least among the employments of Ginger Nut, as well as one which he discharged with the most

---

5. Wine merchant.

alacrity, was his duty as cake and apple purveyor for Turkey and Nippers. Copying law papers being proverbially a dry, husky sort of business, my two scriveners were fain to moisten their mouths very often with Spitzenbergs[6] to be had at the numerous stalls nigh the Custom House and Post Office. Also, they sent Ginger Nut very frequently for that peculiar cake—small, flat, round, and very spicy—after which he had been named by them. Of a cold morning when business was but dull, Turkey would gobble up scores of those cakes, as if they were mere wafers—indeed they sell them at the rate of six or eight for a penny—the scrape of his pen blending with the crunching of the crisp particles in his mouth. Of all the fiery afternoon blunders and flurried rashnesses of Turkey, was his once moistening a ginger-cake between his lips, and clapping it on to a mortgage for a seal. I came within an ace of dismissing him then. But he mollified me by making an oriental bow, and saying—"With submission, sir, it was generous of me to find you in[7] stationery on my own account."

Now my original business—that of a conveyancer and title hunter, and drawer-up of recondite documents of all sorts—was considerably increased by receiving the master's office. There was now great work for scriveners. Not only must I push the clerks already with me, but I must have additional help. In answer to my advertisement, a motionless young man one morning stood upon my office threshold, the door being open, for it was summer. I can see that figure now—pallidly neat, pitiably respectable, incurably forlorn! It was Bartleby.

After a few words touching his qualifications, I engaged him, glad to have among my corps of copyists a man of so singularly sedate an aspect, which I thought might operate beneficially upon the flighty temper of Turkey, and the fiery one of Nippers.

I should have stated before that ground glass folding-doors divided my premises into two parts, one of which was occupied by my scriveners, the other by myself. According to my humor I threw open these doors, or closed them. I resolved to assign Bartleby a corner by the folding-doors, but on my side of them,

6. Variety of apple.
7. Bring you.

so as to have this quiet man within easy call, in case any trifling thing was to be done. I placed his desk close up to a small side-window in that part of the room, a window which originally had afforded a lateral view of certain grimy back-yards and bricks, but which, owing to subsequent erections, commanded at present no view at all, though it gave some light. Within three feet of the panes was a wall, and the light came down from far above, between two lofty buildings, as from a very small opening in a dome. Still further to a satisfactory arrangement, I procured a high green folding screen, which might entirely isolate Bartleby from my sight, though not remove him from my voice. And thus, in a manner, privacy and society were conjoined.

At first Bartleby did an extraordinary quantity of writing. As if long famishing for something to copy, he seemed to gorge himself on my documents. There was no pause for digestion. He ran a day and night line, copying by sunlight and by candlelight. I should have been quite delighted with his application, had he been cheerfully industrious. But he wrote on silently, palely, mechanically.

It is, of course, an indispensable part of a scrivener's business to verify the acccuracy of his copy, word by word. Where there are two or more scriveners in an office, they assist each other in this examination, one reading from the copy, the other holding the original. It is a very dull, wearisome, and lethargic affair. I can readily imagine that to some sanguine temperaments it would be altogether intolerable. For example, I cannot credit that the mettlesome poet Byron would have contentedly sat down with Bartleby to examine a law document of, say, five hundred pages, closely written in a crimpy hand.

Now and then, in the haste of business, it had been my habit to assist in comparing some brief document myself, calling Turkey or Nippers for this purpose. One object I had in placing Bartleby so handy to me behind the screen, was to avail myself of his services on such trival occasions. It was on the third day, I think, of his being with me, and before any necessity had arisen for having his own writing examined, that, being much hurried to complete a small affair I had in hand, I abruptly called to Bartleby. In my haste and natural expectancy of instant compliance, I sat with my head bent over the original on my desk, and my right hand sideways, and somewhat nervously extended with the copy, so that immediately upon emerging from his retreat, Bartleby might snatch it and proceed to business without the least delay.

In this very attitude did I sit when I called to him, rapidly stating what it was I wanted him to do—namely, to examine a small paper with me. Imagine my surprise, nay, my consternation, when without moving from his privacy, Bartleby, in a singularly mild, firm voice, replied, "I would prefer not to."

I sat awhile in perfect silence, rallying my stunned faculties. Immediately it occurred to me that my ears had deceived me, or Bartleby had entirely misunderstood my meaning. I repeated my request in the clearest tone I could assume. But in quite as clear as one came the previous reply, "I would prefer not to."

"Prefer not to," echoed I, rising in high excitement, and crossing the room with a stride. "What do you mean? Are you moonstruck? I want you to help me compare this sheet here—take it," and I thrust it towards him.

"I would prefer not to," said he.

I looked at him steadfastly. His face was leanly composed; his gray eye dimly calm. Not a wrinkle of agitation rippled him. Had there been the least uneasiness, anger, impatience or impertinence in his manner; in other words, had there been anything ordinarily human about him, doubtless I should have violently dismissed him from the premises. But as it was, I should have as soon thought of turning my pale plaster-of-paris bust of Cicero out-of-doors. I stood gazing at him awhile, as he went on with his own writing, and then reseated myself at my desk. This is very strange, thought I. What had one best do? But my business hurried me. I concluded to forget the matter for the present, reserving it for my future leisure. So calling Nippers from the other room, the paper was speedily examined.

A few days after this, Bartleby concluded four lengthy documents, being quadruplicates of a week's testimony taken before me in my High Court of Chancery. It became necessary to examine them. It was an important suit, and great accuracy was imperative. Having all things arranged I called Turkey, Nippers and Ginger Nut from the next room, meaning to place the four copies in the hands of my four clerks, while I should read from the original. Accordingly

Turkey, Nippers and Ginger Nut had taken their seats in a row, each with his document in hand, when I called to Bartleby to join this interesting group.

"Bartleby! quick, I am waiting."

I heard a slow scrape of his chair legs on the uncarpeted floor, and soon he appeared standing at the entrance of his hermitage.

"What is wanted?" said he mildly.

"The copies, the copies," said I hurriedly. "We are going to examine them. There"—and I held toward him the fourth quadruplicate.

"I would prefer not to," he said, and gently disappeared behind the screen.

For a few moments I was turned into a pillar of salt, standing at the head of my seated column of clerks. Recovering myself, I advanced towards the screen, and demanded the reason for such extraordinary conduct.

"*Why* do you refuse?"

"I would prefer not to."

With any other man I should have flown outright into a dreadful passion, scorned all further words, and thrust him ignominiously from my presence. But there was something about Bartleby that not only strangely disarmed me, but in a wonderful manner touched and disconcerted me. I began to reason with him.

"These are your own copies we are about to examine. It is labor saving to you, because one examination will answer for your four papers. It is common usage. Every copyist is bound to help examine his copy. Is it not so? Will you not speak? Answer!"

"I prefer not to," he replied in a flute-like tone. It seemed to me that while I had been addressing him, he carefully revolved every statement that I made; fully comprehended the meaning; could not gainsay the irresistible conclusion; but, at the same time, some paramount consideration prevailed with him to reply as he did.

"You are decided, then, not to comply with my request—a request made according to common usage and common sense?"

He briefly gave me to understand that on that point my judgment was sound. Yes: his decision was irreversible.

It is not seldom the case that when a man is browbeaten in some unprecedented and violently unreasonable way, he begins to stagger in his own plainest faith. He begins, as it were, vaguely to surmise that, wonderful as it may be, all the justice and all the reason is on the other side. Accordingly, if any disinterested persons are present, he turns to them for some reinforcement for his own faltering mind.

"Turkey," said I, "what do you think of this? Am I not right?"

"With submission, sir," said Turkey, with his blandest tone, "I think that you are."

"Nippers," said I, "what do *you* think of it?"

"I think I should kick him out of the office."

(The reader of nice perceptions will here perceive that, it being morning, Turkey's answer is couched in polite and tranquil terms, but Nippers replies in ill-tempered ones. Or, to repeat a previous sentence, Nipper's ugly mood was on duty, and Turkey's off.)

"Ginger Nut," said I, willing to enlist the smallest suffrage in my behalf, "what do *you* think of it?"

"I think, sir, he's a little *luny*," replied Ginger Nut, with a grin.

"You hear what they say," said I, turning towards the screen, "come forth and do your duty."

But he vouchsafed no reply. I pondered a moment in sore perplexity. But once more business hurried me. I determined again to postpone the consideration of this dilemma to my future leisure. With a little trouble we made out to examine the papers without Bartleby, though at every page or two, Turkey deferentially dropped his opinion that this proceeding was quite out of the common; while Nippers, twitching in his chair with a dyspeptic nervousness, ground out between his set teeth occasionally hissing maledictions against the stubborn oaf behind the screen. And for his (Nippers's) part, this was the first and the last time he would do another man's business without pay.

Meanwhile Bartleby sat in his hermitage, oblivious to everything but his own peculiar business there.

Some days passed, the scrivener being employed upon another lengthy work. His late remarkable conduct led me to regard his ways narrowly. I observed that he never went to dinner; indeed that he never went anywhere. As yet I had never of my personal knowledge known him to be outside of my office. He was a perpetual sentry in the corner. At about eleven o'clock though, in the morning, I noticed that Ginger Nut would advance toward the opening in Bartleby's screen, as if silently beckoned thither by a gesture invisible to me where I sat. The boy would then leave the office jingling a few pence, and reappear with a handful of ginger-nuts which he delivered in the hermitage, receiving two of the cakes for his trouble.

He lives, then, on ginger-nuts, thought I; never eats a dinner, properly speaking; he must be vegetarian then; but no; he nevers eats even vegetables, he eats nothing but ginger-nuts. My mind then ran on in reveries concerning the probable effects upon the human constitution of living entirely on ginger-nuts. Ginger-nuts are so called because they contain ginger as one of their peculiar constituents, and the final flavoring one. Now what was ginger? A hot, spicy thing. Was Bartleby hot and spicy? Not at all. Ginger, then, had no effect upon Bartleby. Probably he preferred it should have none.

Nothing so aggravates an earnest person as a passive resistance. If the individual so resisted be of a not inhumane temper, and the resisting one perfectly harmless in his passivity; then, in the better moods of the former, he will endeavor charitably to construe to his imagination what proves impossible to be solved by his judgment. Even so, for the most part, I regarded Bartleby and his ways. Poor fellow! thought I, he means no mischief; it is plain he intends no insolence; his aspect sufficiently evinces that his eccentricities are involuntary. He is useful to me. I can get along with him. If I turn him away, the chances are he will fall in with some less indulgent employer, and then he will be rudely treated, and perhaps driven forth miserably to starve. Yes. Here I can cheaply purchase a delicious self-approval. To befriend Bartleby; to humor him in his strange willfulness, will cost me little or nothing, while I lay up in my soul what will eventually prove a sweet morsel for my conscience. But this mood was not invariable with me. The passiveness of Bartleby sometimes irritated me. I felt strangely goaded on to encounter him in new opposition, to elicit some angry spark from him answerable to my own. But indeed I might as well have essayed to strike fire with my knuckles against a bit of Windsor soap. But one afternoon the evil impulse in me mastered me, and the following little scene ensued:

"Bartleby," said I, "when those papers are all copied, I will compare them with you."

"I would prefer not to."

"How? Surely you do not mean to persist in that mulish vagary?"

No answer.

I threw open the folding-doors near by, and turning upon Turkey and Nippers, exclaimed in an excited manner—

"He says, a second time, he won't examine his papers. What do you think of it, Turkey?"

It was afternoon, be it remembered. Turkey sat glowing like a brass boiler, his bald head steaming, his hands reeling among his blotted papers.

"Think of it?" roared Turkey; "I think I'll just step behind his screen, and black his eyes for him!"

So saying, Turkey rose to his feet and threw his arms into a pugilistic position. He was hurrying away to make good his promise, when I detained him, alarmed at the effect of incautiously rousing Turkey's combativeness after dinner.

"Sit down, Turkey," said I, "and hear what Nippers has to say. What do you think of it, Nippers? Would I not be justified in immediately dismissing Bartleby?"

"Excuse me, that is for you to decide, sir. I think his conduct quite unusual, and indeed unjust, as regards Turkey and myself. But it may only be a passing whim."

"Ah," exclaimed I, "you have strangely changed your mind then— you speak very gently of him now."

"All beer," cried Turkey; "gentleness is effects of beer—Nippers and I dined together today. You see how gentle *I* am, sir. Shall I go and black his eyes?"

"You refer to Bartleby, I suppose. No, not today, Turkey," I replied; "pray, put up your fists."

I closed the doors, and again advanced towards Bartleby. I felt additional incentives tempting me to my fate. I burned to be rebelled against again. I remembered that Bartleby never left the office.

"Bartleby," said I, "Ginger Nut is away; just step round to the Post Office, won't you? (it was but a three minutes' walk,) and see if there is anything for me."

"I would prefer not to."

"You *will* not?"

"I *prefer* not."

I staggered to my desk, and sat there in a deep study. My blind inveteracy returned. Was there any other thing in which I could procure myself to be ignominiously repulsed by this lean, penniless wight?—my hired clerk? What added thing is there, perfectly reasonable, that he will be sure to refuse to do?

"Bartleby!"

No answer.

"Bartleby," in a louder tone.

No answer.

"Bartleby," I roared.

Like a very ghost, agreeably to the laws of magical invocation, at the third summons, he appeared at the entrance of his hermitage.

"Go to the next room, and tell Nippers to come to me."

"I prefer not to," he respectfully and slowly said, and mildly disappeared.

"Very good, Bartleby," said I, in a quiet sort of serenely severe self-possessed tone, intimating the unalterable purpose of some terrible retribution very close at hand. At the moment I half intended something of the kind. But upon the whole, as it was drawing towards my dinner-hour, I thought it best to put on my hat and walk home for the day, suffering much from perplexity and distress of mind.

Shall I acknowledge it? The conclusion of this whole business was, that it soon became a fixed fact of my chambers, that a pale young scrivener, by the name of Bartleby, had a desk there; that he copied for me at the usual rate of four cents a folio (one hundred words); but he was permanently exempt from examining the work done by him, that duty being transferred to Turkey and Nippers, one of compliment doubtless to their superior acuteness; moreover, said Bartleby was never on any account to be dispatched on the most trivial errand of any sort; and that even if entreated to take upon him such a matter, it was generally understood that he would prefer not to—in other words, that he would refuse point-blank.

As days passed on, I became considerably reconciled to Bartleby. His steadiness, his freedom from all dissipation, his incessant industry (except when he chose to throw himself into a standing revery behind his screen), his great stillness, his unalterableness of demeanor under all circumstances, made him a valuable acquisition. One prime thing was this,—*he was always there*,—first in the morning, continually through the day, and the last at night. I had a singular confidence in his honesty. I felt my most precious papers perfectly safe in his hands. Sometimes to be sure I could not, for the very soul of me, avoid falling into sudden spasmodic passions with him. For it was exceeding difficult to bear in mind all the time those strange peculiarities, privileges, and unheard of exemptions, forming the tacit stipulations on Bartleby's part under which he remained in my office. Now and then, in the eagerness of dispatching pressing business, I would inadvertently summon Bartleby, in a short, rapid tone, to put his finger, say, on the incipient tie of a bit of red tape with which I was about compressing some papers. Of course, from behind the screen the usual answer, "I prefer not to," was sure to come; and then, how could a human creature with the common infirmities of our nature, refrain from bitterly exclaiming upon such perverseness—such unreasonableness? However, every added repulse of this sort which I received only tended to lessen the probability of my repeating the inadvertence.

Here it must be said, that according to the custom of most legal gentlemen occupying chambers in densely-populated law buildings, there were several keys to my door. One was kept by a woman residing in the attic, which person weekly scrubbed and daily swept and dusted my apartments. Another was kept by Turkey for convenience sake. The third I sometimes carried in my own pocket. The fourth I knew not who had.

Now, one Sunday morning I happened to go to Trinity Church, to hear a celebrated preacher, and finding myself rather early on the ground, I thought I would walk round to my chambers for a while. Luckily I had my key with me; but upon applying it to the lock, I found it resisted by something inserted from the inside. Quite surprised, I called out; when to my consternation a key was turned from within; and thrusting his lean visage at me, and holding the door ajar, the apparition of Bartleby appeared, in his shirt sleeves, and otherwise in a strangely tattered dishabille, saying quietly that he was sorry, but he was deeply engaged just then, and—preferred not admitting me at present. In a brief word or two, he moreover added, that perhaps I had better walk round the block two or three times, and by that time he would probably have concluded his affairs.

Now, the utterly, unsurmised appearance of Bartleby, tenanting my law-chambers of a Sunday morning, with his cadaverously gentlemanly *nonchalance*, yet withal firm and self-possessed, had such a strange effect upon me, that incontinently I slunk away from my own door, and did as desired. But not without sundry twinges of impotent rebellion against the mild effrontery of this unaccountable scrivener. Indeed, it was his wonderful mildness, chiefly, which not only disarmed me, but unmanned me, as it were. For I consider that one, for the time, is sort of unmanned when he tranquilly permits his hired clerk to dictate to him, and order him away from his own premises. Furthermore, I was full of uneasiness as to what Bartleby could possibly be doing in my office in his shirt sleeves, and in an otherwise dismantled condition of a Sunday morning. Was anything amiss going on? Nay, that was out of the question. It was not to be thought of for a moment that Bartleby was an immoral person. But what could he be doing there?—copying? Nay again, whatever might be his eccentricities, Bartleby was an eminently decorous person. He would be the last man to sit down to his desk in any state approaching to nudity. Besides, it was Sunday; and there was something about Bartleby that forbade the supposition that he would by any secular occupation violate the proprieties of the day.

Nevertheless, my mind was not pacified; and full of a restless curiosity, at last I returned to the door. Without hindrance I inserted my key, opened it, and entered. Bartleby was not to be seen. I looked round anxiously, peeped behind the screen; but it was very plain that he was gone. Upon more closely examining the place, I surmised that for an indefinite period Bartleby must have ate, dressed, and slept in my office, and that too without plate, mirror, or bed. The cushioned seat of a rickety old sofa in one corner bore the faint impress of a lean, reclining form. Rolled away under his desk, I found a blanket under the empty grate, a blacking box and brush; on a chair, a tin basin, with soap and a ragged towel; in a newspaper a few crumbs of ginger-nuts and a morsel of cheese. Yes, thought I, it is evident enough that Bartleby has been making his home here, keeping bachelor's hall all by himself. Immediately then the thought came sweeping across me, What miserable friendlessness and loneliness are here revealed! His poverty is great; but his solitude, how horrible! Think of it. Of a Sunday, Wall Street is deserted as Petra;[8] and every night of every day it is an emptiness. This building too, which of weekdays hums with industry and life, at nightfall echoes with sheer vacancy, and all through Sunday is forlorn. And here Bartleby makes his home; sole spectator of a solitude which he has seen all populous—a sort of innocent and transformed Marius brooding among the ruins of Carthage!

For the first time in my life a feeling of overpowering stinging melancholy seized me. Before, I had never experienced aught but a not-unpleasing sadness. The bond of a common humanity now drew me irresistibly to gloom. A fraternal melancholy! For both I and Bartleby were sons of Adam. I remembered the bright silks and sparkling faces I had seen that day, in gala trim, swan-like sailing down the Mississippi of Broadway; and I contrasted them with the pallid copyist, and thought to myself, Ah, happiness courts the light, so we deem the world is gay; but misery hides aloof, so we deem that misery there is none. These sad fancyings—chimeras, doubtless, of a sick and silly brain—led on to other and more special thoughts, concerning the eccentricities of Bartleby. Presentiments of strange discoveries hovered round me. The scrivener's pale form appeared to me laid out, among uncaring strangers, in its shivering winding sheet.

Suddenly I was attracted by Bartleby's closed desk, the key in open sight left in the lock.

I mean no mischief, seek the gratification of no heartless curiosity, thought I; besides, the desk is mine, and its contents too, so I will make bold to look within. Everything was methodically arranged, the papers smoothly placed. The pigeonholes were deep, and removing the files of documents, I groped into their recesses. Presently I felt something there and dragged it out. It was an old bandanna handkerchief, heavy and knotted. I opened it, and saw it was a savings' bank.

---

8. Ancient, once flourishing Middle Eastern trade center.

I now recalled all the quiet mysteries which I had noted in the man. I remembered that he never spoke but to answer; that though at intervals he had considerable time to himself, yet I had never seen him reading—no, not even a newspaper; that for long periods he would stand looking out, at his pale window behind the screen, upon the dead brick wall; I was quite sure he never visited any refectory or eating house; while his pale face clearly indicated that he never drank beer like Turkey, or tea and coffee even, like other men; that he never went anywhere in particular that I could learn; never went out for a walk, unless indeed that was the case at present; that he had declined telling who he was, or whence he came, or whether he had any relatives in the world; that though so thin and pale, he never complained of ill health. And more than all, I remembered a certain unconscious air of pallid—how shall I call it?—of pallid haughtiness, say, or rather an austere reserve about him, which had positively awed me into my tame compliance with his eccentricities, when I had feared to ask him to do the slightest incidental thing for me, even though I might know, from his long-continued motionlessness, that behind his screen he must be standing in one of those dead-wall reveries of his.

Revolving all these things, and coupling them with the recently discovered fact that he made my office his constant abiding place and home, and not forgetful of his morbid moodiness; revolving all these things, a prudential feeling began to steal over me. My first emotions had been those of pure melancholy and sincerest pity; but just in proportion as the forlornness of Bartleby grew and grew to my imagination, did that same melancholy merge into fear, that pity into repulsion. So true it is, and so terrible too, that up to a certain point the thought or sight of misery enlists our best affections; but, in certain special cases, beyond that point it does not. They err who would assert that invariably this is owing to the inherent selfishness of the human heart. It rather proceeds from a certain hopelessness of remedying excessive and organic ill. To a sensitive being, pity is not seldom pain. And when at last it is perceived that such pity cannot lead to effectual succor, common sense bids the soul be rid of it. What I saw that morning persuaded me that the scrivener was the victim of innate and incurable disorder. I might give alms to his body; but his body did not pain him; it was his soul that suffered, and his soul I could not reach.

I did not accomplish the purpose of going to Trinity Church that morning. Somehow, the things I had seen disqualified me for the time from churchgoing. I walked homeward, thinking what I would do with Bartleby. Finally, I resolved upon this;—I would put certain calm questions to him the next morning, touching his history, &c., and if he declined to answer them openly and unreservedly (and I supposed he would prefer not), then to give him a twenty-dollar bill over and above whatever I might owe him, and tell him his services were no longer required; but that if in any other way I could assist him, I would be happy to do so, especially if he desired to return to his native place, wherever that might be, I would willingly help to defray the expenses. Moreover, if, after reaching home, he found himself at any time in want of aid, a letter from him would be sure of a reply.

The next morning came.

"Bartleby," said I, gently calling to him behind his screen.

No reply.

"Bartleby," said I, in a still gentler tone, "come here; I am not going to ask you to do anything you would prefer not to do—I simply wish to speak to you."

Upon this he noiselessly slid into view.

"Will you tell me, Bartleby, where you were born?"

"I would prefer not to."

"Will you tell me *anything* about yourself?"

"I would prefer not to."

"But what reasonable objection can you have to speak to me? I feel friendly towards you."

He did not look at me while I spoke, but kept his glance fixed upon my bust of Cicero, which as I then sat, was directly behind me, some six inches above my head.

"What is your answer, Bartleby?" said I, after waiting a considerable time for a reply, during which his countenance remained immovable, only there was the faintest conceivable tremor of the white attenuated mouth.

"At present I prefer to give no answer," he said, and retired into his hermitage.

It was rather weak in me I confess, but his manner on this

occasion nettled me. Not only did there seem to lurk in it a certain calm disdain, but his perverseness seemed ungrateful, considering the undeniable good usage and indulgence he had received from me.

Again I sat ruminating what I should do. Mortified as I was at his behavior, and resolved as I had been to dismiss him when I entered my office, nevertheless I strangely felt something superstitious knocking at my heart, and forbidding me to carry out my purpose, and denouncing me for a villain if I dared to breathe one bitter word against this forlornest of mankind. At last, familiarly drawing my chair behind his screen, I sat down and said: "Bartleby, never mind then about revealing your history; but let me entreat you, as a friend, to comply as far as may be with the usages of this office. Say now you will help to examine papers tomorrow or next day: in short, say now that in a day or two you will begin to be a little reasonable:—say so, Bartleby."

"At present I would prefer not to be a little reasonable," was his mildly cadaverous reply.

Just then the folding-doors opened, and Nippers approached. He seemed suffering from an unusually bad night's rest, induced by severer indigestion than common. He overheard those final words of Bartleby.

"*Prefer not*, eh?" gritted Nippers—"I'd *prefer* him, if I were you, sir," addressing me—"I'd prefer him; I'd give him preferences, the stubborn mule! What is it, sir, pray, that he *prefers* not to do now?"

Bartleby moved not a limb.

"Mr. Nippers," said I, "I'd prefer that you would withdraw for the present."

Somehow, of late I had got into the way of involuntarily using this word "prefer" upon all sorts of not exactly suitable occasions. And I trembled to think that my contact with the scrivener had already and seriously affected me in a mental way. And what further and deeper aberration might it not yet produce? This apprehension had not been without efficacy in determining me to summary means.

As Nippers, looking very sour and sulky, was departing, Turkey blandly and deferentially approached.

"With submission, sir," said he, "yesterday I was thinking about Bartleby here, and I think that if he would but prefer to take a quart of good ale every day, it would do much towards mending him and enabling him to assist in examining his papers."

"So you have got the word too," said I, slightly excited.

"With submission, what word, sir?" asked Turkey, respectfully crowding himself into the contracted space behind the screen, and by so doing making me jostle the scrivener. "What word, sir?"

"I would prefer to be left alone here," said Bartleby, as if offended at being mobbed in his privacy.

"*That's* the word, Turkey," said I—"*that's* it."

"Oh, *prefer*? oh yes—queer word. I never use it myself. But, sir, as I was saying, if he would but prefer—"

"Turkey," interrupted I, "you will please withdraw."

"Oh certainly, sir, if you prefer that I should."

As he opened the folding-door to retire, Nippers at his desk caught a glimpse of me, and asked whether I would prefer to have a certain paper copied on blue paper or white. He did not in the least roguishly accent the word *prefer*. It was plain that it involuntarily rolled from his tongue. I thought to myself, surely I must get rid of a demented man, who already has in some degree turned the tongues, if not the heads of myself and clerks. But I thought it prudent not to break the dismission at once.

The next day I noticed that Bartleby did nothing but stand at his window in his dead-wall revery. Upon asking him why he did not write, he said that he had decided upon doing no more writing.

"Why, how now? what next?" exclaimed I, "do no more writing?"

"No more."

"And what is the reason?"

"Do you not see the reason for yourself," he indifferently replied.

I looked steadfastly at him, and perceived that his eyes looked dull and glazed. Instantly it occurred to me, that his unexampled diligence in copying by his dim window for the first few weeks of his stay with me might have temporarily impaired his vision.

I was touched. I said something in condolence with him. I

hinted that of course he did wisely in abstaining from writing for a while; and urged him to embrace that opportunity of taking wholesome exercise in the open air. This, however, he did not do. A few days after this, my other clerks being absent, and being in a great hurry to dispatch certain letters by the mail, I thought that, having nothing else earthly to do, Bartleby would surely be less inflexible than usual, and carry these letters to the post office. But he blankly declined. So, much to my inconvenience, I went myself.

Still added days went by. Whether Bartleby's eyes improved or not, I could not say. To all appearance, I thought they did. But when I asked him if they did, he vouchsafed no answer. At all events, he would do no copying. At last, in reply to my urgings, he informed me that he had permanently given up copying.

"What!" exclaimed I; "suppose your eyes should get entirely well—better than ever before—would you not copy then?"

"I have given up copying," he answered, and slid aside.

He remained, as ever, a fixture in my chamber. Nay—if that were possible—he became still more of a fixture than before. What was to be done? He would do nothing in the office: why should he stay there? In plain fact, he had now become a millstone to me, not only useless as a necklace, but afflictive to bear. Yet I was sorry for him. I speak less than truth when I say that, on his own account, he occasioned me uneasiness. If he would but have named a single relative or friend, I would instantly have written, and urged their taking the poor fellow away to some convenient retreat. But he seemed alone, absolutely alone in the universe. A bit of wreck in the mid-Atlantic. At length, necessities connected with my business tyrannized over all other considerations. Decently as I could, I told Bartleby that in six days' time he must unconditionally leave the office. I warned him to take meaures, in the interval, for procuring some other abode. I offered to assist him in this endeavor, if he himself would but take the first step towards a removal. "And when you finally quit me, Bartleby," added I, "I shall see that you not go away entirely unprovided. Six days from this hour, remember."

At the expiration of that period, I peeped behind the screen, and lo! Bartleby was there.

I buttoned up my coat, balanced myself; advanced slowly towards him, touched his shoulder, and said, "The time has come; you must quit this place; I am sorry for you; here is money; but you must go."

"I would prefer not," he replied, with his back still towards me.

"You *must*."

He remained silent.

Now I had an unbounded confidence in this man's common honesty. He had frequently restored to me sixpences and shillings carelessly dropped upon the floor, for I am apt to be very reckless in such shirt-button affairs. The proceeding then which followed will not be deemed extraordinary.

"Bartleby," said I, "I owe you twelve dollars on account; here are thirty-two; the odd twenty are yours.—Will you take it?" and I handed the bills towards him.

But he made no motion.

"I will leave them here then," putting them under a weight on the table. Then taking my hat and cane and going to the door I tranquilly turned and added—"After you have removed your things from these offices, Bartleby, you will of course lock the door—since everyone is now gone for the day but you—and if you please, slip your key underneath the mat, so that I may have it in the morning. I shall not see you again; so good-bye to you. If hereafter in your new place of abode I can be of any service to you, do not fail to advise me by letter. Good-bye, Bartleby, and fare you well."

But he answered not a word; like the last column of some ruined temple, he remained standing mute and solitary in the middle of the otherwise deserted room.

As I walked home in a pensive mood, my vanity got the better of my pity. I could not but highly plume myself on my masterly management in getting rid of Bartleby. Masterly I call it, and such it must appear to any dispassionate thinker. The beauty of my procedure seemed to consist in its perfect quietness. There was no vulgar bullying, no bravado of any sort, no choleric hectoring, and striding to and fro across the apartment, jerking out vehement commands for Bartleby to bundle himself off with his beggarly traps.[9] Nothing of the kind. Without loudly bidding Bartleby depart—as an inferior genius might have done—I *assumed* the ground that depart he must; and upon that assumption built all I had to say. The more I thought over my procedure, the more I was charmed with it. Nevertheless, next morning, upon awakening, I had my doubts,—I had somehow slept off the fumes of vanity. One of the coolest and wisest hours a man has is just after he awakes in the morning. My procedure seemed as sagacious as ever,—but only in theory. How it would prove in practice—there was the rub. It was truly a beautiful thought to have assumed Bartleby's departure; but, after all, that assumption was simply my own, and none of Bartleby's. The great point was, not whether I had assumed that he would quit me, but whether he would prefer so to do. He was more a man of preferences than assumptions.

After breakfast, I walked downtown, arguing the probabilities *pro* and *con*. One moment I thought it would prove a miserable failure, and Bartleby would be found all alive at my office as usual; the next moment it seemed certain that I should see his chair empty. And so I kept veering about. At the corner of Broadway and Canal Street, I saw quite an excited group of people standing in earnest conversation.

"I'll take odds he doesn't," said a voice as I passed.

"Doesn't go?—done!" said I, "put up your money."

I was instinctively putting my hand in my pocket to produce my own, when I remembered that this was an election day. The words I had overheard bore no reference to Bartleby, but to the success or non-success of some candidate for the mayoralty. In my intent frame of mind, I had, as it were, imagined that all Broadway shared in my excitement, and were debating the same question with me. I passed on, very thankful that the uproar of the street screened my momentary absent-mindedness.

As I had intended, I was earlier than usual at my office door. I stood listening for a moment. All was still. He must be gone. I tried the knob. The door was locked. Yes, my procedure had worked to a charm; he indeed must be vanished. Yet a certain melancholy mixed with this: I was almost sorry for my brilliant success. I was fumbling under the door mat for the key, which

9. Belongings.

Bartleby was to have left there for me, when accidentally my knee knocked against a panel, producing a summoning sound, and in response a voice came to me from within—"Not yet; I am occupied."

It was Bartleby.

I was thunderstruck. For an instant I stood like the man who, pipe in mouth, was killed one cloudless afternoon long ago in Virginia, by summer lightning; at his own warm open window he was killed, and remained leaning out there upon the dreamy afternoon, till some one touched him, when he fell.

"Not gone!" I murmured at last. But again obeying that wondrous ascendancy, which the inscrutable scrivener had over me, and from which ascendancy, for all my chafing, I could not completely escape, I slowly went downstairs and out into the street, and while walking round the block, considered what I should next do in this unheard-of perplexity. Turn the man out by an actual thrusting I could not; to drive him away by calling him hard names would not do; calling in the police was an unpleasant idea; and yet, permit him to enjoy his cadaverous triumph over me,—this too I could not think of. What was to be done? or, if nothing could be done, was there anything further that I could *assume* in the matter? Yes, as before I had prospectively assumed that Bartleby would depart, so now I might retrospectively assume that departed he was. In the legitimate carrying out of this assumption, I might enter my office in a great hurry, and pretending not to see Bartleby at all, walk straight against him as if he were air. Such a proceeding would in a singular degree have the appearance of a home-thrust. It was hardly possible that Bartleby could withstand such an application of the doctrine of assumptions. But upon second thoughts the success of the plan seemed rather dubious. I resolved to argue the matter over with him again.

"Bartleby," said I, entering the office, with a quietly severe expression, "I am seriously displeased. I am pained, Bartleby. I had thought better of you. I had imagined you of such a gentlemanly organization, that in any delicate dilemma a slight hint would suffice—in short, an assumption. But it appears I am deceived. I added, unaffectedly starting, "you have not even touched that money yet," pointing to it, just where I had left it the evening previous.

He answered nothing.

"Will you, or will you not, quit me?" I now demanded in a sudden passion, advancing close to him.

"I would prefer *not* to quit you," he replied, gently emphasizing the *not*.

"What earthly right have you to stay here? Do you pay any rent? Do you pay my taxes? Or is this property yours?"

He answered nothing.

"Are you ready to go on and write now? Are your eyes recovered? Could you copy a small paper for me this morning? or help to examine a few lines? or step round to the post office? In a word, will you do anything at all, to give a coloring to your refusal to depart the premises?"

He silently retired into his hermitage.

I was now in such a state of nervous resentment that I thought it but prudent to check myself at present from further demonstrations. Bartleby and I were alone. I remembered the tragedy of the unfortunate Adams and the still more unfortunate Colt in the solitary office of the latter; and how poor Colt, being dreadfully incensed by Adams, and imprudently permitting himself to get wildly excited, was at unawares hurried into his fatal act—an act which certainly no man could possibly deplore more than the actor himself. Often it had occurred to me in my ponderings upon the subject, that had that altercation taken place in the public street, or at a private residence, it would not have terminated as it did. It was the circumstance of being alone in a solitary office, up stairs, of a building entirely unhallowed by humanizing domestic associations—an uncarpeted office, doubtless, of a dusty, haggard sort of appearance;—this it must have been, which greatly helped to enhance the irritable desperation of the hapless Colt.

But when this old Adam of resentment rose in me and tempted me concerning Bartleby, I grappled him and threw him. How? Why, simply by recalling the divine injunction: "A new commandment give I unto you, that ye love one another." Yes, this it was that saved me. Aside from higher considerations, charity often operates as a vastly wise and prudent principle—a great safeguard to its possessor. Men have committed murder for jealousy's sake, and anger's sake, and hatred's sake, and selfishness' sake, and spiritual pride's sake; but no man that ever I heard of, ever committed a diabolical murder for sweet charity's sake. Mere self-interest, then, if no better motive can be enlisted, should, especially with high-tempered men, prompt all beings to charity and philanthropy. At any rate, upon the occasion in question, I strove to drown my exasperated feelings towards the scrivener by benevolently construing his conduct. Poor fellow, poor fellow! thought I, he don't mean anything; and besides, he has seen hard times, and ought to be indulged.

I endeavored also immediately to occupy myself, and at the same time to comfort my despondency. I tried to fancy that in the course of the morning, at such time as might prove agreeable to him, Bartleby, of his own free accord, would emerge from his hermitage, and take up some decided line of march in the direction of the door. But no. Half-past twelve o'clock came; Turkey began to glow in the face, overturn his inkstand, and become generally obstreperous; Nippers abated down into quietude and courtesy; Ginger Nut munched his noon apple; and Bartleby remained standing at this window in one of his profoundest deadwall reveries. Will it be credited? Ought I to acknowledge it? That afternoon I left the office without saying one further word to him.

Some days now passed, during which, at leisure intervals I looked a little into "Edwards on the Will," and "Priestley on Necessity." Under the circumstances, those books induced a salutary feeling. Gradually I slid into the persuasion that these troubles of mine touching the scrivener, had been all predestinated from eternity, and Bartleby as billeted upon me for some mysterious purpose of an all-wise Providence, which it was not for a mere mortal like me to fathom. Yes, Bartleby, stay there behind your screen, thought I; I shall persecute you no more; you are harmless and noiseless as any of these old chairs; in short, I never feel so private as when I know you are here. At least I see it, I feel it; I penetrate to the predestinated purpose of my life. I am content. Others may have loftier parts to enact; but my mission in this world, Bartleby, is to furnish you with office-room for such period as you may see fit to remain.

I believe that this wise and blessed frame of mind would have continued with me, had it not been for the unsolicited and uncharitable remarks obtruded upon me by my professional friends who visited the rooms. But thus it often is, that the constant friction of illiberal minds wears out at last the best resolves of the more generous. Though to be sure, when I reflected upon it, it was not strange that people entering my office should be struck by the peculiar aspect of the unaccountable Bartleby, and so be tempted to throw out some sinister observations concerning him. Sometimes an attorney having business with me, and calling at my office, and finding no one but the scrivener there, would undertake to obtain some sort of precise information from him touching my whereabouts; but without heeding his idle talk, Bartleby would remain standing immovable in the middle of the room. So after contemplating him in that position for a time, the attorney would depart, no wiser than he came.

Also, when a Reference was going on, and the room full of lawyers and witnesses and business was driving fast; some deeply occupied legal gentleman present, seeing Bartleby wholly unemployed, would request him to run round to his (the legal gentleman's) office and fetch some papers for him. Thereupon, Bartleby would tranquilly decline, and yet remain idle as before. Then the lawyer would give a great stare, and turn to me. And what would I say? At last I was made aware that all through the circle of my professional acquaintance, a whisper of wonder was running round, having reference to the strange creature I kept at my office. This worried me very much. And as the idea came upon me of his possibly turning out a long-lived man, and keep occupying my chambers, and denying my authority; and perplexing my visitors; and scandalizing my professional reputation; and casting a general gloom over the premises; keeping soul and body together to the last upon his savings (for doubtless he spent but half a dime a day), and in the end perhaps outlive me, and claim possession of my office by right of his perpetual occupancy: as all these dark anticipations crowded upon me more and more, and my friends continually intruded their relentless remarks upon the apparition in my room; a great change was wrought in me. I resolved to gather all my faculties together, and forever rid me of this intolerable incubus.

Ere revolving any complicated project, however, adapted to this end, I first simply suggested to Bartleby the propriety of his permanent departure. In a calm and serious tone, I commended the idea to his careful and mature consideration. But having taken three days to meditate upon it, he apprised me that his original determination remained the same; in short, that he still preferred to abide with me.

What shall I do? I now said to myself, buttoning up my coat to the last button. What shall I do? what ought I to do? what does conscience say I *should* do with this man, or rather ghost. Rid myself of him, I must; go, he shall. But how? You will not thrust him, the poor, pale, passive mortal,—you will not thrust such a helpless creature out of your door? you will not dishonor yourself by such cruelty? No, I will not, I cannot do that. Rather would I let him live and die here, and then mason up his remains in the wall. What then will you do? For all your coaxing, he will not budge. Bribes he leaves under your own paperweight on your table; in short, it is quite plain that he prefers to cling to you.

Then something severe, something unusual must be done. What! surely you will not have him collared by a constable, and commit his innocent pallor to the common jail? And upon what ground could you procure such a thing to be done?—a vagrant, is he? What! he a vagrant, a wanderer, who refuses to budge? It is because he will *not* be a vagrant, then, that you seek to count him *as* a vagrant. That is too absurd. No visible means of support: there I have him. Wrong again: for indubitably he *does* support himself, and that is the only unanswerable proof that any man can show of his possessing the means so to do. No more then. Since he will not quit me, I must quit him. I will change my offices; I will move elsewhere; and give him fair notice, that if I find him on my new premises I will then proceed against him as a common trespasser.

Acting accordingly, next day I thus addressed him: "I find these chambers too far from the City Hall; the air is unwholesome. In a word, I propose to remove my offices next week, and shall no longer require your services. I tell you this now, in order that you may seek another place."

He made no reply, and nothing more was said.

On the appointed day I engaged carts and men, proceeded to my chambers, and having but little furniture, everything was removed in a few hours. Throughout, the scrivener remained standing behind the screen, which I directed to be removed the last thing. It was withdrawn; and being folded up like a huge folio, left him the motionless occupant of a naked room. I stood in the entry watching him a moment, while something from within me upbraided me.

I re-entered, with my hand in my pocket—and—and my heart in my mouth.

"Good-bye, Bartleby; I am going—goodbye, and God some way bless you; and take that," slipping something in his hand. But it dropped upon the floor, and then,—strange to say—I tore myself from him whom I had so longed to be rid of.

Established in my new quarters, for a day or two I kept the door locked, and started at every footfall in the passages. When I returned to my rooms after any little absence, I would pause at the threshold for an instant, and attentively listen, ere applying my key. But these fears were needless. Bartleby never came nigh me.

I thought all was going well, when a perturbed-looking stranger visited me, inquiring whether I was the person who had recently occupied rooms at No.——Wall Street.

Full of forebodings, I replied that I was.

"Then sir," said the stranger, who proved a lawyer, "you are responsible for the man you left there. He refuses to do any copying; he refuses to do anything; he says he prefers not to; and he refuses to quit the premises."

"I am very sorry, sir," said I, with assumed tranquillity, but an inward tremor, "but, really, the man you allude to is nothing to me—he is no relation or apprentice of mine, that you should hold me responsible for him."

"In mercy's name, who is he?"

"I certainly cannot inform you. I know nothing about him. Formerly I employed him as a copyist; but he has done nothing for me now for some time past."

"I shall settle him then,—good morning, sir."

Several days passed, and I heard nothing more; and though I often felt a charitable prompting to call at the place and see poor Bartleby, yet a certain squeamishness of I know not what withheld me.

All is over with him, by this time, thought I at last, when through another week no further intelligence reached me. But coming to my room the day after, I found several persons waiting at my door in a high state of nervous excitement.

"That's the man—here he comes," cried the foremost one, whom I recognized as the lawyer who had previously called upon me alone.

"You must take him away, sir, at once," cried a portly person among them, advancing upon me, and whom I knew to be the landlord of No.——Wall Street. "These gentlemen, my tenants, cannot stand it any longer; Mr. B——" pointing to the lawyer, "has turned him out of his room, and he now persists in haunting the building generally, sitting upon the banisters of the stairs by day, and sleeping in the entry by night. Everybody is concerned; clients are leaving the offices; some fears are entertained of a mob; something you must do, and that without delay."

Aghast at this torrent, I fell back before it, and would fain have locked myself in my new quarters. In vain I persisted that Bartleby was nothing to me—no more than to anyone else. In vain:—I was the last person known to have anything to do with him, and they held me to the terrible account. Fearful then of being exposed in the papers (as one person present obscurely threatened) I considered the matter, and at length said, that if the lawyer would give me a confidential interview with the scrivener, in his (the lawyer's) own room, I would that afternoon strive my best to rid them of the nuisance they complained of.

Going upstairs to my old haunt, there was Bartleby silently sitting upon the banister at the landing.

"What are you doing here, Bartleby?" said I.

"Sitting upon the banister," he mildly replied.

I motioned him into the lawyer's room, who then left us.

"Bartleby," said I, "are you aware that you are the cause of great tribulation to me, by persisting in occupying the entry after being dismissed from the office?"

No answer.

"Now one of two things must take place. Either you must do something, or something must be done to you. Now what sort of business would you like to engage in? Would you like to re-engage in copying for someone?"

"No; I would prefer not to make any change."

"Would you like a clerkship in a drygoods store?"

"There is too much confinement about that. No, I would not like a clerkship; but I am not particular."

"Too much confinement," I cried, "why you keep yourself confined all the time!"

"I would prefer not to take a clerkship," he rejoined, as if to settle that little item at once.

"How would a bartender's business suit you? There is no trying of the eyesight in that."

"I would not like it at all; though, as I said before, I am not particular."

His unwonted wordiness inspirited me. I returned to the charge.

"Well then, would you like to travel through the country collecting bills for the merchants? That would improve your health."

"No, I would prefer to be doing something else."

"How then would going as a companion to Europe, to entertain some young gentleman with your conversation,—how would that suit you?"

"Not at all. It does not strike me that there is anything definite about that. I like to be stationary. But I am not particular."

"Stationary you shall be then," I cried, now losing all patience, and for the first time in all my exasperating connection with him fairly flying into a passion. "If you do not go away from these premises before night, I shall feel bound—indeed I *am* bound—to—to—to quit the premises myself!" I rather absurdly concluded, knowing not with what possible threat to try to frighten his immobility into compliance. Despairing of all further efforts, I was precipitately leaving him, when a final thought occurred to me—one which had not been wholly unindulged before.

"Bartleby," said I, in the kindest tone I could assume under such exciting circumstances, "will you go home with me now—not to my office, but my dwelling—and remain there till we can conclude upon some convenient arrangement for you at our leisure? Come, let us start now, right away."

"No: at present I would prefer not to make any change at all."

I answered nothing; but effectually dodging everyone by the suddenness and rapidity of my flight, rushed from the building, ran up Wall Street toward Broadway, and jumping into the first omnibus was soon removed from pursuit. As soon as tranquility returned I distinctly perceived that I had done all that I possibly could, both in respect to the demands of the landlord and his tenants, and with regard to my own desire and sense of duty, to benefit Bartleby, and shield him from rude persecution. I now strove to be entirely carefree and quiescent; and my conscience justified me in the attempt; though indeed it was not so successful as I could have wished. So fearful was I of being again hunted out by the incensed landlord and his exasperated tenants, that, surrendering my business to Nippers, for a few days I drove about the upper part of the town and through the suburbs, in my rockaway; crossed over to Jersey City and Hoboken, and paid fugitive visits to Manhattanville and Astoria. In fact I almost lived in my rockaway for the time.

When again I entered my office, lo, a note from the landlord lay upon the desk. I opened it with trembling hands. It informed me that the writer had sent to the police, and had Bartleby removed to the Tombs as a vagrant. Moreover, since I knew more about him than anyone else, he wished me to appear at that place, and make a suitable statement of the facts. These tidings had a conflicting effect upon me. At first I was indignant; but at last almost approved. The landlord's energetic, summary disposition had led him to adopt a procedure which I do not think I would have decided upon myself; and yet as a last resort, under such peculiar circumstances, it seemed the only plan.

As I afterwards learned, the poor scrivener, when told that he must be conducted to the Tombs, offered not the slightest obstacle, but in his pale unmoving way, silently acquiesced.

Some of the compassionate and curious bystanders joined the party; and headed by one of the constables arm in arm with Bartleby, the silent procession filed its way through all the noise, and heat, and joy of the roaring thoroughfares at noon.

The same day I received the note I went to the Tombs, or to speak more properly, the Halls of Justice. Seeking the right officer, I stated the purpose of my call, and was informed that the individual I described was indeed within. I then assured the functionary that Bartleby was a perfectly honest man, and greatly to be compassionated, however unaccountably eccentric. I narrated all I knew, and closed by suggesting the idea of letting him remain in as indulgent confinement as possible till something less harsh might be done—though indeed I hardly knew what. At all events, if nothing else could be decided upon, the alms-house must receive him. I then begged to have an interview.

Being under no disgraceful charge, and quite serene and harmless in all his ways, they had permitted him freely to wander about the prison, and especially in the inclosed grass-platted yards thereof. And so I found him there, standing all alone in the quietest of the yards, his face towards a high wall, while all around, from the narrow slits of the jail windows, I thought I saw peering out upon him the eyes of murderers and thieves.

"Bartleby!"

"I know you," he said, without looking round,—"and I want nothing to say to you."

"It was not I that brought you here, Bartleby," said I, keenly pained at his implied suspicion. "And to you, this should not be so vile a place. Nothing reproachful attaches to you by being here. And see, it is not so sad a place as one might think. Look, there is the sky, and here is the grass."

"I know where I am," he replied, but would say nothing more, and so I left him.

As I entered the corridor again, a broad meat-like man, in an apron, accosted me, and jerking his thumb over his shoulder said—"Is that your friend?"

"Yes."

"Does he want to starve? If he does, let him live on the prison fare, that's all."

"Who are you?" asked I, not knowing what to make of such an unofficially-speaking person in such a place.

"I am the grub-man. Such gentlemen as have friends here, hire me to provide them with something good to eat."

"Is this so?" said I, turning to the turnkey.

He said it was.

"Well then," said I, slipping some silver into the grub-man's hands (for so they called him). "I want you to give particular attention to my friend there; let him have the best dinner you can get. And you must be as polite to him as possible."

"Introduce me, will you?" said the grub-man, looking at me

with an expression which seemed to say he was all impatience for an opportunity to give a specimen of his breeding.

Thinking it would prove of benefit to the scrivener, I acquiesced; and asking the grub-man his name, went up with him to Bartleby.

"Bartleby, this is Mr. Cutlets; you will find him very useful to you."

"Your sarvant, sir, your sarvant," said the grub-man, making a low salutation behind his apron. "Hope you find it pleasant here, sir;—spacious grounds—cool apartments, sir—hope you'll stay with us some time—try to make it agreeable. May Mrs. Cutlets and I have the pleasure of your company to dinner, sir, in Mrs. Cutlets' private room?"

"I prefer not to dine today," said Bartleby, turning away. "It would disagree with me; I am unused to dinners." So saying he slowly moved to the other side of the inclosure, and took up a position fronting the deadwall.

"How's this?" said the grub-man, addressing me with a stare of astonishment. "He's odd, ain't he?"

"I think he is a little deranged," said I, sadly.

"Deranged? deranged is it? Well now, upon my word, I thought that friend of yourn was a gentleman forger; they are always pale and genteellike, them forgers. I can't help pity 'em—can't help it, sir. Did you know Monroe Edwards?" he added touchingly, and paused. Then, laying his hand pityingly on my shoulder, sighed, "he died of consumption at Sing Sing. So you weren't acquainted with Monroe?"

"No, I was never socially acquainted with any forgers. But I cannot stop longer. Look to my friend yonder. You will not lose by it. I will see you again."

Some few days after this, I again obtained admission to the Tombs, and went through the corridors in quest of Bartleby; but without finding him.

"I saw him coming from his cell not long ago," said a turnkey, "may be he's gone to loiter in the yards."

So I went in that direction.

"Are you looking for the silent man?" said another turnkey passing me. "Yonder he lies—sleeping in the yard there. 'Tis not twenty minutes since I saw him lie down."

The yard was entirely quiet. It was not accessible to the common prisoners. The surrounding walls, of amazing thickness, kept off all sounds behind them. The Egyptian character of the masonry weighed upon me with its gloom. But a soft imprisoned turf grew under foot. The heart of the eternal pyramids, it seemed, wherein, by some strange magic, through the clefts, grass seed, dropped by birds, had sprung.

Strangely huddled at the base of the wall, his knees drawn up, and lying on his side, his head touching the cold stones, I saw the wasted Bartleby. But nothing stirred. I paused; then went close up to him; stooped over, and saw that his dim eyes were open; otherwise he seemed profoundly sleeping. Something prompted me to touch him. I felt his hand, when a tingling shiver ran up my arm and down my spine to my feet.

The round face of the grub-man peered upon me now. "His dinner is ready. Won't he dine today, either? Or does he live without dining?"

"Lives without dining," said I, and closed the eyes.

"Eh!—He's asleep, ain't he?"

"With kings and counsellors," murmured I.

There would seem little need for proceeding further in this history. Imagination will readily supply the meager recital of poor Bartleby's interment. But ere parting with the reader, let me say, that if this little narrative has sufficiently interested him, to awaken curiosity as to who Bartleby was, and what manner of life he led prior to the present narrator's making his acquaintance, I can only reply, that in such curiosity I fully share, but am wholly unable to gratify it. Yet here I hardly know whether I should divulge one little item of rumor, which came to my ear a few months after the scrivener's decease. Upon what basis it rested, I could never ascertain; and hence, how true it is I cannot now tell. But inasmuch as this vague report has not been without a certain strange suggestive interest to me, however sad, it may prove the same with some others; and so I will briefly mention it. The report was this: that Bartleby had been a subordinate clerk in the Dead Letter Office at Washington, from which he had been suddenly removed by a change in the administration. When I think over this rumor, I cannot adequately express the emotions which seize me. Dead letters! does it not sound like dead men? Conceive a man by nature and misfortune prone to a pallid hopelessness, can any business seem more fitted to heighten it than that of continually handling these dead letters, and assorting them for the flames? For by the cartload they are annually burned. Sometimes from out the folded paper the pale clerk takes a ring:—the finger it was meant for, perhaps, molders in the grave; a banknote sent in swiftest charity:—he whom it would relieve, nor eats nor hungers any more; pardon for those who died despairing; hope for those who died unhoping; good tidings for those who died stifled by unrelieved calamities. On errands of life, these letters speed to death.

Ah Bartleby! Ah humanity!

ESSAYS

Jean-Jacques Rousseau (1712–1778)

From Second Discourse

As long as men were content with their rustic huts, as long as they were limited to sewing their clothing of skins with thorns or fish bones, adorning themselves with feathers and shells, painting their bodies with various colors, perfecting or embellishing their bows and arrows, carving with sharp stones a few fishing canoes or a few crude musical instruments; in a word, as long as they applied themselves only to tasks that a single person could do and to arts that did not require the cooperation of several hands, they lived free, healthy, good, and happy insofar as they could be according to their nature, and they continued to enjoy among themselves the sweetness of independent intercourse. But from the moment one man needed the help of another, as soon as they observed that it was useful for a single person to have provisions for two, equality disappeared, property was introduced, labor became necessary; and vast forests were changed into smiling fields which had to be watered with the sweat of men, and in which slavery and misery were soon to germinate and grow with the crops.

Metallurgy and agriculture were the two arts whose invention produced this great revolution. For the poet it is gold and silver, but for the philosopher it is iron and wheat which have civilized men and ruined the human race.

Adam Smith (1723–1790)

From An Inquiry Into the Nature and Causes of the Wealth of Nations

Book I: *Of the Causes of Improvement in the Productive Powers of Labour, and of the Order according to which its Produce is naturally distributed among the different Ranks of the People.*

Chapter I: OF THE DIVISION OF LABOUR

The greatest improvement in the productive powers of labour, and the greater part of the skill, dexterity, and judgment with which it is any where directed, or applied, seem to have been the effects of the division of labour.

The effects of the division of labour, in the general business of society, will be more easily understood, by considering in what manner it operates in some particular manufactures. It is commonly supposed to be carried furthest in some very trifling ones: not perhaps that it really is carried further in them than in others of more importance: but in those trifling manufactures which are destined to supply the small wants of but a small number of people, the whole number of workmen must necessarily be small; and those employed in every different branch of the work can often be collected into the same workhouse, and placed at once under the view of the spectator. In those great manufactures, on the contrary, which are destined to supply the great wants of the great body of the people, every different branch of the work employs so great a number of workmen, that it is impossible to collect them all into the same workhouse. We can seldom see more, at one time, than those employed in one single branch. Though in such manufactures, therefore, the work may really be divided into a much greater number of parts, than in those of a more trifling nature, the division is not near so obvious, and has accordingly been much less observed.

To take an example, therefore, from a very trifling manufacture; but one in which the division of labour has been very often taken notice of, the trade of the pin-maker; a workman not educated to this business (which the division of labour has rendered a distinct trade), nor acquainted with the use of the machinery employed in it (to the invention of which the same division of labour has probably given occasion), could scarce, perhaps, with his utmost industry, make one pin in a day, and certainly could not make twenty. But in the way in which this business is now carried on, not only the whole work is a peculiar trade, but it is divided into a number of branches, of which the greater part are likewise peculiar trades. One man draws out the wire, another straights it, a third cuts it, a fourth points it, a fifth grinds it at the top for receiving the head; to make the head requires two or three distinct operations; to put it on, is a peculiar business, to whiten the pins is another; it is even a trade by itself to put them into the paper; and the important business of making a pin is, in this manner, divided into about eighteen distinct operations, which, in some manufactories, are all performed by distinct hands, though in others the same man will sometimes perform two or three of them. I have seen a small manufactory of this kind where ten men only were employed, and where some of them consequently performed two or three distinct operations. But though they were very poor, and therefore but indifferently accommodated with the necessary machinery, they could, when they exerted themselves, make among them about twelve pounds of pins in a day. There are in a pound upwards of four thousand pins of a middling size. Those ten persons, therefore, could make among them upwards of forty-eight thousand pins in a day. Each person, therefore, making a tenth part of forty-eight thousand pins, might be considered as making four thousand eight hundred pins a day. But if they had all wrought separately and independently, and without any of them having been educated to this peculiar business, they certainly could not each of them have made twenty, perhaps not one pin in a day; that is, certainly, not the two hundred and fortieth, perhaps not the four thousand eight hundredth part of what they are at present capable of performing, in consequence of a proper division and combination of their different operations.

Irwin Edman (1896–1954)

On American Leisure

The best test of the quality of a civilization is the quality of its leisure. Not what the citizens of a commonwealth do when they are obliged to do something by necessity, but what they do when they can do anything by choice, is the criterion of a people's life. One can tell much about a man by noting the objects and pastimes to which he spontaneously turns for joy. The same may be said of a nation. It was a suggestive comment of Maxim Gorky's on visiting Coney Island, "What an unhappy people it must be that turns for happiness here." The most serious criticism leveled against American civilization is not that its work is standardized and its business engulfing, but that its pleasures are mechanical and its leisure slavish. It is not that we have not time. Foreign observers are repeatedly astonished at the number of hours an ever-increasing number of Americans have to themselves. It is not time we lack, but leisure.

Leisure is indeed an affair of mood and atmosphere rather than simply of the clock. It is not a chronological occurrence but a spiritual state. It is unhurried pleasurable living among one's native enthusiasms. Leisure consists of those pauses in our lives when experience is a fusion of stimulation and repose. Genuine leisure yields at once a feeling of vividness and a sense of peace. It consists of moments so clear and pleasant in themselves that one might wish they were eternal.

For traveled Americans, at least, the best illustrations and memories of such experiences will come from abroad. For one it will be the recollection of keen but casual conversation at tea on a lawn in Sussex or Surrey. For another it will be the image of two friends chatting over coffee and liquors at an *al fresco* table on a boulevard in Paris. Another will remember a stroll in an Italian piazza or the long, dignified peace of an evening in a London club.

It is not that one cannot find domestic images, too, of a quality of leisure that seems to be passing almost completely out of the American scene. Many a midddle-aged American, in the midst of a life crowded with social as well as business or professional obligations, will recall some rare hour that in its golden and gratuitous irrelevance seems to belong not in the realm of time but in the careless length of eternity, an afternoon spent browsing without purpose in a library or walking without the thought of time or destination on the quiet windings of an unfrequented country road. One recalls conversations lightly begun after dinner and meandering through wreaths of smoke into unexpected depths and intensities until long after an unnoticed midnight. One remembers some incredibly remote year when one wrote by hand a letter that flowed on as if ink and paper and ideas would never end.

But for Americans the word "leisure" has distinctively Old World associations. That is partly because some Americans have there known it best. Cut off from the pressure and compulsions of their normal occupations at home, they have moved with freedom amid the grace of a leisurely tradition. But there is a deeper reason which lies in the contrast between that European tradition and our own. The quality of leisure in Europe is partly the heritage of a long leisure-class tradition, partly the patience of peoples that have the sense of an age and are not obsessed with hastening toward the new and building the possible in a hurry. In our own civilization, originally and in spirit partly pioneer, there is a working- rather than a leisure-class tradition, and the impress and atmosphere of work have come to control our lives even when we are not working. To be busy has been with us a primary virtue, and even our play has had to find a place for itself as a kind of business.

A number of years ago Professor Veblen in his "Theory of the Leisure Class" tried to point out how the traditions and interests of a leisure class had shaped our tastes and our morals. A quite plausible volume might be written on the thesis that the pursuit of leisure in our civilization is determined by our traditions of work; we carry the morals and ideals of an essentially industrial, essentially business civilization over into our play. Leisure—a quiet and emancipated absorption in things and doings for their own sake—has always seemed to us effeminate and exotic. We wish leisure for relief, for release, for escape; for instruction, enlightenment, or advancement. There is something immoral about moments that are good in themselves. There is probably no other country in the world where idleness is one of the deadly sins.

With us, therefore, leisure has been a melodramatic escape into self-improvement. We oscillate between night clubs and outlines of culture. Every one has at some time or other been present at a determinedly gay party. He has seen ordinarily quiet, intelligent people become wilfully noisy and stupid. He has seen men and women, separately delightful and entertaining, prance about loudly, screaming vulgarities, acting the "grown-up babies of the age." And his pain has been increased by a sense that none of these people cared to do the silly things they were doing. They drank more than they really wished to, and uttered hiccoughing nonsense that they themselves despised.

Every one, likewise, has listened to a group of people at dinner or afterwards, talk with obligatory boredom about the modish books and plays and ideas. Spontaneity, which is of the essence of any truly spiritual life, flies out of the conversation and out of the window, when "culture" becomes deliberate. We settle down as grimly to being serious as we settle down to being silly. Between the foolish and the funereal we have managed to find no middle course.

Of escapes from the pressure of an increasingly mechanized life to occasional outbursts of excitement or triviality there is much to be said. At least it may be said for them that they are natural, perhaps needful, refuges from a world whose tightly woven days would otherwise be unbearable. It is perhaps a sad commentary on the angular and constricted lives we lead that we should have to seek lurid or futile ways to peace. But it is not to be wondered at that, living in such a world of routine, we should plunge ever so often into the loud nonsense of inane parties, wallow in the absurd pathos and comedy of the screen, or fall enraptured victims to successive crazes of footless puzzles and dull games. We may be forgiven our excursions to musical comedies without wit or music, and conversational evenings without humanity or ideas. The contemporary citizen is vexed beyond his own realization by the humdrum unthrilling pressure of his days; he craves naturally now and then an opportunity to be trivial, irresponsible, and absurd.

But the irony of our situation lies in the fact that even when we try to escape into triviality or foolishness we make a serious and standardized business of it. One can pardon occasional madness in a sober civilization, but there is something pathetic, almost ghastly, in soberly making madness a routine. The half-drunken gayety that has become the accompaniment of much respectable social life is a sad determined business. Orgy has become a social obligation; dissipation a prescription to the weary, the repressed, and the disenchanted. It becomes as much a social obligation to play a new game or have a new thrill as to read a new book or wear a current collar or hat. Any number of "nice" people go systematically about becoming on occasion trivial, foolish, or mad. It is as if the American could not stop being efficient when he wanted to, and had to be gay or trivial or ecstatic with the same thoroughness and strained energy with which he might build a business or a skyscraper.

There are other reasons besides our own solemn efficiency that have been transforming our attempts to amuse ourselves into pale and standard routines. The same forces that have gone into the big business of providing our necessities have gone into the big business of providing our amusements. One may glamorously state the possibilities of the radio, the universalization of beautiful music and distinguished thought. One may talk as one will about the possible high art of the moving picture, marvel as one will at the new mechanical perfections of the phonograph. There is no question but that these are at their best mechanical. They turn our leisure into a passive receptivity of standard mediocre amusement. They provide almost nothing of that spontaneous sense of individual living which is part of the repose and stimulation of leisure. It is not pleasant to realize that our leisure is taking on the color—or colorlessness—of the rest of our lives; that we are becoming stereotypes in our play as in our work. The most serious spiritual danger of the Industrial Revolution is that it has come to mechanize and industrialize not merely things but the spirit as well.

When man is at leisure we like to say he is free to be himself, but if his freedom consists in efficiently amusing himself according to the standard formulas or subjecting himself to the passive reception of standard amusements, he is not free at all.

But while leisure has in one direction gone toward conventional amusement and stereotyped triviality, in another direction it has become a kind of elegant overtime work. The latest use we have found for leisure is to make it useful. Its usefulness, which might have been supposed to be that it was a good in itself, has been transformed into its possibility as a means of systematic self-improvement. Correspondence courses, outlines of knowledge, scrapbooks of learning—agencies not always disinterested—have been trying to teach us what we might do with our unharnessed moments if only we would harness them. A little less carousal and a little less bridge, and we might become heirs to all of Western culture, or experts in philosophy or French. There is a revealing irrelevance in the reasons assigned for turning the casual moments of our lives to the pursuit of knowledge. It is not that knowledge will render us self-possessed and whole, that it will give wings to our imagination and give a larger, clearer, and sweeter horizon to our lives. It is that knowledge, or a smattering of it, will make us successful or respected, that a veneer of garbled French will reveal our breeding, or a parade of the names of philosophers testify to our intellectual curiosity. There is possibly no clearer index to the remoteness of a native American culture than the eager indiscriminate voracity with which Americans gobble up tabloid versions of fields of expert knowledge. Far from meaning that we have turned to the love of wisdom, it means that we have turned our idle hours into the hurried business of getting short cuts to knowledge. Outlines simply are a way of applying efficiency to culture as well as to business. Their very essence is to say that here is all philosophy or history or literature for those who have not the patience or sympathy to explore any corner of any of them with disinterested delight. Worst of all, they have taken from leisure its saving essence—the sense of doing some lovely thing for its own lovable sake.

There are aristocratic pessimists in our midst who hold that leisure in the sense of a fine spontaneous use of free time is increasingly impossible in America. They point to the facts cited in the foregoing and to other equally distressing social habits. The omnipresence of the automobile is not simply a temptation to literal speed, but has come to be a symbol for speed in spiritual matters as well. The only excitement in any activity, even in the pursuit of truth, is the excitement of going fast. It is for that reason, they insist, that there is no country where ideas become popular so fast as in America, no country where, half-learned, they are so quickly outmoded and forgotten. A book is the book of a month or at most a season, and the rapid-transit reader comes to forswear books for the reviews of them, and forswear reviews for excerpts from them in a synthetic magazine.

It is pointed out again, and with justice, that the multiplication of physical luxuries and physical distractions is a constant intruder upon that collectedness of spirit in which alone leisure can come to being. Serenity and integrity are menaced as much by the telephone as by any single invention of the last century. Long quiet waves of time have become almost impossible in evenings shattered by radios, by movies, and by the constant seduction and noise of the automobile. Speculation begins in a dreaming fantasy; meditation in reverie. In our contemporary urban world one almost never has a chance to achieve the half-drowsy detachment in which fantasy and reveries begin. We are kept too wide-awake ever to be really at peace or in thought. Finally, in a country where there is still a glamorous sense of unlimited opportunity, the desire for first place makes almost impossible that freedom and detachment, which leave one free to follow an impulse for its own self-rewarding delight.

The desire for speed, the desire for luxury, the desire for first place—these are indeed three deadly enemies of leisure. In the current movement of American life there is not much prospect of radically overcoming them. But there are portents of a change in our point of view that may portend a radical change in our practice.

There are growing evidences of a hunger for quiet and unhurried living among an increasing number of Americans. One cannot—nor would one—abolish the telephone or the automobile. There is no use in sighing for an anachronistic Paradise. It is impossible to transform life in New York in the twentieth century into the retirement of a rectory in Kent in the eighteenth. One cannot in the noise and hurry of a Western metropolitan winter pretend one is living in the timeless unconcern of an Eastern tropical island.

But part of our difficulty lies not in the impossibility of our circumstances, but in the blindness of our philosophy. If we once learned to rediscover the values of quiet spaces in our lives we should find a way to find them. There is time to be had even in New York or Chicago, and solitude even among crowds. One need not follow Thoreau into the wilderness to practice his isolation, nor Buddha into the desert to achieve his meditation. There is peace in a city apartment if one will but stay at home an evening to find it, and Nirvana to be found at home in one's own mind.

Ultimately the lack of leisure is lack of spiritual integration. We flee to society, dull though it be, through the fear of the greater dullness of being alone. We hurtle along at a breakneck speed, physically and spiritually, for fear of the drabness and futility we might feel if we slowed down. Any number of people are suddenly becoming aware of that situation and honest with themselves; are beginning to realize how much leisure one might have if one had enough faith in one's own resources. One need not let life be shattered into a splintered busyness by a routine absorption into social evenings which give one a standard good time. The rediscovery of solitude is being made by Americans, and with that rediscovery come many other delightful things: the chance to do nothing at all, not even talk, and the chance out of that interlude to follow a fancy or meditate a dream. Many a good citizen, given a chance to be alone with himself for an evening, might discover for the first time the quality of his own character, the contours of taste and interest that make him a personality as well as a jobholder and taxpayer. In such an interval a man may discover a hobby that will be for him a substitute for creative genius. He may not paint, write, or compose, but he may learn to do something indelibly himself and make something incredibly his own.

But in the golden days of leisure, in the spacious and graceful society of the Renaissance or the English country house, obviously men and women did not retire into their own souls away from the stimulation of other people. Good conversation is certainly one of the most enlivening ways of leisure, and good conversation is something between solemnity and absurdity. In America, of late, we have had to choose between talking on "subjects" solemnly and schematically, or babbling nonsense, doing anything rather than talk. We are, I think, beginning to learn again the joy of conversation, a light and easy play of minds and tempers over common human themes. We have grown a little weary of talk that is all smart and burnished; we have grown tired, too, of talk that sounds like the overflow program of a literary club. We are learning again that the meeting of minds and moods is one of the sweetest and most amiable fruits of human society. It has its own novelties and excitements no less than the automobile, radio, and bridge.

Not but that these last have their own special value as the pure gold of leisure. Even the mania for speed has about it something of the quality of poetry. No one who on some moonlight night has sped along a country road will deny the sheer poetical appeal there is in the ease and freedom of speed. But the automobile has made the more peaceful kind of leisure possible as it never was before. It has brought the city dweller within easy reach of green and solitude. It has made neighbors of involuntary hermits. The radio, too, for all its blare of tawdry music, has put millions within the reach of formerly impossible musical beauty. It has brought Beethoven to the farmer and to apartment dwellers who could never be lured to Carnegie Hall. And bridge, sniffed at by the cultured moralist, has its own justification. It is a diverting and harmless adventure of the mind and has for its devotees its own glories of wonder and conflict and surprise. If all these things are less interesting ultimately than conversation it is because we are social minds rather than aleatory machines.

There is, paradoxically enough, an incredible romanticism in our efficient impatience with leisure. We chase as madly as any early nineteenth-century German poet the Blue Flower of Happiness always beyond the hill. It is for that reason that we cannot take our idleness for the happiness it is; we try to turn it into an instrument toward the happiness it may bring. It may bring all knowledge into our province, or all salaries into our reach. It is for that reason that we have turned to outlines of knowledge and courses in success. But here, too, a change in spirit is notable.

There are men one knows who have made the surprised and delighted discovery that it is possible, if not to become hastily omniscient at least to become patiently at home in some small field of knowledge or some tiny technic or art. It is not easy or particularly joyous to go into the whole vague history of mankind; but it is possible with pleasure to know one period or one decade of American history, or the story of one man or one movement. Only an octogenarian genius can master the whole of comparative literature; but any one can carve out a little pathway of poetry or prose, make one author, one genre, one theme his own, be it Trollope or sonnets, whaling or ballades. It is not possible for every man to be an artist; but almost any one can learn to draw or model, to play an instrument or plant a garden. In England one meets omniscient people no more than in America; nor are artists in every lane. But there are thousands of unpretentious lawyers or business men who have made some intimate little field of knowledge or thought their own, or learned to do one modest small hobby well.

We may talk much about the future of America, and think to measure its destiny by statistics of its educational, economic, or political changes. But the outlook for our country lies in the quality of its idleness almost as much as anything else.

Shall we then always alternate between trivial escapes into foolishness and solemn plunges into exploitation of our moments of repose? For us, as for Aristotle, there must be a golden mean. We may learn still to be at peace long enough to think and dream after our own fashion. We may learn to be together and be gay without being rowdy. We may learn to be expert in some little territory of art or thought or science without losing the amateur touch. We may still find time to live rather than time to kill.

If we do, we shall have learned what the spiritual life really means. For it means nothing more than those moments in experience when we have some free glint of life for its own sake, some lovely unforced glimmer of laughter or reason or love.

VIEWPOINTS

Robert Hessen

The Effects of the Industrial Revolution on Women and Children

Child Labor and the Industrial Revolution

The least understood and most widely misrepresented aspect of the history of capitalism is child labor.

One cannot evaluate the phenomenon of child labor in England during the Industrial Revolution of the late eighteenth and early nineteenth century, unless one realizes that the introduction of the factory system offered a livelihood, a means of survival, to tens of thousands of children who would not have lived to be youths in the pre-capitalistic eras.

The factory system led to a rise in the general standard of living, to rapidly falling urban death rates and decreasing infant mortality—and produced an unprecedented population explosion.

In 1750, England's population was six million; it was nine million in 1800 and twelve million in 1820, a rate of increase without precedent in any era. The age distribution of the population shifted enormously; the proportion of children and youths increased sharply. "The proportion of those born in London dying before five years of age" fell from 74.5 percent in 1730–49 to 31.8 percent in 1810–29.[1] Children who hitherto would have died in infancy now had a chance for survival.

Both the rising population and the rising life expectancy give the lie to the claims of socialist and fascist critics of capitalism that the conditions of the laboring classes were progressively deteriorating during the Industrial Revolution.

1. Mabel C. Buer, *Health, Wealth, and Population in the Early Days of the Industrial Revolution, 1760–1815* (London: George Routledge & Sons, 1926), p. 30.

One is both morally unjust and ignorant of history if one blames capitalism for the condition of children during the Industrial Revolution, since, in fact, capitalism brought an enormous improvement over their condition in the preceding age. The source of that injustice was ill-informed, emotional novelists and poets, like Dickens and Mrs. Browning; fanciful medievalists, like Southey; political tract writers posturing as economic historians, like Engels and Marx. All of them painted a vague, rosy picture of a lost "golden age" of the working classes, which, allegedly, was destroyed by the Industrial Revolution. Historians have not supported their assertions. Investigation and common sense have deglamorized the pre-factory system of domestic industry. In that system, the worker made a costly initial investment, or paid heavy rentals, for a loom or frame, and bore most of the speculative risks involved. His diet was drab and meager, and even subsistence often depended on whether work could be found for his wife and children. There was nothing romantic or enviable about a family living and working together in a badly lighted, improperly ventilated, and poorly constructed cottage.

How did children thrive before the Industrial Revolution? In 1697, John Locke wrote a report for the Board of Trade on the problem of poverty and poor-relief. Locke estimated that a laboring man and his wife in good health could support no more than two children, and he recommended that *all children over three years of age* should be taught to earn their living at working schools for spinning and knitting, where they would be given food. "What they can have at home, from their parents," wrote Locke, "is seldom more than bread and water, and that very scantily too."

Professor Ludwig von Mises reminds us:

> The factory owners did not have the power to compel anybody to take a factory job. They could only hire people who were ready to work for the wages offered to them. Low as these wage rates were, they were nonetheless much more than these paupers could earn in any other field open to them. It is a distortion of facts to say that the factories carried off the housewives from the nurseries and the kitchen and the children from their play. These women had nothing to cook with and to feed their children. These children were

destitute and starving. Their only refuge was the factory. It saved them, in the strict sense of the term, from death by starvation.[2]

Factory children went to work at the insistence of their parents. The children's hours of labor were very long, but the work was often quite easy—usually just attending a spinning or weaving machine and retying threads when they broke. It was not on behalf of such children that the agitation for factory legislation began. The first child labor law in England (1788) regulated the hours and conditions of labor of the miserable children who worked as chimney sweeps—a dirty, dangerous job which long antedated the Industrial Revolution, and which was not connected with factories. The first Act which applied to factory children was passed to protect those who had been sent into virtual slavery by the parish authorities, *a government body*: they were deserted or orphaned pauper children who were legally under the custody of the poor-law officials in the parish, and who were bound by these officials into long terms of unpaid apprenticeship in return for a bare subsistence.

Conditions of employment and sanitation are acknowledged to have been best in the larger and newer factories. As successive Factory Acts, between 1819 and 1846, placed greater and greater restrictions on the employment of children and adolescents, the owners of the larger factories, which were more easily and frequently subject to visitation and scrutiny by the factory inspectors, increasingly chose to dismiss children from employment rather than be subjected to elaborate, arbitrary, and ever-changing regulations on how they might run a factory which employed children. The result of legislative intervention was that these dismissed children, who needed to work in order to survive, were forced to seek jobs in smaller, older, and more out-of-the-way factories, where the conditions of employment, sanitation, and safety were markedly inferior. Those who could not find new jobs were reduced to the status of their counterparts a hundred years before, that is, to irregular agricultural labor, or worse in the

---

2. Ludwig van Mises, *Human Action* (New Haven, Connecticut: Yale University Press, 1949), p. 615.

words of Professor von Mises—to "infest the country as vagabonds, beggars, tramps, robbers and prostitutes."

Child labor was not ended by legislative fiat; child labor ended when it became economically unnecessary for children to earn wages in order to survive—when the income of their parents became sufficient to support them. The emancipators and benefactors of those children were not legislators or factory inspectors, but manufacturers and financiers. Their efforts and investments in machinery led to a rise in real wages, to a growing abundance of goods at lower prices, and to an incomparable improvement in the general standard of living.

The proper answer to the critics of the Industrial Revolution is given by Professor T. S. Ashton:

> There are today on the plains of India and China men and women, plague-ridden and hungry, living lives little better, to outward appearance, than those of the cattle that toil with them by day and share their places of sleep by night. Such Asiatic standards, and such unmechanized horrors, are the lot of those who increse their numbers without passing through an industrial revolution.[3]

Let me add that the Industrial Revolution and its consequent prosperity were the achievement of capitalism and cannot be achieved under any other politico-economic system. As proof, I offer you the spectacle of Soviet Russia which combines industrialization—and famine.

Women and the Industrial Revolution

To condemn capitalism one must first misrepresent its history. The notion that industrial capitalism led to nothing but misery and degradation for women is an article of faith among critics of capitalism. It is as prevalent as the view that children were victimized and exploited by the Industrial Revolution—and it is as false.

---

3. T. S. Ashton, *The Industrial Revolution,* 1760-1830 (London: Oxford University Press, 1948), p. 161.

Let us examine the source of this view. To appreciate the benefits that capitalism brought to women, one must compare their status under capitalism with their condition in the preceding centuries. But the nineteenth-century critics of capitalism did not do this; instead, they distorted and falsified history, glamorizing the past and disparaging everything modern by contrast.

For instance, Richard Oastler, one of the most fanatical nineteenth-century enemies of capitalism, claimed that everyone was better off spiritually and materially in the Middle Ages than in the early nineteenth century. Describing medieval England, Oastler rhapsodized about the lost golden age: "Oh, what a beautiful ship was England once! She was well built, well manned, well provisioned, well rigged! All were then merry, cheerful and happy on board."

This was said of centuries in which "the bulk of the population were peasants in a servile condition, bound by status, not free to change their mode of life or to move from their birthplace"[4]— when people had only the promise of happiness in the life beyond the grave to succor them against decimating plagues, recurring famines and at best half-filled stomachs—when people lived in homes so infested with dirt and vermin that one historian's verdict about these cottages is: "From a health point of view the only thing to be said in their favor was that they burnt down very easily!"[5]

Oastler represented the viewpoint of the medievalists. The socialists, who agreed with them, were equally inaccurate historians.

For example, describing the conditions of the masses in the pre-industrial seventeenth and early eighteenth centuries, Friedrich Engels alleged: "The workers vegetated throughout a passably comfortable existence, leading a righteous and peaceful life in all piety and probity; and their material position was far better off than their successors."

This was written of an age characterized by staggeringly high mortality rates, especially among children—crowded towns and villages untouched by sanitation—notoriously high gin consumption. The working-class diet consisted mainly of oatmeal, milk, cheese, and beer; while bread, potatoes, coffee, tea, sugar,

4. Buer, p. 250.
5. Ibid., p. 88.

and meat were still expensive luxuries. Bathing was infrequent and laundering a rarity because soap was so costly, and clothing—which had to last a decade or generation—would not last if washed too often.

The most rapid change wrought by the Industrial Revolution was the shifting of texile production out of the home and into the factory. Under the previous system, called "domestic industry," the spinning and weaving was done in the workers's own home with the aid of his wife and children. When technological advances caused the shifting of textile production into factories, this led, said one critic of capitalism, "to the breakup of the home as a social unit."[6]

Mrs. Neff writes approvingly that "under the system of domestic industry the parents and the children had worked together, the father the autocratic head, pocketing the family earnings and directing their expenditure." Her tone turns to condemnation when she recounts: "But under the factory system the members of the family all had their own earnings, they worked in separate departments of the mill, coming home only for food and sleep. The home was little but a shelter."

The factories were held responsible, by such critics, for every social problem of that age, including promiscuity, infidelity, and prostitution. Implicit in the condemnation of women working in the factories was the notion that a woman's place is in the home and that her only proper role is to keep house for her husband and to rear his children. The factories were blamed simultaneously for removing girls from the watchful restraints of their parents and for encouraging early marriages; and later, for fostering maternal negligence and incompetent housekeeping, as well as for encouraging lack of female subordination and the desire for luxuries.

It is a damning indictment of the pre-factory system to consider what kind of "luxuries" the Industrial Revolution brought within reach of the working-class budget. Women sought such luxuries as shoes instead of clogs, hats instead of shawls, "delicacies" (like coffee, tea, and sugar) instead of "plain food."

Critics denounced the increasing habit of wearing ready-made

---

6. Wanda Neff, *Victorian Working Women* (New York: Columbia University Press, 1920), p. 51.

clothes, and they viewed the replacement of wools and linens by inexpensive cottons as a sign of growing poverty. Women were condemned for not making by hand that which they could buy more cheaply, thanks to the revolution in textile production. Dresses no longer had to last a decade—women no longer had to wear coarse petticoats until they disintegrated from dirt and age; cheap cotton dresses and undergarments were a revolution in personal hygiene.

The two most prevalent nineteenth-century explanations of why women worked in the factories were: (a) that their "husbands preferred to remain home idle, supported by their wives," and (b) that the factory system "displaced adult men and imposed on women the 'duty and burden of supporting their husbands and families.'" These charges are examined in *Wives and Mothers in Victorian Industry*, a definitive study by Dr. Margaret Hewitt of the University of Exeter. Her conclusion is: "Neither of these assumptions proves to have any statistical foundation whatsoever."[7]

In fact, women worked in the factories for far more conventional reasons. Dr. Hewitt enumerates them: many women worked because "their husbands' wages were insufficient to keep the home going"; others were widowed or deserted; others were barren, or had grown-up children; some had husbands who were unemployed, or employed in seasonal jobs; and a few chose to work in order to earn money for extra comforts in the home, although their husbands' wages were sufficient to cover necessities.[8]

What the factory system offered these women was—*not* misery and degradation—but a means of survival, of economic independence, of rising above the barest subsistence. Harsh as nineteenth-century factory conditions were, compared to twentieth-century conditions, women increasingly preferred work in the factories to any other alternatives open to them, such as domestic service, or back-breaking work in agricultural gangs, or working as haulers and pullers in the mines; moreover, if a woman could support herself, she was was not driven into early marriage.

7. London: Rockliff, 1958, p. 190.
8. Ibid., pp. 192, 194.

Even Professor Trevelyan, who persistently disparaged the factories and extolled "the good old days," admitted:

> ... the women who went to work in the factories though they lost some of the best things in life [Trevelyan does not explain what he means], gained independence. ... The money they earned was their own. The factory hand acquired an economic position personal to herself, which in the course of time other women came to envy.

And Trevelyan concluded: "The working class home often became more comfortable, quiet and sanitary by ceasing to be a miniature factory."[9]

Critics of the factory system still try to argue that the domestic spinners or weavers could have a creator's pride in their work, which they lost by becoming mere cogs in a huge industrial complex. Dr. Dorothy George easily demolishes this thesis: "It seems unlikely that the average weaver, toiling hour after hour throwing the shuttle backwards and forwards on work which was monotonous and exhausting, had the reactions which would satisfy a modern enthusiast for peasant arts."[10]

Finally, it was charged that factory work made women too concerned with material comforts at the expense of spiritual considerations.

The misery in which women lived before capitalism, might have made them cherish the New Testament injunction: "Love not the world, nor the things that are in the world." But the productive splendor of capitalism vanquished that view. Today, the foremost champions of that viewpoint are Professor Galbraith and the austerity-preachers behind the Iron Curtain.

---

9. George M. Trevelyan, *English Social History* (New York and London: Longmans, Green & Company, 1942), p. 487.
10. M. Dorothy George, *England in Transition: Life and Work in the Eighteenth Century* (London: Penguin, 1953), p. 139.

Report of a Special Task Force to the Secretary of Health, Education, and Welfare

Albert Camus wrote that "Without work all life goes rotten. But when work is soulless, life stifles and dies." Our analysis of work in America leads to much the same conclusion: Because work is central to the lives of so many Americans, either the absence of work or employment in meaningless work is creating an increasingly intolerable situation. The human costs of this state of affairs are manifested in worker alienation, alcoholism, drug addiction, and other symptoms of poor mental health. Moreover, much of our tax money is expended in an effort to compensate for problems with at least a part of their genesis in the world of work. A great part of the staggering national bill in the areas of crime and delinquency, mental and physical health, manpower and welfare are generated in our national policies and attitudes toward work. Likewise, industry is paying for its continued attachment to Tayloristic[1] practices through low worker productivity and high rates of sabotage, absenteeism, and turnover. Unions are paying through the faltering loyalty of a young membership that is increasingly concerned about the apparent disinterest of its leadership in problems of job satisfaction. Most important, there are the high costs of lost opportunities to encourage citizen participation: the discontent of women, minorities, blue-collar workers, youth, and older adults would be considerably less were these Americans to have an active voice in the decisions in the workplace that most directly affect their lives.

Our analysis of health, education, welfare, and manpower programs from the unique perspective of work indicates that to do nothing about these problems in the short run is to increase costs to society in the long run. Much of the capital needed to redesign jobs, increase worker mobility, and create new jobs can be directed to these activities through trade-offs with existing

---

1. Frederick W. Taylor, management scientist of the early twentieth century, supposedly promoted technical expertise without considering human factors in job design.

expenditures. More capital can be obtained by lowering the waste of unemployment and through increasing worker productivity. But the essential first step toward these goals is the commitment on the part of policy makers in business, labor, and government to the improvement of the quality of working life in America.

Robert Gilpin

Exporting the Technological Revolution

Ours has always been a technological civilization. No prior civilization or empire has been so closely identified with research-and-development as has the American. The influence and inspiration that we have radiated throughout the world have been largely technological and have demonstrated what machines can do to make men free and prosperous. In contrast, the Greek inspiration was political and cultural. The Romans were soldiers and law-givers. Though the British were the initiators of the Industrial Revolution and of industrial civilization, as the 19th century wore on, they gave up technology for finance and the political management of empire. The French and the Russians have given the modern world great literature, art, and science but little technology. And although the Germans led the way with respect to the technologies of the second phase of the Industrial Revolution—electricity, organic chemistry, steel, and the internal-combustion engine—America achieved the full potential of these technologies for reshaping society and the lives of men. It has been from America that these technologies have made their continuing impact on the world.

The American technological impulse was there at the very beginning. Benjamin Franklin and Thomas Jefferson took pride in their inventions, and George Washington was by profession a surveyor. In the world's first written constitution, one of the few powers given to the federal government was "to promote the progress of science and useful arts, by securing for limited times to authors and inventors the exclusive rights to their respective writings and discoveries." Our folk heroes and the Americans best known abroad have been our inventors: Thomas Edison, the Wright brothers, and an inventor of a different sort, Henry Ford. *Popular Mechanics* remains one of America's most widely read magazines. Nor is it without significance, as others have noted, that in addition to the signing of our Declaration of Independence, two other important events took place abroad in 1776 that were to affect deeply America's economy and its impact on the world. These events were the invention of the separate-condenser steam engine, which provided the motive power for the Industrial Revolution, and the publication of Adam Smith's *Wealth of Nations*. These three moments in history symbolize the fusion of political liberty, technology, and a free economy that has been central to the American historical experience.

* * *

Whereas earlier empires had conquered through superior military technology, America's thrust outward was based on its industrial and technological supremacy. First through trade and then via the establishment of foreign subsidiaries, America's gigantic corporations took the offensive against an unprepared world. As early as the 1890s, British and continental writers began to develop a theme that would be echoed in our time by Jean-Jacques Servan-Schreiber's best-selling *The American Challenge*—that American corporations, through their expansionism and the foreign response it inspired, were helping to change the world.

The American technological advances affected the world in three broad areas. First, from Isaac Singer's sewing machine and Cyrus McCormick's reaper to modern electronic computers, the American inventive genius expressed itself in the form of machines that save labor, increase productivity, and raise the general standard of living. As Joseph Schumpeter pointed out in defense of industrial capitalism, the beneficiaries of technological advance have been the great mass of the world's population.

Second, the United States has given the world a new way of integrating man with machine. Invented by Eli Whitney, perfected by Henry Ford, and satirized by Charlie Chaplin, the techniques of interchangeable parts and mass production revolutionized manufacturing processess. But before Ford or Chaplin, the American efficiency expert Frederick Winslow Taylor, the father of scientific management, had in theory carried the logic of mass production to its logical conclusion—the conversion of man on the assembly line into a machine himself. For Lenin—one of the founders of that other powerful technological civilization, Soviet Russia—Taylor was the foremost prophet of the 20th century, an innovator who held the key to the reorganization of Russian society if communism were to surpass the productive accomplishments of capitalism.

America's third great contribution was the systematic harnessing of science to the advancement of technology. The first phase of the Industrial Revolution, which had its origins in Great Britain, owed little to science. James Watt, the inventor of the separate-condenser steam engine, was inspired by the trial-and-error method of science. But scientific theory itself contributed little. In the latter part of the 19th century, the Germans were the first to exploit scientific theory in the founding of the electrical and organic-chemical industries, the pivotal industries during the second phase of the Industrial Revolution. But it was the United States that carried this development one critical step forward. The founding of giant research laboratories by American corporations and particularly—owing to the experience of the Second World War—the recognition by the federal government of basic science as the ultimate natural resource represented major advances. Modern electronics, atomic energy, and aerospace technologies were the fruit of this massive joint exploitation of science by industry and government. Henceforth, the capacity to advance and utilize science for technological purposes became the hallmark of any advanced, modernized society.

4
Organization as a Religion

> Are you to pay for what you have
> With all you are?
> —E. A. ROBINSON

It has often been observed that Marxism is a "secular religion." Democratic societies do not usually think of themselves as parties to the "blind faith and inflexible doctrine" images called forth by the mention of Marxism and its variants. Instead they almost always praise independent thinking (and even occasionally heed it).

Some independent thinkers, including a number of writers, believe that in freer societies a new faith and worship are developing, but not in any formal religion. The faith is in the Good Life, and the worship is of the institutions and organizations that promise to lead us to the Good Life, or at least save us from some earthly hell.

More often than not, the Good Life is associated with material goods and services; moral and intellectual progress are given only a cursory salute. One might properly argue that people would be hard-pressed to develop their minds, their values, and their appreciation of the aesthetic if they were penniless and hungry. But a prime concern of most writers is that there seem to be no restraints on material pursuits and on the emphasis on "success" created in such pursuits.

The views of many writers appear thusly: Material possessions and success dominate our thinking and measure our "worth." Any organizational arrangement and any organizational authority that increases this worth is acceptable. We promote efficiency to the detriment of other values. People defer to institutions and organizations that may strip humans of imagination, dignity, and personal morals. Other writers express concern about the adulation of personal success. People turn to leaders in government, industry, unions, even the entertainment world to show the way. Personality cults develop; we wait for guidance from the great ones in "important" organizations. Even unappealing or incompetent leaders are accepted because "they made it to the top in their business." Football clubs that purposely maim opponents, union leaders who intimidate, and business leaders who hide facts about their products are idolized because "they're number one!" Even unidentified "royalty" are followed blindly: a university student recently expressed a faith that "they" will find a solution to expiring resources, overpopulation, and pollution. Summarizing, some writers fear that organizations and their leaders may become deified, a condition not without precedent in primitive societies. They may come to be worshiped for what they provide and what they promise—and little questioned for the harm they may do.

On the other hand, some writers take a very positive view of modern organizations and technology. For example, "To a Locomotive in Winter" and "The Hammer" celebrate the tools of humankind. "The Iron Messiah," a Russian poem, worships unequivocally.

Are many of the works that follow too enthusiastic or too glum, or are their observations accurate? Are organizations taking on the aspects of a religion, as some people fear? If this fear is based on fact, what is to be done? What would we do without strong political/economic systems? Calleo and Rowland write: "The nation-state may all too seldom speak the voice of reason. But it remains the only serious alternative to chaos."[1] Perhaps strong organizations and strong leaders provide answers to questions about the quality of life. Perhaps MacLeish's great leaders do far more good than harm. Perhaps we are quite capable and willing to keep technological advances as "tools" to serve humankind, as Saint-Exupéry suggests. Or, as Steinbeck implies,

---

1. David Calleo and Benjamin Rowland, *America and the World Political Economy* (Bloomington: Indiana University Press, 1973), p. 191.

perhaps some organizations have grown beyond our control. Perhaps we have new organization "kings," as Sandburg suggests. Are we really at the altar of a new religion, with new messiahs, praying to organizations for deliverance in a world that is continuously threatening, confounding, and incoherent?

POEMS

William Wordsworth (1770–1850)

The World Is Too Much With Us

The world is too much with us; late and soon,
Getting and spending, we lay waste our powers:
Little we see in Nature that is ours;
We have given our hearts away, a sordid boon!
This Sea that bares her bosom to the moon;
The winds that will be howling at all hours,
And are up-gathered now like sleeping flowers;
For this, for everything, we are out of tune;
It moves us not.—Great God! I'd rather be
A Pagan suckled in a creed outworn;
So might I, standing on this pleasant lea,
Have glimpses that would make me less forlorn;
Have sight of Proteus[1] rising from the sea;
Or hear old Triton[1] blow his wreathèd horn.

1. Sea deities of classical mythology.

Arthur Hugh Clough (1819–1861)

The Latest Decalogue[1]

Thou shalt have one God only; who
Would be at the expense of two?
No graven images may be
Worshipped, except the currency:
Swear not at all; for, for thy curse

1. A basic and binding set of rules, such as the Ten Commandments.

Thine enemy is none the worse:
At church on Sunday to attend
Will serve to keep the world thy friend:
Honour thy parents; that is, all
From whom advancement may befall;
Thou shalt not kill; but need'st not strive
Officiously to keep alive:
Do not adultery commit;
Advantage rarely comes of it:
Thou shalt not steal; an empty feat,
When it's so lucrative to cheat:
Bear not false witness; let the lie
Have time on its own wings to fly:
Thou shalt not covet, but tradition
Approves all forms of competition.

WALT WHITMAN (1819–1892)

To a Locomotive in Winter

Thee for my recitative,
Thee in the driving storm even as now, the snow, the winter-day declining,
Thee in thy panoply, thy measur'd dual throbbing and thy beat convulsive,
Thy black cylindric body, golden brass and silvery steel,
Thy ponderous side-bars, parallel and connecting rods, gyrating, shuttling at thy sides,
Thy metrical, now swelling pant and roar, now tapering in the distance,
Thy great protruding head-light fix'd in front,
Thy long, pale, floating vapor-pennants, tinged with delicate purple,
The dense and murky clouds out-belching from thy smoke-stack,
Thy knitted frame, thy springs and valves, the tremulous twinkle of thy wheels,

Thy train of cars behind, obedient, merrily following,
Through gale or calm, now swift, now slack, yet steadily
    careering;
Type of the modern—emblem of motion and power—pulse
    of the continent,
For once come serve the Muse and merge in verse, even as
    here I see thee,
With storm and buffeting gusts of wind and falling snow,
By day thy warning ringing bell to sound its notes,
By night thy silent signal lamps to swing.

Fierce-throated beauty!
Roll through my chant with all thy lawless music, thy
    swinging lamps at night,
Thy madly-whistled laughter, echoing, rumbling like an
    earthquake, rousing all,
Law of thyself complete, thine own track firmly holding,
(No sweetness debonair of tearful harp or glib piano thine,)
Thy trills of shrieks by rocks and hills return'd
Launch'd o'er the prairies wide, across the lakes,
To the free skies unpent and glad and strong.

EDWIN ARLINGTON ROBINSON
(1869–1935)

Cassandra[1]

I heard one who said "Verily,
    What word have I for children here?
Your Dollar is your only Word,
    The wrath of it your only fear.

---

1. From classical mythology. Cassandra was granted the gift of prophecy by the god Apollo. Later, in anger, Apollo placed a curse on her by causing none of her prophecies to be believed. Her name has become associated with prophets of doom whose warnings are ignored.

"You build it altars tall enough
   To make you see, but you are blind;
You cannot leave it long enough
   To look before you or behind.

"When Reason beckons you to pause,
   You laugh and say that you know best;
But what it is you know, you keep
   As dark as ingots in a chest.

"You laugh and answer, 'We are young;
   O leave us now, and let us grow.'—
Not asking how much more of this
   Will Time endure or Fate bestow.

"Because a few complacent years
   Have made your peril of your pride,
Think you that you are to go on
   Forever pampered and untried?

"What lost eclipse of history,
   What bivouac of the marching stars,
Has given the sign for you to see
   Millenniums and last great wars?

"What unrecorded overthrow
   Of all the world has ever known,
Or ever been, has made itself
   So plain to you, and you alone?

"Your Dollar, Dove and Eagle made
   A Trinity that even you
Rate higher than you rate yourselves;
   It pays, it flatters, and it's new.

"And though your very flesh and blood
   Be what your Eagle eats and drinks,
You'll praise him for the best of birds,
   Not knowing what the Eagle thinks.

"The power is yours, but not the sight;
   You see not upon what you tread;
You have the ages for your guide,
   But not the wisdom to be led.

"Think you to tread forever down
   The merciless old verities?
And are you never to have eyes
   To see the world for that it is?

"Are you to pay for what you have
   With all you are?"—No other word
We caught, but with a laughing crowd
   Moved on. None heeded, and few heard.

Anonymous

John Henry

When John Henry was a little fellow,
   You could hold him in the palm of your hand,
He said to his pa, "When I grow up
   I'm gonna be a steel-driving man.
      Gonna be a steel-driving man."

When John Henry was a little baby,
   Setting on his mammy's knee,
He said "The Big Bend Tunnel on the C.&O. Road
   Is gonna be the death of me,
      Gonna be the death of me."

One day his captain told him,
   How he had bet a man
That John Henry would beat his steam drill down,
   Cause John Henry was the best in the land,
      John Henry was the best in the land.

John Henry kissed his hammer,
   White man turned on the steam,
Shaker held John Henry's trusty steel,
   Was the biggest race the world had ever seen,
      Lord, biggest race the world ever seen.

John Henry on the right side
   The steam drill on the left,
"Before I'll let your steam drill beat me down,
   I'll hammer my fool self to death,
      Hammer my fool self to death."

John Henry walked in the tunnel,
   His captain by his side,
The mountain so tall, John Henry so small,
   He laid down his hammer and he cried,
      Laid down his hammer and he cried.

Captain heard a mighty rumbling,
   Said "The mountain must be caving in,"
John Henry said to the captain,
   "It's my hammer swinging in de wind,
      My hammer swinging in de wind."

John Henry said to his shaker,
   "Shaker, you'd better pray;
For if ever I miss this piece of steel,
   Tomorrow'll be your burial day,
      Tomorrow'll be your burial day."

John Henry said to his shaker,
   "Lordy, shake it while I sing,
I'm pulling my hammer from my shoulders down,
   Great Gawdamighty, how she ring,
      Great Gawdamighty, how she ring!"

John Henry said to his captain,
  "Before I ever leave town,
Gimme one mo' drink of dat tom-cat gin,
  And I'll hammer dat steam driver down,
    I'll hammer dat steam driver down."

John Henry said to his captain,
  "Before I ever leave town,
Gimme a twelve-pound hammer wid a whale-bone handle,
  And I'll hammer dat steam driver down,
    I'll hammer dat steam drill on down."

John Henry said to his captain,
  "A man ain't nothin' but a man,
But before I'll let dat steam drill beat me down,
  I'll die wid my hammer in my hand,
    Die wid my hammer in my hand."

The man that invented the steam drill
  He thought he was mighty fine,
John Henry drove down fourteen feet,
  While the steam drill only made nine,
    Steam drill only made nine.

"Oh, lookaway over yonder, captain,
  You can't see like me,"
He gave a long and loud and lonesome cry,
  "Lawd, a hammer be the death of me,
    A hammer be the death of me!"

John Henry had a little woman,
  Her name was Polly Ann,
John Henry took sick, she took his hammer,
  She hammered like a natural man,
    Lawd, she hammered like a natural man.

John Henry hammering on the mountain
   As the whistle blew for half-past two,
The last words his captain heard him say,
   "I've done hammered my insides in two,
     Lawd, I've hammered my insides in two."

The hammer that John Henry swung
   It weighed over twelve pound,
He broke a rib in his left hand side
   And his intrels fell on the ground,
     And his intrels fell on the ground.

John Henry, O, John Henry,
   His blood is running red,
Fell right down with his hammer to the ground,
   Said, "I beat him to the bottom but I'm dead,
     Lawd, beat him to the bottom but I'm dead."

When John Henry was laying there dying,
   The people all by his side,
The very last words they heard him say,
   "Give me a cool drink of water 'fore I die,
     Cool drink of water 'fore I die."

John Henry had a little woman,
   The dress she wore was red,
She went down the track, and she never looked back,
   Going where her man fell dead,
     Going where her man fell dead.

John Henry had a little woman,
   The dress she wore was blue,
De very last words she said to him,
   "John Henry, I'll be true to you,
     John Henry, I'll be true to you."

"Who's gonna shoes yo' little feet,
   Who's gonna glove yo' hand.
Who's gonna kiss yo' pretty, pretty cheek,
   Now you done lost yo' man?
     Now you done lost yo' man?"

"My mammy's gonna shoes my little feet,
   Pappy gonna glove my hand,
My sister's gonna kiss my pretty, pretty cheek,
   Now I done lost my man,
     Now I done lost my man."

They carried him down by the river,
   And buried him in the sand,
And everybody that passed that way,
   Said, "There lies that steel-driving man,
     There lies a steel-driving man."

They took John Henry to the river,
   And buried him in the sand,
And every locomotive come a-roaring by,
   Says, "There lies that steel-drivin' man,
     Lawd, there lies a *steel*-drivin' man."

Some say he came from Georgia,
   And some from Alabam,
But it's wrote on the rock at the Big Bend Tunnel,
   That he was an East Virginia man,
     Lord, Lord, an East Virginia man.

CARL SANDBURG (1878–1967)

The Hammer

I have seen
The old gods go
And the new gods come.

Day by day
And year by year
The idols fall
And the idols rise.

Today
I worship the hammer.

Vladimir Timofeevich Kirillov
(1889–1943)

The Iron Messiah

There he is—the saviour, the lord of the earth,
The master of titanic forces—
In the roar of countless steel machinery,
In the sparkle of suns of electricity.

We thought he would appear in a starry stole,
With a nimbus of divine mystery,
But he came to us clad in black smoke
From the suburbs, foundries, factories.

We thought he would appear in glory and glitter,
Meek, blessing and gentle,
But he, like the molten lava,
Came—multifaced and turbulent . . . .

There he walks o'er the abyss of seas,
All of steel, unyielding and impetuous;
He scatters sparks of rebellious thoughts,
And the purging flames are pouring forth.

Wherever his masterful call is heard,
The world's bosom is bared,
The mountains give way before him,
The earth's poles together are brought.

Wherever he walks, he leaves a trail
Of ringing iron rail;
He brings joy and light to us,
A desert he strews with blossoms.

To the world he brings the New Sun,
He destroys the thrones and prisons.
He calls the peoples to eternal fraternity,
And wipes out boundary lines.

His crimson banner is symbol of struggle;
For the oppressed it is the guiding beacon;
With it we shall crush the yoke of destiny,
We shall conquer the enchanting world.

Louis Untermeyer (1885–1977)

Portrait of a Machine

What nudity is beautiful as this
Obedient monster purring at its toil;
These naked iron muscles dripping oil;
And the sure-fingered rods that never miss.
This long and shiny flank of metal is
Magic that greasy labor cannot spoil;
While this vast engine that could rend the soil
Conceals its fury with a gentle hiss.

It does not vent its loathing, does not turn
Upon its makers with destroying hate.
It bears a deeper malice; throbs to earn
Its master's bread and lives to see this great
Lord of the earth, who rules but cannot learn,
Become the slave of what his slaves create.

CARL SANDBURG   (1878–1967)

Prayers of Steel

Lay me on an anvil, O God.
Beat me and hammer me into a crowbar.
Let me pry loose old walls.
Let me lift and loosen old foundations.

Lay me on an anvil, O God.
Beat me and hammer me into a steel spike.
Drive me into the girders that hold a skyscraper together.
Take red-hot rivets and fasten me into the central girders.
Let me be the great nail holding a skyscraper through blue nights
    into white stars.

VASILI VASILIEVICH KAZIN (1898–   )

The Heavenly Factory

It is high and it is wide—
This blue stone factory.
Hark! The gusty blast
Calls with a dusty voice
And from all corners hurry
In thick sooty overalls
Throngs of stalwart smiths
Whom the windy blast has united.
Darker and darker are the vaults:
The black throngs meet
And quickly
They've kindled
The furnace of lightning
With sultry heat,
And with the roaring thunder
The factory walls shudder.

Robert Frost (1874–1963)

Why Wait for Science

Sarcastic Science, she would like to know,
In her complacent ministry of fear,
How we propose to get away from here
When she has made things so we have to go
Or be wiped out. Will she be asked to show
Us how by rocket we may hope to steer
To some star off there, say, a half light-year
Through temperature of absolute zeró?
Why wait for Science to supply the how
When any amateur can tell it now?
The way to go away should be the same
As fifty million years ago we came—
If anyone remembers how that was.
I have a theory, but it hardly does.

Reed Whittemore (1919–)

A Projection

I wish they would hurry up their trip to Mars,
Those rocket gentlemen.
We have been waiting too long; the fictions of little men
And canals,
And of planting and raising flags and opening markets
For beads, cheap watches, perfume and plastic jewelry—
All these begin to be tedious; what we need now
Is the real thing, a thoroughly bang-up voyage
Of discovery.

Led by Admiral Byrd
In the *Nina*, *Pinta* and *Santa Maria*
With a crew of hundreds of experts
In physics, geology, war and creative writing,
The expedition should sail with a five-year supply
Of Pemmican, Jello, Moxie,
Warm woolen socks and jars of Gramma's preserves.

Think of them out there,
An ocean of space before them, using no compass,
Guiding themselves by speculative equations,
Looking,
Looking into the night and thinking now
There are no days, no seasons, time
Is only on watches,
                      and landing on Venus
Through some slight error, bearing

Proclamations of friendship,
Declarations of interstellar faith,
Acknowledgments of American supremacy,
And advertising matter.

I wonder,
Out in the pitch of space, having worlds enough,
If the walled-up, balled-up self could from its alley
Sally.
I wish they would make provisions for this,
Those rocket gentlemen.

Jesse Stuart (1907–1984)

Appalachian Suicide

I

This is the place of desolation here,
The mines have fallen, tracks have rusted red;
The lizards, rabbits, crows are left to care
Where shacks have tumbled and the damp is dead.
Life was once here: one couldn't ask for more;
Mole-men, fat checks, for mining our black gold
Stepped sprightly all night on the dance-hall floor,
Unmindful that tomorrow's camp would fold.
What of tomorrow when there was today,
And hell with those who spoke of waste and sin;
John-L was god who upped their take-home pay,
They whored and fought and drank highridge and gin.
Then, unexpectedly there came the blight,
An economic fungus over all;
There came Depression's endless lonely night
Recorded by the blacksnake's writhing scrawl.

II

Portrait:
Rockcastle County

Apathetic hills,
Scrub-timber covered;
Apathetic shacks
On yellow-clay banks,
Tar-paper covered.

Apathetic fields,
Scrub pine encircled
On rugged slopes;
Maturing corn waist-high
With thumb-sized ears

Compensation for
Digging with hoes
And plowing with
A skinny mule
And cutter plow.

Can the people win?
Backbreaking toil
And salty sweat!
Children, children,
Like flitting swarms
Of butterflies.

Parents broken
Before their time
In body and spirit.
Apathetic people!
My people!

III

Bell County
(a lonesome ballad)

Churches, churches everywhere,
Many denominations;
They thrive and vie in rivalry,
Each with its definitions!

Heaven, Heaven so exciting,
Idyllic, far away
From hellhole scars of mining
And blue-slate dumps of clay.

Heaven has all for comforting,
Housing with food and heat;
Then why not be preparing
To conquer mine defeat!

Billboards without conformity
Have warned us to prepare,
Rush on to Heaven singing,
Escaping what is here.

IV

A one-product people
We lived on coal;
We groveled under mountains
With picks, augers, shovels.
This was our black gold,
We groveled by carbide lamps
In the semidark ill-ventilated holes,
Outside the mine the sunlight hurt our eyes
And burned our cool, sallow, coal-mine faces.

When black gold was a product
For which there was a great demand
We received our wonderfully fat checks,
Bought everything from the company store,
Even to refrigerators for our front porches
Of our shotgun company shacks!
We were the first families
With two cars for one garage.

But our one product didn't last!
Expensive labor,
Priced our black gold from the market.

Our rugged land
Produces no other product
That will sustain us here.
People and land are poor,
People and land are hungry too.
Our land can't walk away,
Nor can it ride away,
But we the people can
Ride away or walk away
To where, to what
Strange land and people?

We leave dark gaping mouths,
With decaying mine-post teeth,
We leave the blue-slate dumps,
These only monuments of our having been
Here once to leave our contributions
For tourists yet unborn to see.

We leave our hungry land we love
That cannot say *good-bye* to us
Then we depart,
Broken in spirit,
Famished for food
And sick at heart.

V

The New Classes

The Middlings and
The Higher-ups
Will leave behind
Their empty cups

For North, for South,
For East for West,
For anyplace
They live the best,

Forgetting foul
Polluted water,
Deserted mines
And drunken laughter,

Forgetting hunger
And the dance-hall floor,
Cheap booze and music
And the company store.

Progressives leave,
Politicos stay
And vote it right
For more handouts
And the easy way.

VI

His shaggy hair and brows, miners adored,
Atrocious manners, dictatorial king
Who brushed off Presidents and told the world;
His Shakespeare quoting was another thing
Where mountains of black gold rose to the skies.
He ruled his Union with an iron hand
Until his Empire sank before his eyes
When prices rose and there was no demand.
There came cold facts that blue recessions make
That brought more ghost towns than old Genghis Khan,
World conqueror, brought in his whirlwind wake
And those ingredients politicians feed upon.

Czar John-L left his marks on mountain brow
And in deep valleys of our mountain earth
Where loyal subjects have deserted now
And stunned they speculate about his worth.

VII

When Czar John-L becomes a heavenly sprite
And over his clay temple daisies grow,
When he has gone to meet his endless night,
Who'll weep for him with heads in grief bowed low?
His power and his oratory gone
Into that lonesome cell of his last mine,
Will a miner's widow grieve for him alone?
Beside his bier will miners stand in line?
His going into his eternity
Will leave ten thousand monuments behind;
Deserted coal camps where the wind blows free
Will speak for him at peace and out of mind.
His bubble brilliant as a buttercup
Dew-pearled in sunlight of an April spring,
But too much power blew his bubble up
And then it burst into an ugly thing.

VIII

Finis

When a whirlybird dropped from the skies
To an humble shack in the vale below,
"'Poor people" were not taken by surprise,
Photographers were there "ready to go."
A tall man with Disciples of his Creed
Swarmed in like flies to shake "poor peoples'"
    hands,

Cameras clicked, the tall man spoke of need:
No poverty like this in all the land,
A billion dollars will cure all your ills.
For thirty years his Party had had power
And Poverty was found among our hills
In this contact and in his glory hour.
So handsome, clean, above all mortal sin,
This soft-voiced man who never did a wrong
Walked to his whirlybird and climbed therein,
So simple and all poverty was gone.

CARL SANDBURG (1878–1967)

Name Us a King

Name us a king
who shall live forever—
a peanut king, a potato king,
a gasket king, a brass-tack king,
a wall-paper king with a wall-paper crown
and a wall-paper queen with wall-paper jewels.

Name us a king
so keen, so fast, so hard,
he shall last forever—
and all the yes-men square shooters
telling the king, "Okay Boss, you shall
   last forever! and then some!"
telling it to an onion king, a pecan king,
a zipper king or a chewing gum king,
any consolidated amalgamated syndicate king—
listening to the yes-men telling him
he shall live forever, he is so keen,
   so fast, so hard,

an okay Boss who shall never bite the dust,
never go down and be a sandwich for the worms
   like us—the customers,
   like us—the customers.

Kenneth Fearing   (1902–1961)

Dirge[1]

1-2-3 was the number he played but today the number came 3-2-1;
Bought his Carbide at 30 and it went to 29; had the favorite at
   Bowie but the track was slow—

O executive type, would you like to drive a floating-power, knee-
   action, silk-upholstered six? Wed a Hollywood star? Shoot
   the course in 58? Draw to the ace, king, jack?
O fellow with a will who won't take no, watch out for three
   cigarettes on the same, single match; O democratic voter
   born in August under Mars, beware of liquidated rails—

Denouement[2] to denouement, he took a personal pride in the certain, certain way he lived his own, private life,
But nevertheless, they shut off his gas; nevertheless, the bank fore-
   closed; nevertheless, the landlord called; nevertheless, the
   radio broke,

And twelve o'clock arrived just once too often,
Just the same he wore one gray tweed suit, bought one straw hat,
   drank one straight Scotch, walked one short step, took one
   long look, drew one deep breath,
Just one too many,

1. A song or hymn of grief accompanying funeral rites.
2. The final outcome of a sequence of events.

And wow he died as wow he lived,
Going whop to the office and blooie home to sleep and biff got
married and bam had children and oof got fired,
Zowie did he live and zowie did he die,

With who the hell are you at the corner of his casket, and where
the hell're we going on the right-hand silver knob, and
who the hell cares walking second from the end with an
American Beauty wreath from why the hell not,

Very much missed by the circulation staff of the New York Evening Post; deeply, deeply mourned by the B.M.T.[3]

Wham, Mr. Roosevelt; pow, Sears Roebuck; awk, big dipper;
bop, summer rain;
Bong, Mr., bong, Mr., bong, Mr., bong.

3. A public transportation system.

FENTON JOHNSON (1888–1958)

The Daily Grind

If Nature says to you,
"I intend you for something fine,
For something to sing the song
That only my whirling stars can sing,
For something to burn in the firmament
With all the fervor of my golden sun,
For something to moisten the parched souls
As only my rivulets can moisten the parched,"

What can you do?

If the System says to you,
"I intend you to grind and grind
Grains of corn beneath millstones;
I intend you to shovel and sweat
Before a furnace of Babylon;
I intend you for grist and meat
To fatten my pompous gods
As they wallow in an alcoholic nectar,"

What can you do?

Naught can you do
But watch that eternal battle
Between Nature and the System.
You cannot blame God,
You cannot blame man;
For God did not make the System,
Neither did man fashion Nature.
You can only die each morning,
And live again in the dreams of the night.
If Nature forgets you,
If the System forgets you,
God has blest you.

NORMAN NATHAN (1915–)

Investment

Vending myself,
A once machine,
I'm worth more dead,
With parts alive,
If my heart beats
For someone else,
My cornea sees
In another's eye.

Lungs, kidneys, blood,
My unscarred skin
Is above sex
Or next of kin;
They're hardly me,
Or so he says
Who chews my tongue,
Prays on my knees.

As noble thoughts
Caress all minds,
My lips may kiss
My cheeks when I'm
Scattered upon
A dozen forms
Or a club who share
Bits of my prime.

John Ciardi   (1916–1986)

Back Through the Looking Glass to This Side

Yesterday, in a big market, I made seven thousand dollars
while I was flying to Dallas to speak to some lunch group
and back for a nightcap with my wife. A man from Dallas
sat by me both ways, the first from Campbell's Soup,
the other from some labeled can of his own, mostly water,
and Goldwater at that. Capt. J.J. Slaughter

of Untied Airlines kept us all in smooth air and well
and insistently informed me of our progress. Miss G. Klaus
brought us bourbon on ice, and snacks. At the hotel
the lunch grouped and the group lunched. I was,
if I may say so, perceptive, eloquent, sincere.
Then back to the airport with seventeen minutes to spare.

Capt. T.V. Ringo took over with Miss P. Simbus
and that Goldwater oaf. We made it to Newark at nine
plus a few minutes lost in skirting cumulonimbus
in our descent at the Maryland-Delaware line.
"Ticker runs late," said the horoscope page. "New highs
posted on a broad front."—So the good guys

had won again! Fat, complacent, a check
for more than my father's estate in my inside pocket,
with the launched group's thanks for a good day's work,
I found my car in the lot and poked it
into the lunatic aisles of U.S.1,
a good guy coming home, the long day done.

ALICE ROSE GEORGE (1944–   )

Success

Somehow the days take care of themselves.
Desire that feels as if it will scorch
The skin of wanting doesn't get fulfilled
And somehow we don't die—though we want to.
We have learned to dwell on the world condition,
To have consciousness even as we rape the child
Of any decent future—and this isn't just pessimism
    talking.
These are long, hard days we spend breathing
With an unnatural knowledge of what is meant by the word
Aloneness. The collective we is friends obsessed
With busy routines, the electing body, family unseen
For years, identities broken, the chain broken,
Words breaking our hearts, but then we straighten up
And go on pretending it never happened, we are so
    strong.

Irony, cynicism, gossip are appropriate, they fit
Our times—the spread out page of a newspaper
Telling us what we are better than a real God,
Who can't talk, ever could. We find
Ourselves over Sunday brunch bad mouthing
Our very sadness so that even the sun loses validity,
Proof of our days is invalid, but we talk on as though
Some answer were kicking under the dining room table.
If not a meal, then a party where drunks can let down
   their hair,

Be natural with pain that comes up like vomit,
No longer thinking control; the desire to be loved,
So unnatural for our world, dances like a whore
Before our eyes, in us, ashamed we go home
Alone, naked for the stars only.
The only way to survive is to act—so,
Days fly by with their demands and only a few moments
Of desire and despair slip past the censors
And they don't kill us—yet.
We are ok, we are concerned, we reassure one another.

Adrienne Rich (1929–   )

Power

Living   in the earth-deposits   of our history

Today a backhoe divulged   out of a crumbling flank of earth
one bottle   amber   perfect   a hundred-year-old
cure for fever   or melancholy   a tonic
for living on this earth   in the winters of this climate

Today I was reading about Marie Curie:[1]
she must have known she suffered   from radiation sickness
her body bombarded for years   by the element
she had purified
It seems she denied to the end
the source of the cataracts on her eyes
the cracked and suppurating skin   of her finger-ends
till she could no longer hold   a test-tube or a pencil

She died   a famous woman   denying
her wounds
denying
her wounds   came   from the same source as her power

1. Physicist and chemist (1867–1934) who, with her husband, Pierre, discovered radium.

Byron Rufus Newton (1861–1938)

Owed to New York—1906

Vulgar of manner, overfed,
Overdressed and underbred,
Heartless, Godless, hell's delight,
Rude by day and lewd by night;
Bedwarfed the man, o'ergrown the brute,
Ruled by boss and prostitute:
Purple-robed and pauper-clad,
Raving, rotting, money-mad;
A squirming herd in Mammon's mesh,
A wilderness of human flesh;
Crazed by avarice, lust and rum,
New York, thy name's "Delirium."

Liz Sohappy Bahe (1947–)

Printed Words

I stared at the printed words
hazed, blurred, they became grey.
I trailed down the page
to a picture shouting what I read.

I thought about my people
up North—
far from here.
My land, the hot dry basin,
the pine on the mountain ranges
and the snowcapped peaks.

I thought of the killing word:
Civilization.
The steel buildings stabbing the earth,
stabbing old religions
now buried on the hilltop,
to have their tears drip black
from Industry's ash clouds.

I thought of the unseen tears
in eyes watching our valley
gashed by plows,
proud trees uprooted, dragged aside,
giving way to smothering tar roads.
And river veins pumped away
never knowing the path to the Columbia River.

Howard Nemerov (1920–)

BOOM!
Sees Boom in Religion, Too

Atlantic City, June 23, 1957 (AP)—
President Eisenhower's pastor said tonight
that Americans are living in a period of
"unprecedented religious activity" caused
partially by paid vacations, the
eight-hour day and modern conveniences.
"These fruits of material progress,"
said the Rev. Edward L.R. Elson of the
National Presbyterian Church,
Washington, "have provided the leisure,
the energy, and the means for a level of
human and spiritual values never before
reached."

Here at the Vespasian-Carlton, it's just one
religious activity after another; the sky
is constantly being crossed by cruciform
airplanes, in which nobody disbelieves
for a second, and the tide, the tide
of spiritual progress and prosperity
miraculously keeps rising, to a level
never before attained. The churches are full,
the beaches are full, and the filling-stations
are full, God's great ocean is full
of paid vacationers praying an eight-hour day
to the human and spiritual values, the fruits,
the leisure, the energy, and the means, Lord,
the means for the level, the unprecedented level,
and the modern conveniences, which also are full.
Never before, O Lord, have the prayers and praises
from belfry and phonebooth, from ballpark and barbecue
the sacrifices, so endlessly ascended.

It was not thus when Job in Palestine
sat in the dust and cried, cried bitterly;
when Damien kissed the lepers on their wounds
it was not thus; it was not thus
when Francis worked a fourteen-hour day
strictly for the birds; when Dante took
a week's vacation without pay and it rained
part of the time, O Lord, it was not thus.

But now the gears mesh and the tires burn
and the ice chatters in the shaker and the priest
in the pulpit, and Thy Name, O Lord,
is kept before the public, while the fruits
ripen and religion booms and the level rises
and every modern convenience runneth over,
that it may never be with us as it hath been
with Athens and Karnak and Nagasaki,
nor Thy sun for one instant refrain from shining
on the rainbow Buick by the breezeway
or the Chris Craft with the uplift life raft;
that we may continue to be the just folks we are,
plain people with ordinary superliners and
disposable diaperliners, people of the stop'n'shop
'n'pray as you go, of hotel, motel, boatel,
the humble pilgrims of no deposit no return
and please adjust thy clothing, who will give to Thee,
if Thee will keep us going, our annual
Miss Universe, for Thy Name's Sake, Amen.

DELMORE SCHWARTZ (1913–1966)

The True-Blue American

Jeremiah Dickson was a true-blue American,
For he was a little boy who understood America, for he
    felt that he must
Think about *everything*; because that's *all* there is to
    think about,

Knowing immediately the intimacy of truth and comedy,
Knowing intuitively how a sense of humor was a necessity
For one and for all who live in America. Thus, natively,
    and
Naturally when on an April Sunday in an ice cream
    parlor Jeremiah
Was requested to choose between a chocolate sundae
    and a banana split
He answered unhesitatingly, having no need to think of it
Being a true-blue American, determined to continue as
    he began:
Rejecting the either-or of Kierkegaard, and many another
    European;
Refusing to accept alternatives, refusing to believe the
    choice of between;
Rejecting selection; denying dilemma; electing absolute
    affirmation: knowing
  in his breast

    The infinite and the gold
    Of the endless frontier, the deathless West.

"Both: I will have them both!" declared this true-blue
    American
In Cambridge, Massachusetts, on an April Sunday, in-
    structed
  By the great department stores, by the Five-and-Ten,
Taught by Christmas, by the circus, by the vulgarity and
    grandeur of
  Niagara Falls and the Grand Canyon,
Tutored by the grandeur, vulgarity, and infinite appetite
    gratified and
  Shining in the darkness, of the light
On Saturdays at the double bills of the moon pictures,
The consummation of the advertisements of the imagina-
    tion of the light
Which is as it was—the infinite belief in infinite hope—of
    Columbus,
  Barnum, Edison, and Jeremiah Dickson.

FICTION

ÉMILE ZOLA (1840–1902)

From L'Assommoir[1]

One autumn afternoon, Gervaise, on her way back from the Rue des Portes-Blanches, where she had been taking some clothes to a customer, found herself at the bottom of the Rue des Poissonniers just as the light was fading. It had rained that morning, the air was soft, an odour rose from the damp pavement; and the laundress, hampered by her big basket, breathed heavily, dragging her feet a little, her body drooping, making her way up the street with a sort of vaguely sensual desire, bred of her lassitude. She would have liked to have something nice to eat. Then, as she raised her eyes, she saw the name of the Rue Marcadet on the corner of the street, and the idea suddenly occurred to her to go and see Goujet at his forge. Twenty times he had asked her to step over some day when she would like to see how iron was worked. Besides, before the other workmen, she would ask for Étienne, she would seem to have come merely to see her son.

The manufactory of bolts and rivets must be in that direction, at that end of the Rue Marcadet, she did not quite know where; especially as the numbers were often wanting, along the buildings, separated by open spaces. It was a street in which she would not have lived for worlds, a big, dirty street, black with coal-dust from the manufactories all round, with dilapidated pavements, and ruts in which the water lay in puddles. At each end was a row of sheds, great workshops with glass windows, grey elevations, unfinished-looking, their bricks and timbers bare, a confusion of tumble-down masonry with great gaps between, with

1. To club or hit. Also, a dive or bar.

dubious lodging-houses and low taverns on either side. She only remembered that the manufactory was near an old rag and iron store, a sort of open sewer, in which slept hundreds of thousands of francs' worth of merchandise, Goujet had told her. And she tried to find her way in the midst of the roar of factories: thin chimneys on the roof poured out great clouds of steam; a steam-saw sounded out with a continuous screech, like the sharp tearing of a piece of calico; button manufactories shook the soil with the roll and tic-tac of their machines. As she gazed towards Montmartre, undecided, not knowing whether to go on further, a puff of wind blew down the soot from a tall chimney, filling the street with stench; and she closed her eyes, half suffocated, when she heard a rhythmical sound of hammers; without knowing it, she was right opposite the manufactory, which she recognized by the hole at the side, full of old rags.

Nevertheless she still hesitated, not knowing where to find an entrance. A broken-down fencing opened up a passage that seemed to lose itself in the rubbish of a house that was being pulled down. As a pool of muddy water barred the way, two planks had been laid across. At last she ventured upon the planks, turned to the left, and found herself lost in a strange forest of old carts, lying with their shafts in the air—ruined hovels whose beams still remained standing. At the end, like a bit of day in the midst of this dark and dismal night, a red light burned. The noise of hammers had ceased. She advanced cautiously towards the light, when a workman passed her close by, his face blackened with coal and covered with a bristling beard; he gave her a sidelong glance out of his pale eyes as he passed.

"Monsieur," she asked, "it is here, isn't it, that a boy called Étienne works? It is my boy."

"Étienne, Étienne," said the workman, huskily, swaying to and fro. "Étienne—no, don't know him."

When he opened his mouth, he exhaled an odour of alcohol like that which comes from a newly-opened cask of old brandy. And as he was beginning to be rather familiar, meeting a woman like that in a dark corner, Gervaise recoiled, murmuring,—

"It is here, though, that Monsieur Goujet works?"

"Ah! Goujet, yes!" said the workman; "I know Goujet. If it is Goujet you want to see, go right to the end."

And turning he shouted with his voice, that sounded like cracked brass,—

"I say, Gueule-d'Or,[2] a lady for you!"

But the shout was lost in a clatter of iron. Gervaise went right to the end. She reached a great door, and looked in. It was a huge building in which she could at first distinguish nothing. The forge, as if extinct, shone in a corner with the pale brilliancy of a star, beating back the darkness about it. Great shadows floated around; and from moment to moment black masses were to be seen passing in front of the fire, blocking up this last patch of light—men of incredible size, whose huge proportions one guessed at. Gervaise dared not venture in; she called out softly from the door,—

"Monsieur Goujet! Monsieur Goujet!"

Suddenly the place was all lit up. The bellows had begun to work, and a jet of white flame issued. The shed was now visible, closed in by great planks, with holes roughly plastered, and corners consolidated with brick-work. The coal dust, flying in every direction, covered the place with a sort of greyish soot. Cobwebs hung from the beams, like rags hung out to dry, heavy with years of accumulated dirt. About the walls, lying on shelves, hung on nails, or thrown in dark corners, a pell-mell of old irons and implements, huge tools, were strewn about, standing out in sharp, hard outline. And the white flame still rose dazzlingly, falling like a ray of sunlight on the beaten soil, where the polished steel of four anvils, fixed in their blocks, looked like silver dotted with gold.

Then Gervaise recognized Goujet beside the forge, by his yellow beard. Étienne was blowing the bellows, and there were two other workmen there. She only saw Goujet, and she went forward and stood in front of him.

"What! Madame Gervaise!" he cried, his face beaming, "what a good surprise!"

But, as his fellow-workmen looked very quizzical, he drew Étienne over to his mother, and went on,—

"You have come to see the boy. He gets on very well; he is getting a famous wrist of his own."

---

2. Literal translation is "snout of gold," from Goujet's golden beard.

"Well, well!" she said, "it isn't easy to get here. I thought I had got to the end of the world."

And she told him how she had come. Then she asked why the name of Étienne was not known there. Goujet laughed; he explained to her that everyone called him little Zouzou, because his hair was cropped close, like that of a Zouave.[3] While they were talking, Étienne stopped blowing the bellows, and the flame of the forge went down, the rosy light dwindled away into the darkness of the shed. The blacksmith looked tenderly at Gervaise, who stood there smiling, bringing so fresh an aspect into that artificial light. Then, as neither of them spoke, standing there together in the darkness, he seemed to recollect himself, and broke the silence,—

"Excuse me, Madame Gervaise, I have something to finish. Stay there; you are not in anybody's way."

She stood there, Étienne had returned to the bellows. The forge flamed, sending up rockets of sparks; especially as the boy, wanting to shew off his strength before his mother, let loose a perfect whirlwind. Goujet stood watching a bar of iron which was heating; he waited, pincers in hand. He was in the full blaze of the light. His shirt sleeves were rolled up, his collar was open at the neck, leaving bare his arms and his chest, a rosy skin like that of a girl, on which curled little blonde hairs; and, with his head bowed on his huge shoulders, on which the muscles stood out in knots, his face attentive, his pale eyes fixed steadily on the flame, he looked like a giant in repose, tranquil in his strength. When the bar was white-hot, he seized it with the pincers, and with his hammer cut it off into regular sections on the anvil, as if he had been breaking bits of glass, with little taps. Then he put the bits back in the fire, taking them out again one by one, to work them into shape. He was forging six-sided rivets. He put the ends in a heading-frame, hammered down the iron at the top, flattened the six sides, and then threw the finished rivets, still red-hot, on the ground, where they went out in darkness; and he hammered away without a pause, swinging in his right hand a hammer weighing five pounds, finishing off some detail at every blow, turning and manipulating his iron so deftly,

---

3. Soldier in the French service in Algeria.

that he could go on talking and looking about all the time. The anvil rang out its silvery chime, and the blacksmith, without a drop of sweat, quite at his ease, hammered away as composedly, and apparently with as little effort, as when he was cutting out his figures at home in the evening.

"Oh, that—it's only a small rivet, twenty millimetres," he said, in answer to Gervaise's questions. "One could do three hundred a day. But it needs practice, because one's arm soon gets tired."

When she asked him if his wrist was not stiff by night, he had a good laugh. Did she think he was a young lady? His wrist had seen some hard work since he was fifteen; it had turned to iron with pulling about so many tools. However, she was right enough; a gentleman who had never forged a rivet or a bolt, and who tried to play with his hammer of five pounds' weight, would get a pretty stroke of lumbago at the end of two hours. It looked nothing at all, but it often cleaned out a good solid chap in a few years. Meanwhile the other workmen went on hammering away, all together. Their huge shadows danced in the light, the red gleam of the iron as it was taken out of the fire flashed into the darkness, a splutter of sparks flew out under the blows of the hammers, shining like suns, almost on the level of the anvils. And Gervaise seemed to be caught up into the wind of the forge, happy to be there, without a wish to be going. She made a large *détour* in order to get near Étienne without risk of getting her hands burnt, when she saw the dirty-bearded workman, whom she had spoken to outside, come in.

"So you found him, Madame?" said he, with his bantering, drunken air. "Gueule-d'Or, you know it was I who told the lady where to find you."

He was called Bec-Salé,[4] otherwise Boit-sans-Soif,[5] a bolt-maker of great dash, as strong as a horse, who rinced his irons in a pint of brandy a day. He had gone out for a drop then, unable to wait till six o'clock. When he found out that Zouzou was called Étienne, he thought it very droll; and he laughed, showing his discoloured teeth. Then he recognized Gervaise. Only the day

---

4. Literal translation is "salty snout," perhaps referring to his sassy tongue.
5. Literal translation is "he who drinks without thirst," probably referring to his attachment to alcohol.

before, he had had a glass with Coupeau. You might mention Bec-Salé, otherwise Boit-sans-Soif, to Coupeau; he would say at once, he's a good fellow! That chap Coupeau was a good sort, he stood treat oftener than his turn.

"I am very glad to know you are his wife," he went on. "He deserves a pretty wife. I say, Gueule-d'Or, she is pretty, isn't she?"

He came close to her with a gallant air, and she had to take up her basket, and hold it in front of her, in order to keep him at a distance. Goujet was vexed, knowing that his fellow-workman wanted to tease him on account of his friendly relations with Gervaise, and he shouted,—

"I say, lazy-bones! when are we to do the forty millimetres? Are you game now, now that you've got your belly full, you damned bibber?"

The blacksmith referred to an order for big bolts, which needed two strikers at the anvil.

"Right away, if you will, big baby!" replied Bec-Salé, otherwise Boit-sans-Soif. "Sucks its thumb, it does, and thinks itself a man! I've eaten others as big as you!"

"All right, straight away! Come along, us two!"

"Right you are, old joker!"

The presence of Gervaise had put them both on their metal. Goujet put the pieces of iron, ready cut, into the fire; then he fixed on the anvil a large sized heading-frame. The other workman had taken from against the wall two huge sledge-hammers of twenty pounds, the two big sisters, Fifine and Dédèle. And he bragged away, telling of a half-gross of rivets that he had forged for the Dunkerque lighthouse, regular jewels, things to put in a museum, so prettily he had worked them. What the blazes! he wasn't the man to fear competition; you might hunt all over the city without finding another like him. Oh, it was going to be a joke; now we shall see what we shall see.

"The lady shall decide," he said, turning to Gervaise.

"Enough chatter!" cried Goujet. "At it, Zouzou. There's no heat there, my lad!"

But Bec-Salé, otherwise Boit-sans-Soif, asked again,—

"Do we both strike together?"

"Not at all! a bolt each, old man!"

The proposition caused a sensation, and the other workman,

despite his cheek, felt his mouth turn dry. Bolts of forty millimetres made by one man? such a thing had never been heard of, especially as the bolts had to be rounded at the top—a deuce of a piece of work, a regular poser. The three other workmen had left their work to look on; a big lean fellow wagered a bottle of wine that Goujet would be beaten. Meanwhile the two blacksmiths each took a sledge-hammer, choosing them with eyes closed, for Fifine weighed half a pound more than Dédèle. Bec-Salé, otherwise Boit-sans-Soif, had the good luck to lay hands on Dédèle; Gueule-d'Or took Fifine. And the former, as he waited for the iron to get white-hot, stood before the anvil, throwing tender glances in the direction of Gervaise; then he put himself in position, tapping his foot like one who is ready for the fight, already swaying Dédèle lightly in the air. Damn it all! he was all there; he'd make a cake of the Vendôme Column![6]

"Now, at it!" said Goujet, placing in the heading-frame one of the bits of iron, as big as a girl's wrist.

Bec-Salé, otherwise Boit-sans-Soif, leant back, and whirled Dédèle into the air with both hands. Small and lean, with his stubbly beard, and his wolfish eyes shining under his matted crop of hair, he made a tremendous exertion at every blow of the hammer, leaping off the ground as if carried away by his own fury. He went at it desperately, fighting with his iron, wroth with it for being so hard; and he gave a grunt when he had given it a good sound box. Brandy might weaken the arms of others, but he had need of it in his veins instead of blood; the last drop he had drunk warmed his carcase like a boiler, he felt as damned strong as a steam-hammer. And the iron feared him that day; he beat it flatter than a quid of tobacco. And didn't Dédèle waltz! She cut capers, heels in the air, like a little baggage at the Elyseé-Montmartre shewing off her under-things; for it is no good dawdling, iron is such a brute, it cools in no time, with one hammer. In thirty strokes Bec-Salé, otherwise Boit-sans-Soif, had formed the head of his bolt, But he was panting, his eyes starting out of their sockets; and he was seized with a furious anger when he heard his joints crack. Then, dancing and grimacing, he delivered two more blows, simply to revenge

[6]. A famous monument in Paris.

himself for his discomfort. When he took it out of the heading-frame, the bolt was deformed, the head on one side like a hunchback's.

"Well, does that look neat?" said he, with his usual self-confidence, presenting his work to Gervaise.

"I am not well up in it, monsieur," she answered, with an air of reserve.

But she saw clearly enough on the head of the bolt the mark of Dédèle's last two kicks, and she was awfully pleased. She put her lips together so as not to laugh, for Goujet now had all the chances on his side.

It was Gueule-d'Or's turn. Before beginning, he threw Gervaise a look full of confidence and of tenderness. Then, without hurrying, he measured his distance and brought down the hammer in steady, downward, regular strokes. His stroke was classic, correct, measured, supple. Fifine, in his hands, danced to low *chahut*,[7] her legs outside her petticoat; she rose and fell rhythmically, like a noble lady leading a grave and ancient minuet. Fifine's heels beat the measure solemnly, sinking into the red-hot iron on the head of the bolt with a deliberate skill, first flattening the metal in the middle, then modelling it with a series of strokes, each delivered with perfect precision. Sure enough, it was not brandy that Gueule-d'Or had in his veins; it was blood, pure blood, whose mighty beats made themselves felt in the very hammer, marking time. What a splendid fellow he was for work! He stood full in face of the whole heat of the forge. His short hair, curling over his low forehead, his fine golden beard, with its close ringlets, were lit up, they shone all golden, a very head of gold, in truth. And he had a neck like a pillar, white as the neck of a child; an immense breadth of chest, wide enough for a woman to lie across it; shoulders and arms that seemed to belong to some sculptured giant in a museum. When he put forth all his strength, his muscles swelled, mountains of flesh rolling and hardening under the skin; his shoulders, neck, and chest distended, he cast a light all around him, he was strong and mighty as a god. Twenty times already he had brought down Fifine, his eyes fixed on the iron, drawing in his breath at each stroke, with only two large drops of sweat

---

7. Wild and rowdy dancing.

trickling over his forehead. He counted: twenty-one, twenty-two, twenty-three. Fifine continued tranquilly her lordly reverences.

"What a prig!" muttered sneeringly Bec-Salé, otherwise Boit-sans-Soif.

And Gervaise, standing opposite to Gueule-d'Or, gazed at him with an affectionate smile. Good Lord! what fools men were! Were not those two hammering away on their bolts in order to pay court to her? Oh, she saw well enough that they were disputing over her, they and their hammers; they were like two great crested cocks shewing off before a little white hen. It was an odd contrivance, wasn't it? Still, people sometimes make love in a very strange manner. Yes, it was for her, this thunder of Dédèle and Fifine on the anvil; it was for her, all this battering of iron; it was for her, this forge in motion, flaming like a conflagration, sending out showers of sparks. They were fashioning their love for her, and it was for that they disputed with each other, seeing who could fashion it the best. And, truly, she was glad at heart; for what woman does not love compliments? The hammering of Gueule-d'Or, in particular, spoke to her heart; it rang out a clear music on the anvil, as if in accompaniment to the beating of her own blood. Folly as it seems, she felt as if that drove something home in her, something solid, like bolt-iron. That evening, on her way home, along the damp pavement, she had had a vague desire, a longing after something good to eat; now she was satisfied, as if the strokes of Gueule-d'Or's hammer had sufficed her. Oh! she had no doubt of his success. It was to him that she was destined to fall. Bec-Salé, otherwise Boit-sans-Soif, was too hideous in his dirty workman's things, skipping about like an escaped monkey. And she waited, flushed and yet happy in the intense heat, delighting to be shaken from head to foot by the last strokes of Fifine.

Goujet still went on counting.

"And twenty-eight," he said at last, resting the hammer on the ground. "It is finished; you can look at it."

The head of the bolt was smooth, flawless, without a crease, a regular bit of jeweller's work, round as a billiard ball made in a mould. The workmen gazed at it, wagging their heads; there was not a word to be said, one might go on one's knees to it. Bec-Salé, otherwise Boit-sans-Soif, tried to turn it off as a joke; but he found nothing to say, and he went back to his anvil with his tail between his legs. Meanwhile, Gervaise pressed against Goujet, as if to see better. Étienne had left the bellows, the forge was once more sunk in shadow, like a red sunset falling all at once into the sheer darkness of night. And to the blacksmith and the laundress it seemed delicious to be there, with this night about them, in the shed black with soot and iron filings, full of the smell of old iron; they would not have seemed more alone in the Bois de Vincennes, if they had had a rendezvous in mid-forest. He took her hand as if he had won her.

But outside, they had not a word to say. He could think of nothing; except that she might have taken Étienne along with her if he had not had another half-hour's work to do. She was on the point of going, when he called her back again, trying to keep her with him a few minutes longer.

"Come, you haven't seen everything. Really it is very curious."

He took her to the right, into another shed, where there was a machine-manufactory belonging. On the threshold she hesitated, taken with an instinctive fear. The great building, shaken by all these machines, trembled; and huge shadows waved in the air, streaked with vivid fire. But he reassured her, smiling, swearing that there was nothing to fear; she must only be careful not to let her skirts go too near the cog-wheels. He went first, she following, in a deafening din where all sorts of noises hissed and rumbled, in the midst of smoke peopled with vague beings, black hurrying men, machines with waving arms, which she could not distinguish from one another. The passages were very narrow, one had to step over obstacles, get out of the way of holes, step aside to make way for a cart. They could not hear each other speak. As yet she saw nothing; all danced before her eyes. Then, as she felt a sensation above her head like a great flutter of wings, she looked up, and stood still to watch the straps running along the ceiling like a gigantic spider's web, every thread going in a different direction; the motor steam-engine was hidden away in a corner, behind a little brick wall; and the straps seemed to run of their own accord, coming swiftly out of the shadowy distance, with a regular soft, continuous, gliding motion, like a bird of the night. But she nearly fell, striking her foot against one of the ventilating pipes, which crossed in all directions on the beaten soil, sending out their little sharp breath of wind on all the little forges beside the machines. And first of all he shewed her that: he let loose the air on one of the furnaces; large sheets of fan-shaped flames spread from all four sides, a circle of indentated flames, dazzlingly, turning to a deep red; the light was so strong that the workmen's small lamps looked like spots of shadow on the sun. Then he raised his voice to explain things to her, he shewed her the machines, mechanical scissors which cut up bars of iron, severing a piece at each bite, spitting out the ends at the back, one by one; bolt and rivet machines, big and complicated, forging the heads with a single pressure of their powerful screw; the shearing machines with cast-iron fly-wheels, an iron ball which struck the air furiously at every piece they trimmed; the worming-machines, manipulated by women, worming the bolts and their spiral screws, with the tic-tac of their wheel-work of steel, shining under the grease with which they had been oiled. She could thus follow the whole series, from the block-iron leaning against the walls, to the finished bolts and rivets, heaped up in cases in every corner. She understood it all now, and she smiled and nodded; but she was a little nervous all the same, nervous at being so small and frail among all these rugged metal-workers; turning, now and again, her blood curdling, at the dull noise of a shearing-machine. She grew accustomed to the dim light, could see into the recesses where men, standing motionless, regulated the panting dance of fly-wheels, when a furnace suddenly let loose the vivid illumination of its circle of flame. And, in spite of herself, it was constantly to the ceiling that she turned back, to the very life-blood of the machines, the flexile flight of leathern straps above her, with their huge and silent force passing in the vague night of the rafters.

  Meanwhile, Goujet had stopped before one of the rivetting machines. He stood there, looking down with fixed eyes, absorbed in a reverie. The machine forged rivets of forty millimetres with the tranquil ease of a giant. And nothing, indeed, could be more simple. The stoker took the piece of iron from the furnace; the striker placed it in the heading-frame, on which a stream of water was constantly running in order to preserve the temper of the steel; and it was done, the screw came down, the bolt fell to the ground with its head as round as if it had been placed in a mould. In twelve hours this infernal machine turned out hundreds of kilogrammes. Goujet, little disposed as he was to malevolence, felt at certain moments as if he would gladly have brought down Fifine on all that apparatus of iron, whose arms were so far more powerful than his own. It caused him a huge annoyance, even when he reasoned that flesh and blood could not fight against iron. One day, for certain, the machine would put an end to the workman; already their day's wages had fallen from twelve to nine francs, and there was talk of reducing them yet further; and they were not pretty at all, those great beasts that made rivets and bolts as if they were making sausages. He gazed at the machines for three good minutes without speaking; he frowned, and his golden beard bristled threateningly. Then a resigned and composed air came slowly back to his features. He turned towards Gervaise, who pressed up against him, and said with a sad smile,—

"Well, it takes us down a peg! But perhaps one day it will be for the general good."

Gervaise laughed at the "general good." The machine-made bolts seem to her badly made.

"You know what I mean!" she cried, excitedly, "they are too well made. I like yours better. There one feels the artist's hand."

It was a great joy to him to hear her say that, for he was wondering if she would despise him after having seen the machines. Lord! if he were stronger than Bec-Salé, otherwise Boit-sans-Soif, the machines were stronger than he. When at last he left her in the court-yard, he squeezed her hands nearly hard enough to break them, in his delight.

John Steinbeck   (1902–1969)

From The Grapes of Wrath

The owners of the land came onto the land, or more often a spokesman for the owners came. They came in closed cars, and they felt the dry earth with their fingers, and sometimes they drove big earth augers into the ground for soil tests. The tenants, from their sun-beaten dooryards, watched uneasily when the closed cars drove along the fields. And at last the owner men drove into the dooryards and sat in their cars to talk out of the windows. The tenant men stood beside the cars for a while, and then squatted on their hams and found sticks with which to mark the dust.

In the open doors the women stood looking out, and behind them the children—corn-headed children, with wide eyes, one bare foot on top of the other bare foot, and the toes working. The women and the children watched their men talking to the owner men. They were silent.

Some of the owner men were kind because they hated what they had to do, and some of them were angry because they hated to be cruel, and some of them were cold because they had long ago found that one could not be an owner unless one were cold. And all of them were caught in something larger than themselves. Some of them hated the mathematics that drove them, and some were afraid, and some worshiped the mathematics because it provided a refuge from thought and from feeling. If a bank or a finance company owned the land, the owner man said, the Bank—or the Company—needs—wants—insists—must have—as though the Bank or the Company were a monster, with thought and feeling, which had ensnared them. These last would take no responsibility for the banks or the companies because they were men and slaves, while the banks were machines and masters all at the same time. Some of the owner men were a little proud to be slaves to such cold and powerful masters. The owner men sat in the cars and explained. You know the land is poor. You've scrabbled at it long enough, God knows.

The squatting tenant men nodded and wondered and drew

figures in the dust, and yes, they knew, God knows. If the dust only wouldn't fly. If the top would only stay on the soil, it might not be so bad.

The owner men went on leading to their point: You know the land's getting poorer. You know what cotton does to the land; robs it, sucks all the blood out of it.

The squatters nodded—they knew, God knew. If they could only rotate the crops they might pump blood back into the land.

Well, it's too late. And the owner men explained the workings and the thinkings of the monster that was stronger than they were. A man can hold land if he can just eat and pay taxes; he can do that.

Yes, he can do that until his crops fail one day and he has to borrow money from the bank.

But—you see, a bank or a company can't do that, because those creatures don't breathe air, don't eat side-meat. They breathe profits; they eat the interest on money. If they don't get it, they die the way you die without air, without side-meat. It is a sad thing, but it is so. It is just so.

The squatting men raised their eyes to understand. Can't we just hang on? Maybe the next year will be a good year. God knows how much cotton next year. And with all the wars—God knows what price cotton will bring. Don't they make explosives out of cotton? And uniforms? Get enough wars and cotton'll hit the ceiling. Next year, maybe. They looked up questioningly.

We can't depend on it. The bank—the monster has to have profits all the time. It can't wait. It'll die. No, taxes go on. When the monster stops growing, it dies. It can't stay one size.

Soft fingers began to tap the sill of the car window, and hard fingers tightened on the restless drawing sticks. In the doorways of the sun-beaten tenant houses, women sighed and then shifted feet so that the one that had been down was now on top, and the toes working. Dogs came sniffing near the owner cars and wetted on all four tires one after another. And chickens lay in the sunny dust and fluffed their feathers to get the cleansing dust down to the skin. In the little sties the pigs grunted inquiringly over the muddy remnants of the slops.

The squatting men looked down again. What do you want us to do? We can't take less share of the crop—we're half starved now. The kids are hungry all the time. We got no clothes, torn an' ragged. If all the neighbors weren't the same, we'd be ashamed to go to meeting.

And at last the owner men came to the point. The tenant system won't work any more. One man on a tractor can take the place of twelve or fourteen families. Pay him a wage and take all the crop. We have to do it. We don't like to do it. But the monster's sick. Something's happened to the monster.

But you'll kill the land with cotton.

We know. We've got to take cotton quick before the land dies. Then we'll sell the land. Lots of families in the East would like to own a piece of land.

The tenant men looked up alarmed. But what'll happen to us? How'll we eat?

You'll have to get off the land. The plows'll go through the dooryard.

And now the squatting men stood up angrily. Grampa took up the land, and he had to kill the Indians and drive them away. And Pa was born here, and he killed weeds and snakes. Then a bad year came and he had to borrow a little money. An' we was born here. There in the door—our children born here. And Pa had to borrow money. The bank owned the land then, but we stayed and we got a little bit of what we raised.

We know that—all that. It's not us, it's the bank. A bank isn't like a man. Or an owner with fifty thousand acres, he isn't like a man either. That's the monster.

Sure, cried the tenant men, but it's our land. We measured it and broke it up. We were born on it, and we got killed on it, died on it. Even if it's no good, it's still ours. That's what makes it ours—being born on it, working it, dying on it. That makes ownership, not a paper with numbers on it.

We're sorry. It's not us. It's the monster. The bank isn't like a man.

Yes, but the bank is only made of men.

No, you're wrong there—quite wrong there. The bank is something else than men. It happens that every man in a bank hates what the bank does, and yet the bank does it. The bank is something more than men, I tell you. It's the monster. Men made it, but they can't control it.

The tenants cried, Grampa killed Indians, Pa killed snakes for the land. Maybe we can kill banks—they're worse than Indians and snakes. Maybe we got to fight to keep our land, like Pa and Grampa did.

And now the owner men grew angry. You'll have to go.

But it's ours, the tenant men cried. We—

No. The bank, the monster owns it. You'll have to go.

We'll get our guns, like Grampa when the Indians came. What then?

Well—first the sheriff, and then the troops. You'll be stealing if you try to stay, you'll be murderers if you kill to stay. The monster isn't men, but it can make men do what it wants.

But if we go, where'll we go? How'll we go? We got no money.

We're sorry, said the owner men. The bank, the fifty-thousand-acre owner can't be responsible. You're on land that isn't yours. Once over the line maybe you can pick cotton in the fall. Maybe you can go on relief. Why don't you go on west to California? There's work there, and it never gets cold. Why, you can reach out anywhere and pick an orange. Why, there's always some kind of crop to work in. Why don't you go there? And the owner men started their cars and rolled away.

The tenant men squatted down on their hams again to mark the dust with a stick, to figure, to wonder. Their sunburned faces were dark, and their sun-whipped eyes were light. The women moved cautiously out of the doorways toward their men, and the children crept behind the women, cautiously, ready to run. The bigger boys squatted beside their fathers, because that made them men. After a time the women asked, What did he want?

And the men looked up for a second, and the smolder of pain was in their eyes. We got to get off. A tractor and a superintendent. Like factories.

Where'll we go? the women asked.

We don't know. We don't know.

And the women went quickly, quietly back into the houses and herded the children ahead of them. They knew that a man so hurt and so perplexed may turn in anger, even on people he loves. They left the men alone to figure and to wonder in the dust.

After a time perhaps the tenant man looked about—at the

pump put in ten years ago, with a goose-neck handle and iron flowers on the spout, at the chopping block where a thousand chickens had been killed, at the hand plow lying in the shed, and the patent crib hanging in the rafters over it.

The children crowded about the women in the houses. What we going to do, Ma? Where we going to go?

The women said, We don't know, yet. Go out and play. But don't go near your father. He might whale you if you go near him. And the women went on with the work, but all the time they watched the men squatting in the dust—perplexed and figuring.

The tractors came over the roads and into the fields, great crawlers moving like insects, having the incredible strength of insects. They crawled over the ground, laying the track and rolling on it and picking it up. Diesel tractors, puttering while they stood idle; they thundered when they moved, and then settled down to a droning roar. Snubnosed monsters, raising the dust and sticking their snouts into it, straight down the country, across the country, through fences, through dooryards, in and out of gullies in straight lines. They did not run on the ground, but on their own roadbeds. They ignored hills and gulches, water courses, fences, houses.

The man sitting in the iron seat did not look like a man; gloved, goggled, rubber dust mask over nose and mouth, he was a part of the monster, a robot in the seat. The thunder of the cylinders sounded through the country, became one with the air and the earth, so that earth and air muttered in sympathetic vibration. The driver could not control it—straight across country it went, cutting through a dozen farms and straight back. A twitch at the controls could swerve the cat', but the driver's hands could not twitch because the monster that built the tractors, the monster that sent the tractor out, had somehow got into the driver's hands, into his brain and muscle, had goggled him and muzzled him— goggled his mind, muzzled his speech, goggled his perception, muzzled his protest. He could not see the land as it was, he could not smell the land as it smelled; his feet did not stamp the clods or feel the warmth and power of the earth. He sat in an iron seat and stepped on iron pedals. He could not cheer or beat or curse or encourage the extension of his power, and because of this he could not cheer or whip or curse or encourage himself. He did not know or own or trust or beseech the land. If a seed dropped did not germinate, it was nothing. If the young thrusting plant withered in drought or drowned in a flood of rain, it was no more to the driver than to the tractor.

He loved the land no more than the bank loved the land. He could admire the tractor—its machined surfaces, its surge of power, the roar of its detonating cylinders; but it was not his tractor. Behind the tractor rolled the shining disks, cutting the earth with blades—not plowing but surgery, pushing the cut earth to the right where the second row of disks cut it and pushed it to the left; slicing blades shining, polished by the cut earth. And pulled behind the disks, the harrows combing with iron teeth so that the little clods broke up and the earth lay smooth. Behind the harrows the long seeders—twelve curved iron penes erected in the foundry, orgasms set by gears, raping methodically, raping without passion. The driver sat in his iron seat and he was proud of the straight lines he did not will, proud of the tractor he did not own or love, proud of the power he could not control. And when that crop grew, and was harvested, no man had crumbled a hot clod in his fingers and let the earth sift past his fingertips. No man had touched the seed, or lusted for the growth. Men ate what they had not raised, had no connection with the bread. The land bore under iron, and under iron gradually died; for it was not loved or hated, it had no prayers or curses.

At noon the tractor driver stopped sometimes near a tenant house and opened his lunch: sandwiches wrapped in wax paper, white bread, pickle, cheese, Spam, a piece of pie branded like an engine part. He ate without relish. And tenants not yet moved away came out to see him, looked curiously while the goggles were taken off, and the rubber dust mask, leaving white circles around the eyes and a large white circle around nose and mouth. The exhaust of the tractor puttered on, for fuel is so cheap it is more efficient to leave the engine running than to heat the Diesel nose for a new start. Curious children crowded close, ragged children who ate their fried dough as they watched. They watched hungrily the unwrapping of the sandwiches, and their hunger-sharpened noses smelled the pickle, cheese, and Spam. They didn't speak to the driver. They watched his hand as it carried food to his mouth. They did not watch him chewing; their eyes followed the hand that held the sandwich. After a while the tenant who could not leave the place came out and squatted in the shade beside the tractor.

"Why, you're Joe Davis's boy!"

"Sure," the driver said.

"Well, what you doing this kind of work for—against your own people?"

"Three dollars a day. I got damn sick of creeping for my dinner—and not getting it. I got a wife and kids. We got to eat. Three dollars a day, and it comes every day."

"That's right," the tenant said, "But for your three dollars a day fifteen or twenty families can't eat at all. Nearly a hundred people have to go out and wander on the roads for your three dollars a day. Is that right?"

And the driver said, "Can't think of that. Got to think of my own kids. Three dollars a day, and it comes every day. Times are changing, mister, don't you know? Can't make a living on the land unless you've got two, five, ten thousand acres and a tractor. Crop land isn't for little guys like us any more. You don't kick up a howl because you can't make Fords, or because you're not the telephone company. Well, crops are like that now. Nothing to do about it. You try to get three dollars a day someplace. That's the only way."

The tenant pondered. "Funny thing how it is. If a man owns a little property, that property is him, it's part of him, and it's like him. If he owns property only so he can walk on it and handle it and be sad when it isn't doing well, and feel fine when the rain falls on it, that property is him, and some way he's bigger because he owns it. Even if he isn't successful he's big with his property. That is so."

And the tenant pondered more. "But let a man get property he doesn't see, or can't take time to get his fingers in, or can't be there to walk on it—why, then the property is the man. He can't do what he wants, he can't think what he wants. The property is the man, stronger than he is. And he is small, not big. Only his possessions are big—and he's the servant of his property. That is so, too."

The driver munched the branded pie and threw the crust away.

"Times are changed, don't you know? Thinking about stuff like that don't feed the kids. Get your three dollars a day, feed your kids. You got no call to worry about anybody's kids but your own. You get a reputation for talking like that, and you'll never get three dollars a day. Big shots won't give you three dollars a day if you worry about anything but your three dollars a day."

"Nearly a hundred people on the road for your three dollars. Where will we go?"

"And that reminds me," the driver said, "you better get out soon. I'm going through the dooryard after dinner."

"You filled in the well this morning."

"I know. Had to keep the line straight. But I'm going through the dooryard after dinner. Got to keep the lines straight. And—well, you know Joe Davis, my old man, so I'll tell you this. I got orders wherever there's a family not moved out—if I have an accident—you know, get too close and cave the house in a little—well, I might get a couple of dollars. And my youngest kid never had no shoes yet."

"I built it with my hands. Straightened old nails to put the sheathing on. Rafters are wired to the stringers with baling wire. It's mine. I built it. You bump it down—I'll be in the window with a rifle. You even come too close and I'll pot you like a rabbit."

"It's not me. There's nothing I can do. I'll lose my job if I don't do it. And look—suppose you kill me? They'll just hang you, but long before you're hung there'll be another guy on a tractor, and he'll bump the house down. You're not killing the right guy."

"That's so," the tenant said. "Who gave the orders? I'll go after him. He's the one to kill."

"You're wrong. He got his orders from the bank. The bank told him, 'Clear those people out or it's your job.'"

"Well, there's a president of the bank. There's a board of directors. I'll fill up the magazine of the rifle and go into the bank."

The driver said, "Fellow was telling me the bank gets orders from the East. The orders were, 'Make the land show profit or we'll close you up.'"

"But where does it stop? Who can we shoot? I don't aim to starve to death before I kill the man that's starving me."

"I don't know. Maybe there's nobody to shoot. Maybe the thing isn't men at all. Maybe like you said, the property's doing it. Anyway I told you my orders."

"I got to figure," the tenant said. "We all got to figure. There's some way to stop this. It's not like lightning or earthquakes. We've got a bad thing made by men, and by God that's something we can change." The tenant sat in his doorway, and the driver thundered his engine and started off, tracks falling and curving, harrows combing, and the phalli of the seeder slipping into the ground. Across the dooryard the tractor cut, and the hard, foot-beaten ground was seeded field, and the tractor cut through again; the uncut space was ten feet wide. And back he came. The iron guard bit into the housecorner, crumbled the wall, and wrenched the little house from its foundation so that it fell sideways, crushed like a bug. And the driver was goggled and a rubber mask covered his nose and mouth. The tractor cut a straight line on, and the air and the ground vibrated with its thunder. The tenant man stared after it, his rifle in his hand. His wife was beside him, and the quiet children behind. And all of them stared after the tractor.

Heinrich Böll (1917–)

The Laugher

When someone asks me what business I am in, I am seized with embarrassment: I blush and stammer, I who am otherwise known as a man of poise. I envy people who can say: I am a bricklayer. I envy barbers, bookkeepers and writers the simplicity of their avowal, for all these professions speak for themselves and need no lengthy explanation, while I am constrained to reply to such questions: I am a laugher. An admission of this kind demands another, since I have to answer the second question: "Is that how you make your living?" truthfully with "Yes." I actually do make a living at my laughing, and a good one too, for my laughing is—commercially speaking—much in demand. I am a good laugher, experienced, no one else laughs as well as I do, no one else has such command of the fine points of my art. For a long time, in order to avoid tiresome explanations, I called myself an actor, but my talents in the field of mime and elocution are so meager that I felt this designation to be too far from the truth: I love the truth, and the truth is: I am a laugher. I am neither a clown nor a comedian. I do not make people gay, I portray gaiety: I laugh like a Roman emperor, or like a sensitive schoolboy, I am as much at home in the laughter of the seventeenth century as in that of the nineteenth, and when occasion demands I laugh my way through all the centuries, all classes of society, all categories of age: it is simply a skill which I have acquired, like the skill of being able to repair shoes. In my breast I harbor the laughter of America, the laughter of Africa, white, red, yellow laughter—and for the right fee I let it peal out in accordance with the director's requirement.

I have become indispensable; I laugh on records, I laugh on tape, and television directors treat me with respect. I laugh mournfully, moderately, hysterically; I laugh like a streetcar conductor or like a helper in the grocery business; laughter in the morning, laughter in the evening, nocturnal laughter and the laughter of twilight. In short: wherever and however laughter is required—I do it.

It need hardly be pointed out that a profession of this kind is tiring, especially as I have also—this is my specialty—mastered the art of infectious laughter; this has also made me indispensable to third- and fourth-rate comedians, who are scared—and with good reason—that their audiences will miss their punch lines, so I spend most evenings in night clubs as a kind of discreet claque, my job being to laugh infectiously during the weaker parts of the program. It has to be carefully timed: my hearty, boisterous laughter must not come too soon, but neither must it come too late, it must come just at the right spot: at the pre-arranged moment I burst out laughing, the whole audience roars with me, and the joke is saved.

But as for me, I drag myself exhausted to the checkroom, put on my overcoat, happy that I can go off duty at last. At home I usually find telegrams waiting for me: "Urgently require your laughter. Recording Tuesday," and a few hours later I am sitting on an overheated express train bemoaning my fate.

I need scarcely say that when I am off duty or on vacation I have little inclination to laugh: the cowhand is glad when he can forget the cow, the bricklayer when he can forget the mortar, and carpenters usually have doors at home which don't work or drawers which are hard to open. Confectioners like sour pickles, butchers like marzipan, and the baker prefers sausage to bread; bullfighters raise pigeons for a hobby, boxers turn pale when their children have nose-bleeds: I find all this quite natural, for I never laugh off duty. I am a very solemn person, and people consider me—perhaps rightly so—a pessimist.

During the first years of our married life, my wife would often say to me: "Do laugh!" but since then she has come to realize that I cannot grant her this wish. I am happy when I am free to relax my tense face muscles, my frayed spirit, in profound solemnity. Indeed, even other people's laughter gets on my nerves, since it reminds me too much of my profession. So our marriage is a quiet, peaceful one, because my wife has also forgotten how to laugh: now and again I catch her smiling, and I smile too. We converse in low tones, for I detest the noise of the night clubs, the noise that sometimes fills the recording studios. People who do not know me think I am taciturn. Perhaps I am, because I have to open my mouth so often to laugh.

I go through life with an impassive expression, from time to time permitting myself a gentle smile, and I often wonder whether I have ever laughed. I think not. My brothers and sisters have always known me for a serious boy.

So I laugh in many different ways, but my own laughter I have never heard.

Antoine De Saint-Exupéry
(1900–1944)

The Tool

And now, having spoken of the men born of the pilot's craft, I shall say something about the tool with which they work—the airplane. Have you looked at a modern airplane? Have you followed from year to year the evolution of its lines? Have you ever thought, not only about the airplane but about whatever man builds, that all of man's industrial efforts, all his computations and calculations, all the nights spent over working draughts and blueprints, invariably culminate in the production of a thing whose sole and guiding principle is the ultimate principle of simplicity?

It is as if there were a natural law which ordained that to achieve this end, to refine the curve of a piece of furniture, or a ship's keel, or the fuselage of an airplane, until gradually it partakes of the elementary purity of the curve of a human breast or shoulder, there must be the experimentation of several generations of craftsmen. In anything at all, perfection is finally attained not when there is no longer anything to add, but when there is no longer anything to take away, when a body has been stripped down to its nakedness.

It results from this that perfection of invention touches hands with absence of invention, as if that line which the human eye will follow with effortless delight were a line that had not been invented but simply discovered, had in the beginning been hidden by nature and in the end been found by the engineer. There is an ancient myth about the image asleep in the block of marble until it is carefully disengaged by the sculptor. The sculptor must himself feel that he is not so much inventing or shaping the curve of the breast or shoulder as delivering the image from its prison.

In this spirit do engineers, physicists concerned with thermodynamics, and the swarm of preoccupied draughtsmen tackle their work. In appearance, but only in appearance, they seem to be polishing surfaces and refining away angles, easing this joint or stabilizing that wing, rendering these parts invisible, so that in the end there is no longer a wing hooked to a framework but a form flawless in its perfection, completely disengaged from its matrix, a sort of spontaneous whole, its parts mysteriously fused together and resembling in their unity a poem.

Meanwhile, startling as it is that all visible evidence of invention should have been refined out of this instrument and that there should be delivered to us an object as natural as a pebble polished by the waves, it is equally wonderful that he who uses this instrument should be able to forget that it is a machine.

There was a time when a flyer sat at the centre of a complicated works. Flight set us factory problems. The indicators that oscillated on the instrument panel warned us of a thousand dangers. But in the machine of today we forget that motors are whirring: the motor, finally, has come to fulfil its function, which is to whirr as a heart beats—and we give no thought to the beating of our heart. Thus, precisely because it is perfect the machine dissembles its own existence instead of forcing itself upon our notice.

And thus, also, the realities of nature resume their pride of place. It is not with metal that the pilot is in contact. Contrary to the vulgar illusion, it is thanks to the metal, and by virtue of it, that the pilot rediscovers nature. As I have already said, the machine does not isolate man from the great problems of nature but plunges him more deeply into them.

Numerous, nevertheless, are the moralists who have attacked the machine as the source of all the ills we bear, who, creating a fictitious dichotomy, have denounced the mechanical civilization as the enemy of the spiritual civilization.

If what they think were really so, then indeed we should have to despair of man, for it would be futile to struggle against this new advancing chaos. The machine is certainly as irresistible in its advance as those virgin forests that encroach upon equatorial domains. A congeries of motives prevents us from blowing up our spinning mills and reviving the distaff. Gandhi had a try at this sort of revolution: he was as simple-minded as a child trying to empty the sea on to the sand with the aid of a teacup.

It is hard for me to understand the language of these pseudo-dreamers. What is it makes them think that the ploughshare torn from the bowels of the earth by perforating machines, forged, tempered, and sharpened in the roar of modern industry, is nearer to man than any other tool of steel? By what sign do they recognize the inhumanity of the machine?

Have they ever really asked themselves this question? The central struggle of men has ever been to understand one another, to join together for the common weal. And it is this very thing that the machine helps them to do! It begins by annihilating time and space.

To me, in France, a friend speaks from America. The energy that brings me his voice is born of dammed-up waters a thousand miles from where he sits. The energy I burn up listening to him is dispensed in the same instant by a lake formed in the River Yser which, four thousand miles from him and five hundred from me, melts like snow in the action of the turbines. Transport of the mails, transport of the human voice, transport of flickering pictures—in this century as in others our highest accomplishments still have the single aim of bringing men together. Do our dreamers hold that the invention of writing, of printing, of the sailing ship, degraded the human spirit?

It seems to me that those who complain of man's progress confuse ends with means. True, that man who struggles in the unique hope of material gain will harvest nothing worth while. But how can anyone conceive that the machine is an end? It is a tool. As much a tool as is the plough. The microscope is a tool. What disservice do we do the life of the spirit when we analyze the universe through a tool created by the science of optics, or seek to bring together those who love one another and are parted in space?

"Agreed!" my dreamers will say, "but explain to us why it is that a decline in human values has accompanied the rise of the machine?" Oh, I miss the village with its crafts and its folksongs as much as they do! The town fed by Hollywood seems to me, too, impoverished despite its electric street lamps. I quite agree that men lose their creative instincts when they are fed thus without raising a hand. And I can see that it is tempting to accuse industry of this evil.

But we lack perspective for the judgment of transformations that go so deep. What are the hundred years of the history of the machine compared with the two hundred thousand years of the history of man? It was only yesterday that we began to pitch our camp in this country of laboratories and power stations, that we took possession of this new, this still unfinished, house we live in. Everything round us is new and different—our concerns, our working habits, our relations with one another.

Our very psychology has been shaken to its foundations, to its most secret recesses. Our notions of separation, absence, distance, return are reflections of a new set of realities, though the words themselves remain unchanged. To grasp the meaning of the world of today we use a language created to express the world of yesterday. The life of the past seems to us nearer our true natures, but only for the reason that it is nearer our language.

Every step on the road of progress takes us farther from habits which, as the life of man goes, we had only recently begun to acquire. We are in truth emigrants who have not yet founded our homeland. We Europeans have become again young peoples, without tradition or language of our own. We shall have to age somewhat before we are able to write the folksongs of a new epoch.

Young barbarians still marveling at our new toys—that is what we are. Why else should we race our planes, give prizes to those who fly highest, or fastest? We take no heed to ask ourselves why we race: the race itself is more important than the object.

And this holds true of other things than flying. For the colonial soldier who founds an empire, the meaning of life is conquest. He despises the colonist. But was not the very aim of his conquest the settling of this same colonist?

In the enthusiasm of our rapid mechanical conquests we have overlooked some things. We have perhaps driven men into the service of the machine, instead of building machinery for the service of man. But could anything be more natural? So long as we were engaged in conquest, our spirit was the spirit of conquerors. The time has now come when we must be colonists, must make this house habitable which is still without character.

Little by little the machine will become part of humanity. Read the history of the railways in France, and doubtless elsewhere too: they had all the trouble in the world to tame the people of our villages. The locomotive was an iron monster. Time had to pass before men forgot what it was made of. Mysteriously, life began to run through it, and now it is wrinkled and old. What is it today for the villager except a humble friend who calls every evening at six?

The sailing vessel itself was once a machine born of the calculations of engineers, yet it does not disturb our philosophers. The sloop took its place in the speech of men. There is a poetry of sailing as old as the world. There have always been seamen in recorded time. The man who assumes that there is an essential difference between the sloop and the airplane lacks historic perspective.

Every machine will gradually take on this patina[1] and lose its identity in its function.

Air and water, and not machinery, are the concern of the hydroplane pilot about to take off. The motors are running free and the plane is already ploughing the surface of the sea. Under the dizzying whirl of the scythelike propellers, clusters of silvery water bloom and drown the flotation gear. The element smacks the sides of the hull with a sound like a gong, and the pilot can sense this tumult in the quivering of his body. He feels the ship charging itself with power as from second to second it picks up speed. He feels the development, in these fifteen tons of matter, of a maturity that is about to make flight possible. He closes his hands over the controls, and little by little in his bare palms he receives the gift of this power. The metal organs of the controls, progressively as this gift is made him, become the messengers of the power in his hands. And when his power is ripe, then, in a gesture gentler than the culling of a flower, the pilot severs the ship from the water and establishes it in the air.

---

1. A look or sheen acquired with age or use.

ESSAYS

Matthew 25:14–30

The Parable of Talents

14. For *the kingdom of heaven is* as a man travelling into a far country, *who* called his own servants, and delivered unto them his goods.

15. And unto one he gave five talents, to another two, and to another one; to every man according to his several ability; and straightway took his journey.

16. Then he that had received the five talents went and traded with the same, and made *them* other five talents.

17. And likewise he that *had received* two, he also gained other two.

18. But he that had received one went and digged in the earth, and hid his lord's money.

19. After a long time the lord of those servants cometh, and reckoneth with them.

20. And so he that had received five talents came and brought other five talents, saying, Lord, thou deliveredst unto me five talents: behold, I have gained beside them five talents more.

21. His lord said unto him, Well done, *thou* good and faithful servant: thou hast been faithful over a few things, I will make thee ruler over many things: enter thou into the joy of thy lord.

22. He also that had received two talents came and said, Lord, thou deliveredst unto me two talents: behold, I have gained two other talents beside them.

23. His lord said unto him, Well done, good and faithful servant; thou hast been faithful over a few things, I will make thee ruler over many things: enter thou into the joy of thy lord.

24. Then he which had received the one talent came and said, Lord, I knew thee that thou art an hard man, reaping where thou hast not sown, and gathering where thou has not strawed:

25. And I was afraid, and went and hid thy talent in the earth: lo *there* thou hast *that is* thine.

26. His lord answered and said unto him, T*hou* wicked and slothful servant, thou knewest that I reap where I sowed not, and gather where I have not strawed:

27. Thou oughtest therefore to have put my money to the exchangers, and *then* at my coming I should have received mine own with usury.

28. Take therefore the talent from him, and give *it* unto him which hath ten talents.

29. For unto every one that hath shall be given, and he shall have abundance: but from him that hath not shall be taken away even that which he hath.

30. And cast ye the unprofitable servant into outer darkness: there shall be weeping and gnashing of teeth.

Thomas Carlyle (1795–1881)

Labour

For there is a perennial nobleness, and even sacredness, in Work. Were he never so benighted, forgetful of his high calling, there is always hope in a man that actually and earnestly works: in Idleness alone is there perpetual despair. Work, never so Mammonish, mean, *is* in communication with Nature; the real desire to get Work done will itself lead one more and more to truth, to Nature's appointments and regulations, which are truth.

The latest Gospel in this world is, Know thy work and do it. 'Know thyself:' long enough has that poor 'self' of thine tormented thee; thou wilt never get to 'know' it, I believe! Think it not thy business, this of knowing thyself; thou art an unknowable individual: know what thou canst work at; and work at it, like a Hercules! That will be thy better plan.

It has been written, 'an endless significance lies in Work;' a man perfects himself by working. Foul jungles are cleared away, fair seedfields rise instead, and stately cities; and withal the man himself first ceases to be a jungle and foul unwholesome desert thereby. Consider how, even in the meanest sorts of Labour, the whole soul of a man is composed into a kind of real harmony, the instant he sets himself to work! Doubt, Desire, Sorrow, Remorse, Indignation, Despair itself, all these like helldogs lie beleaguering the soul of the poor dayworker, as of every man: but he bends himself with free valour against his task, and all these are stilled, all these shrink murmuring far off into their caves. The man is now a man. The blessed glow of Labour in him, is it not as purifying fire, wherein all poison is burnt up, and of sour smoke itself there is made bright blessed flame!

Destiny, on the whole, has no other way of cultivating us. A formless Chaos, once set it *revolving*, grows round and ever rounder; ranges itself, by mere force of gravity, into strata, spherical courses; is no longer a Chaos, but a round compacted World. What would become of the Earth, did she cease to revolve? In the poor old Earth, so long as she revolves, all inequalities, irregularities disperse themselves; all irregularities are incessantly becoming regular. Hast thou looked on the Potter's wheel,—one of the venerablest objects; old as the Prophet Ezechiel and far older? Rude lumps of clay, how they spin themselves up, by mere quick whirling, into beautiful circular dishes. And fancy the most assiduous Potter, but without his wheel; reduced to make dishes, or rather amorphous botches, by mere kneading and baking! Even such a Potter were Destiny, with a human soul that would rest and lie at ease, that would not work and spin! Of an idle unrevolving man the kindest Destiny, like the most assiduous Potter without wheel, can bake and knead nothing other than a botch; let her spend on him what expensive colouring, what gilding and enamelling she will, he is but a botch. Not a dish; no, a bulging, kneaded, crooked, shambling, squint-cornered, amorphous botch,— a mere enamelled vessel of dishonour! Let the idle think of this.

Blessed is he who has found his work; let him ask no other blessedness. He has a work, a life-purpose; he has found it, and will follow it! How, as a free-flowing channel, dug and torn by noble force through the sour mud-swamp of one's existence, like an ever-deepening river there, it runs and flows;—draining-off the sour festering water, gradually from the root of the remotest grassblade; making, instead of pestilential swamp, a green fruitful meadow with its clear-flowing stream. How blessed for the meadow itself, let the stream and *its* value be great or small! Labour is Life: from the inmost heart of the Worker rises his god-given Force, the sacred celestial Life-essence breathed into him by Almighty God; from his inmost heart awakens him to all nobleness,—to all knowledge, 'self-knowledge' and much else, so soon as Work fitly begins. Knowledge? The knowledge that will hold good in working, cleave thou to that; for Nature herself accredits that, says Yea to that. Properly thou hast no other knowledge but what thou hast got by working: the rest is yet all a hypothesis of knowledge; a thing to be argued of in schools, a thing floating in the clouds, in endless logic-vortices, till we try it and fix it. 'Doubt, of whatever kind, can be ended by Action alone.'

ELLEN GOODMAN (1941–)

Our High-tech Hardware Will Have to Learn to Live With the 'Human Factor'

In technical terms, I am what is known as the "human factor." So are you.

Once upon a time we were just plain people. But that was before we began having relationships with mechanical systems. Get involved with a machine and sooner or later you are reduced to a factor.

Today, for example, I am interacting (this is what it's called) with a word processor and an entire computerized system. No matter how perfect this setup is, I have the power to botch up the results. From the point of view of the machine, I am the loose cannon, the dubious and somewhat unpredictable human factor in its life.

If the processor that I write on had a separate existence, it would probably send messages to its colleagues saying, "You won't believe what my human factor did today. Coffee! Right down the old keyboard!" But on the whole, I am not very dangerous to the wider world. Indeed, the most common evil I spew forth from this machine into the environment is a grammatical error.

But what about the other human factors out there? Last week, the National Research Council reported with alarm that there is virtually no safety research being done by the Nuclear Regulatory Commission on the "human factors." The focus has been on the physical plants, they said, and not on the "people who design, operate, maintain and manage" nuclear plants. I suspect that it's like that almost everywhere.

The disaster at Chernobyl, the near-disaster at Three Mile Island, each had its human factor and yet most of the original attention focused in on the buildings, the systems. The Challenger explosion one year ago initially was billed as a technological disaster. It was a while before the inquiry shifted from the state of the O-rings to the state of the decision-makers.

At Bhopal, India, where some 1,700 people died, and at Basel, Switzerland, where the Rhine River was poisoned, we heard first of chemical leaks and spills, and impersonal safety "procedures." We heard only secondarily of workers who may not have sounded alarms or known enough not to hose chemicals. Even in the recent low-tech Amtrak disaster, the attention was first on the state of signals and only then on the signal-readers.

I suppose there's a reason for our reluctance to focus on the human factors. During recent decades, we have all become more conscious of the centralization of danger. We know that more lives hinge on fewer "things": on nuclear missiles and plants, on chemicals and computers. It may be easier to think of "systems" that can be perfected than on people who aren't perfectible.

But it is human factors who read nuclear-plant blueprints backwards. Human factors who cut corners to meet deadlines and use lower-grade concrete to save money. Human factors who try to cover up errors. Human factors who make those errors. Human factors who get cranky, careless, tired. Sometimes even fall asleep on the job. And when we try to design plants and procedures that guard against human error, it is humans who design them.

In my 3-o'clock-in-the-morning fantasies of nuclear war, I have one that features a series of improbable mistakes in some silo deep under the North Dakota earth. I have another that shows a light going on in the White House and a single man who must, without a shower, without a cup of coffee, without time for consultation or double-checking, decide whether or not to send the missiles up. Such fantasies are not reassuring.

But during the daylight hours, most of us choose to think of the human role in our sophisticated technological society as a minor part of the equation. We accept a walk-on part in the modern world and give the machines, the systems, the lead.

Again and again, in the wake of a catastrophe, we look for solutions that will correct "it" rather than "us." The risks we live with, particularly those of chemicals and atoms, are so enormous that it is comforting to believe people can people-proof their lives. But it is illusory.

Consult my computer if you must, but no machine is more trustworthy than the humans who made it and operate it. So we are stuck. Stuck here in the high-tech, high-risk world with our own low-tech species. Like it or not, no mechanical system can ever be more perfect than the sum of its very human factors.

VIEWPOINTS

J. Bronowski

The Drive for Power

Power is a new preoccupation, in a sense a new idea, in science. The Industrial Revolution, the English revolution, turned out to be the great discoverer of power. Sources of energy were sought in nature: wind, sun, water, steam, coal. And a question suddenly became concrete: Why are they all one? What relation exists between them? That had never been asked before. Until then science had been entirely concerned with exploring nature as she is. But now the modern conception of transforming nature in order to obtain power from her, and of changing one form of power into another, had come up to the leading edge of science. In particular, it grew clear that heat is a form of energy, and is converted into other forms at a fixed rate of exchange. In 1824 Sadi Carnot, a French engineer, looking at steam engines, wrote a treatise on what he called "la puissance motrice du feu," in which he founded, in essence, the science of thermodynamics—the dynamics of heat. Energy had become a central concept in science; and the main concern in science now was the unity of nature, of which energy is the core.

And it was a main concern not only in science. You see it equally in the arts, and the surprise is there. While this is going on, what is going on in literature? The uprush of romantic poetry round about the year 1800. How could the romantic poets be interested in industry? Very simply: the new concept of nature as the carrier of energy took them by storm. They loved the word "storm" as a synonym for energy, in phrases like *Sturm und Drang*, "storm and thrust." The climax of Samuel Taylor Coleridge's *Rime of the Ancient Mariner* is introduced by a storm that breaks the deadly calm and releases life again.

> The upper air burst into life!
> And a hundred fire-flags sheen,
> To and fro they were hurried about!
> And to and fro, and in and out,
> The wan stars danced between.
>
> The loud wind never reached the ship,
> Yet now the ship moved on!
> Beneath the lightning and the Moon
> The dead men gave a groan.

A young German philosopher, Friedrich von Schelling, just at this time in 1799, started a new form of philosophy which has remained powerful in Germany, *Naturphilosophie*—philosophy of nature. From him Coleridge brought it to England. The Lake Poets had it from Coleridge, and the Wedgwoods, who were friends of Coleridge's and indeed supported him with an annuity. Poets and painters were suddenly captured by the idea that nature is the fountain of power, whose different forms are all expressions of the same central force, namely energy.

And not only nature. Romantic poetry says in the plainest way that man himself is the carrier of a divine, at least a natural, energy. The Industrial Revolution created freedom (in practice) for men who wanted to fulfil what they had in them—a concept inconceivable a hundred years earlier. But hand in hand, romantic thought inspired those men to make of their freedom a new sense of personality in nature. It was said best of all by the greatest of the romantic poets, William Blake, very simply: "Energy is Eternal Delight."

Gilbert Burck

The Hazards of "Corporate Responsibility"

Every Friday evening, Walter Fackler, professor of economics at the University of Chicago's Graduate School of Business, has been addressing a class of seventy-five high-ranking executives on the problems of public policy and corporate social responsibility. A more appropriate and exigent activity these days is hard to imagine. Fackler says he has never seen businessmen so confused and defensive. The doctrine that business has responsibilities "beyond business," which began to gather momentum a dozen or so years ago, is still picking up steam. Never before has the U.S. business establishment been confronted with such a bewildering variety of animad-version, such a Vanity Fair of conflicting demands and prescriptions. A detailed inventory of the "social" demands being made on business would fill several volumes; reconciling the numerous and conflicting prescriptions would baffle a synod of Solomons.

Perhaps because businessmen are so defensive, they themselves have not done much talking back to those who are making all the demands. When businessmen essay to discuss their role in society these days, they all too often sound like young ladies fifty years ago talking about sex. They cough and clear their throats and come up with moralistic platitudes. The back talk has come principally from economists—notably from some, like Milton Friedman and Henry Manne, who have generally been identified with the classical school. These "strict constructionists" argue that business serves society best when it minds its business well, and that it should take part in social activities only to the extent that these are necessary to its own well-being.

Fackler himself manages to sound like a strict constructionist much of the time. The great, the dominant, the indispensable *social* role of business, he tells his executive students, is a familiar one. In this most uncertain world, their prime job is to evaluate risks wisely, to allocate the nation's resources prudently, and to use them with optimum efficiency. Business fulfills its real social role by striving endlessly to take in more money than it pays out, or, as some of its critics would put the case, by lusting incessantly after the Almighty Dollar.

Arrayed on the other side of the argument are social-responsibility advocates—those who want an enlarged social role for industry. For all the immense variety of their prescriptions, these advocates agree on one general proposition: business ought to accept social responsibilities *that go beyond the requirements of the law.* In addition to mere compliance with the law, say the advocates, business should actively initiate measures to abate pollution, to expand minority rights, and in general to be an exemplary citizen, and should cheerfully accept all the costs associated with this good citizenship.

Suppressing the Controversy

Many of the most vocal social-responsibility advocates, including those affiliated with one or another band of Nader's raiders, tend to extreme forms of self-righteousness. Their proposals are often couched in rather general terms; they imply that the justice of their ideas is self-evident and that only a moral delinquent, or a businessman consumed by greed, could resist them. The notion that some schemes for implementing the proposals might actually be controversial, or that there might be serious questions of equity involved in asking corporate executives to tackle social problems with money belonging to other people (i.e., their stockholders)—these thoughts often seem to be suppressed in the advocates' minds.

But there is also a more sophisticated version of the social-responsibility proposition. According to this version, corporate executives who are strict constructionists at heart, and who harbor powerful lusts for Almighty Dollars, might nevertheless conclude that an activist social posture was good for their companies. They might decide, in other words, that social activism was good public relations. They might agree with Paul Samuelson, the Nobel laureate, who takes a simple view of the new demands on corporations. "A large corporation these days," he says, "not only may engage in social responsibility; it had damn well better try to do so."

A similarly pragmatic view of the matter has been propounded by Professor Neil Jacoby of the Graduate School of Management at the University of California, Los Angeles. Jacoby has been a dean of the school, a member of the Council of Economic Advisers under Eisenhower, a fellow of the Center for the Study of Democratic Institutions, and a member of the Pay Board. His forthcoming book, *Corporate Power and Social Responsibility*, describes corporate social involvement as a fact of life. "I don't really ask companies to do a single thing that isn't profitable," Jacoby remarked recently. "But political forces are just as real as market forces, and business must respond to them, which means it often must be content with optimizing and not maximizing immediate profits."

Corporations Do It Better

Professor Henry Wallich of Yale has also advanced a rather sophisticated case for corporate social responsibility. Writing in *Fortune* last year (Books & Ideas, March, 1972), Wallich made the point that corporations can perform some social activities better than can government; and in undertaking to do more than the law requires, they are shifting activities from the public to the private sector. When one corporation undertakes social obligations not borne by its competitors, it would, of course, be at a disadvantage. Therefore, Wallich proposes, companies in an industry should be allowed to work together toward social goals without fear of antitrust action.

Some serious economists regard the social-responsibility movement as a harbinger of major changes in the business environment. Professor George Steiner of the U.C.L.A. Graduate School of Management, for instance, believes the movement implies "a new area of voluntarism" that will change large corporations' basic operating style. Generally speaking, Steiner says, the old authoritarian way of running a company will give way to permissive and statesmanlike methods; the single-minded entrepreneur will be succeeded by the broad-gauge "renaissance" manager. Centralized decision making will be accompanied, if not largely superseded, by decision making in small groups. Financial accounting will be augmented by human-resources accounting, and the "social" costs of production will be increasingly internalized. Inevitably, government and business planning will complement each other. "We are," says Steiner prophetically, "in the process of redefining capitalism."

How Supreme Life Got the Business

A few companies are beginning to act as if they believe Steiner. One is Standard Oil Co. (Indiana), which is spending about $40 million a year on pollution control—far more than it legally has to. It also boasts a long list of other social achievements, including efforts on behalf of Chicago's schools and a determined program to hire and promote minority employees and to help minority suppliers and businessmen. Recently, for example, Standard arranged with Chicago's Supreme Life Insurance Co. of America, a company owned by blacks, to insure two plants of its Amoco chemical subsidiary in California. Standard's policy is to use not only qualified but "qualifiable" minority suppliers—i.e., it helps some to qualify.

The company's director of public affairs these days is Phillip Drotning, author of three books on the black movement in the U.S., and an advocate of a high level of corporate involvement. If Drotning has his way—and so far he has been backed by top management—the promotion of executives will depend not only on their cost and profit records but on their approach to social objectives. Managers will be supplied with the information they need to evaluate the social consequences of their decisions, and they will plan strategies that benefit both the company and society. "The heads of the company," says Drotning, "will exercise leadership among their peers in the broad business community and the public at large, to generate support for the far-reaching, long-range changes in social policy that must occur."

The goals of Chicago's CNA Financial Corp., an insurance-centered company with revenues of $1.6 billion, are pretty ambitious too. Last year the company spent close to $660,000 on dozens of selected social projects, compelled its insurance subsidiaries to demand that their clients take "corrective action" on a variety of pollution problems, and insisted on a 30 percent minority representation among the workers erecting its new headquarters building.

CNA's vice president in charge of social policy is a former social-agency administrator named David Christensen, who argues that companies typically go through several phases in the perception of their social responsibilities. First there is the "do-good" phase, in which the company builds libraries with its name on them—but goes right on dumping waste in the lake. Later comes a more systematic effort to coordinate public relations and corporate involvement in, say, urban affairs. Finally the company gets to the phase of genuine corporate responsibility, in which it is concerned less with public relations than with developing responsible ways to improve society. Conscience money is no longer needed, because the company doesn't have a bad conscience.

Nobody Talks About Cost

Christensen says that CNA is just now entering the third phase. To guide it in this period he has helped the company develop an elaborate manual on corporate responsibility—a document that details just how CNA proposes to involve all its executives in social goals, and how they in turn should involve their charges. The whole opus has a somewhat evangelical tone, suggesting the marching orders for an all-out war on the devil. What it all will cost and who will finally pay for it are matters nobody seems to talk about. Presumably, however, CNA can afford it. That is to say, CNA, unlike many less opulent and more price-competitive companies, can absorb the costs—i.e., reduce the profits of its shareholders.

Given the natural inclination of managers to demand records and evaluations, it is not surprising that many businessmen who are interested in being socially responsible are also interested in what is known as the "social audit." Just as a conventional audit sums up a company's financial performance, a social audit would describe its social performance. Hundreds of articles, pamphlets, and books have already been written about the social audit, scores of workshops and seminars have been held to discuss it, and some sizable companies are experimenting with ways to implement the idea.

So far, it is fair to say, little has come of the effort. The problem, says Professor S. Prakash Sethi of the University of California at Berkeley, is that nobody has yet drawn up an objective definition of socially responsible behavior; hence nobody has succeeded in measuring it consistently. And who, in any case, would certify that the accounting was accurate? Professor Raymond Bauer of the Harvard Graduate School of Business Administration says, "We still need to learn how to get on the learning curve."

The social-audit concept has been scoffed at even by some of the most ardent advocates of corporate social responsibility. Milton Moskowitz, a financial columnist who edits a crusading biweekly sheet called *Business & Society*, derides the social-audit concept as "nonsense, redemption through mathematics, and useful to companies only as a laundry list." F. Thomas Juster, until recently a senior economist at the National Bureau of Economic Research, has been exploring social and economic measurement. "Given the state of the art," says Juster, "we're all kidding ourselves if we think we can measure [social] output. One reason is that real outputs are very long range. . . . We can't measure that, not now . . . probably can't measure it in ten years."

One of the most insistent of all recent efforts to develop a social audit was present in the Winter 1972–73 issue of the quarterly *Business and Society Review*, in an article by David Linowes, a partner in the accounting firm of Laventhol Krekstein Horwath & Horwath. Linowes, who likes to be alluded to as the father of socioeconomic accounting, presents a model of a social audit. The model differentiates, logically, between mandatory and voluntary corporate outlays, and proposes to put dollar figures on the employee time, the facilities, the training, etc., that a company voluntarily invests in social areas. Linowes anticipates that *Fortune*'s 500 list will someday include a corporate responsibility rating. In the same issue of the review, however, six friendly critics who were asked to comment on Linowes' suggestions raise a host of substantive and technical objections. As one puts it,

Linowes tries "to shoehorn ... into the framework of the orthodox income statement model" what are essentially nonfiscal data containing highly subjective determinations.

Meanwhile, the social-audit enthusiasts seem determined to find a way of making the thing work. A host of consultants who specialize in advising companies on the art and mystery of carrying out their responsibilities to society have got behind the idea of the social audit. "Anytime there is money to be made in some area requiring newly developed expertise," says Ralph Lewis, editor of the *Harvard Business Review*, "a new breed of consultants seems to arise." Several serious enterprises are also showing interest in the social-responsibility audit. Abt Associates Inc., a contract research organization, publishes an annual report accompanied by its version of a social audit. Meanwhile, imaginative newspapermen are setting themselves up as experts, and social audits seem to be giving the public-relations profession a new lease on life.

The Great Social Increment

All this may sound highly laudable at best and harmless enough at worst. But in some circumstances it might be very harmful indeed. It could very well threaten the phenomenon known as rising productivity.

Perhaps because most people are so used to the phrase, they often forget what a stupendous phenomenon it describes. Last year American business produced more than $900 billion worth of goods and services, more than two-thirds of which were accounted for by corporations. Owing in large part to the corporations' striving to make money, national productivity rose by 4 percent. (Corporations earned some $88 billion before taxes, $41 billion of which was taxed away for government and other social needs.)

That 4 percent figure means that business turned out roughly $36 billion *more* of goods and services than it would have if it had maintained only the productivity level of the year before. This great social increment, fluctuating from year to year but expanding at an average of about 3 percent a year, is the very foundation of the nation's way of life; these gains afford the only basis on which a better society can be built. Rising productivity alone made possible the first eight-hour day more than eighty years ago, just as rising productivity has more recently brought higher real pay, shorter hours, and larger fringe benefits. And rising productivity alone will enable the U.S. to achieve without inordinate sacrifice the benefits that the advocates of social responsibility are now demanding.

This is so important a matter that it deserves to be viewed from another perspective. Suppose productivity ceased to rise, or that it even fell a little. Unless more people worked longer, the average living standard would then remain constant or decline. The costs associated with cleaner air, training for minorities, and other socially desirable programs would increase the total price of other things by precisely the amount of those costs. Every benefit would be offset by a sacrifice. If productivity did not rise, one man's gain would be another man's loss.

It's the Consumer Who Pays

Productivity, however, rises only when a business manages to innovate successfully and when it manages to cut costs, either by using fewer resources to make a product or by turning out a better product with the same resources. As the man in charge of costs, the businessman is the agent of what might be called the "consumer at large." When the businessman wastes resources on a bad risk, it is this consumer who principally pays (although the stockholders are presumably losers too). When he reduces his costs or innovates successfully, it is the consumer who benefits.

And so, precisely because the businessman's drive for profitability is identical with his drive for lower costs, his profit is a pretty good measure of social welfare. Suppose two companies make similar products and sell them at about the same price. Company A nets $10 million, but Company B nets twice as much because it is run by a tough crew of hardheaded, no-nonsense, endlessly striving managers motivated by abundant bonuses—the kind of men corporate critics often like to describe as s.o.b.'s. To an individual consumer, the two companies might seem to offer little choice. But so far as society at large is concerned, Company B has done a much better job, because it has used $10 million less of our resources, i.e., raw material and manpower, in doing the same job. So, obviously, the s.o.b.'s have been better for society than easygoing and irresolute managers would have been. As the Lord remarked of Faust, "He who strives endlessly, him we can redeem."

It is just possible, then, that the U.S. could use more endless strivers, redeemed or not. The advocates of corporate social responsibility, indeed, seem to have overlooked what may be the real case against U.S. business: it may be using too many resources for what it turns out. Suppose, at all events, that U.S. corporations had managed to turn out that 1972 volume for 2 percent less than they actually spent. The incremental profit would have amounted to $11 billion, enough to eliminate, over the years, practically all pollution. "If the responsibility buffs really want to promote national welfare," one strict constructionist observed recently, "they should be complaining that companies aren't making *enough* money."

And so it seems reasonable to ask what effect the businessman's increasing preoccupation with those other social "responsibilities" will have on his endless striving to elevate productivity. Thirty-one years ago the late Joseph Schumpeter predicted that, as corporations grew bigger, businessmen would cease to behave like aggressive entrepreneurs, and would degenerate into mere bureaucrats. Schumpeter's prediction hasn't come true, but some now worry that it may. They fear that the new emphasis on Good Works will sicken the businessman o'er with the pale cast of thought, vitiate his drive to innovate and cut costs, and gradually convert him and his fellows into the kind of bureaucrats that infest so many marble halls of government.

Our Socially Responsible Monopolists

These are the kinds of considerations that bother Milton Friedman when he contemplates the contentions in favor of social responsibility. Friedman likes to dramatize his position by making the superficially shocking statement that the businessman's *only* social responsibility is to increase profits. He is against the acceptance of social responsibilities, because it implicitly expresses the socialist view that political, and not market, considerations should govern the allocation of resources, and over the long run this means reduced efficiency. What's more, Friedman says, "no businessman has money to spend on social responsibility unless he has monopoly power. Any businessman engaged in social responsibility ought to be immediately slapped with an antitrust suit."

In the same vein, Professor Harold Demsetz of U.C.L.A. insists that the word "responsibility" is being misused: "The only responsibility of businessmen or anyone else is to obey the laws of the land, no more, no less." If our society wants business to set up day-care centers for employees' children, for example, then it should pass a law to that effect, so that the burden will be shared by all business enterprises.

The problem of sharing that burden is one that most social-responsibility advocates seem not to have thought through. One trouble with leaving good deeds up to individual executives is that not all of their companies are equally prosperous. Now that the Kaiser empire is in trouble, for example, Edgar Kaiser is taking a hard line on demands for "responsibility" in his companies. "Not to husband resources," Kaiser says with considerable feeling, "would be social irresponsibility of the highest order." Hard-pressed companies obviously cannot undertake the social programs supported by companies with strong market power, such as utilities (whose regulated rates are based on costs). And healthily profitable companies like Standard of Indiana and CNA obviously have a great advantage over companies that are constantly battling to stay in the black.

Even companies that have the resources to undertake socially responsible projects do not necessarily possess the skills to solve most complex social problems. "The job of the public and government," says F. Thomas Juster, "is to tell business what the appropriate social objectives are; they shouldn't want business messing around with its own set of social objectives." Professor Paul Heyne of Southern Methodist University, a strict constructionist, argues that the economic system is not a playground in which businessmen should be exercising their own preferences.

"Any economic system," he explains, "ought to be a social mechanism for picking up the preferences of everyone, matching these against available resources, and obtaining from what we have a maximum of what we want. The market is a mechanism of almost incredible effectiveness in the accomplishment of this task. The market works effectively because those who have command over resources continually reallocate them in response to the signals provided by relative prices. The businessman who wants to behave in a socially responsible way must depend heavily, overwhelmingly, on this information."

Just Like Embezzlement

Probably no economist has given more thought to corporate social responsibility than Henry Manne, professor of law at the University of Rochester, who began writing about the subject a dozen years ago. He observed that most companies maintained enough reserves to meet unforeseen contingencies and to offset unintended mistakes, and so could *temporarily* spend some money on social activities that raise costs without raising revenues or income. So far as consumers and employees are concerned, Manne has observed, somewhat caustically, this spending is indistinguishable in its effects from simple inefficiency or outright embezzlement.

Manne believes that the whole concept of corporate responsibility suits government officials and intellectuals—particularly intellectuals who deride and even hate the idea of a free market. It also goes down just fine with bloviating businessmen who don't mind casting themselves as members of the divine elect. Of course, businessmen often interpret "socially responsible" policies as long-term profit maximization, i.e., "in the long run we make more money by spending to be good citizens now." Manne doesn't object to this line of reasoning so long as the spending really does maximize profits in the long run—and helps the firms survive in a free market. He says, however, that voluntary corporate altruism has never made a significant dent in any but insignificant problems. Manne has developed his own economic model of corporate responsibility—the first of its kind—and reports that it can accommodate a little, but not much, corporate giving; he finds it impossible to justify a model of substantial corporate social action.

Above all, Manne avers, any such action will result in more government controls. It implies that business and government should work together to promote social progress. "Corporate social responsibility, a doctrine offered by many as a scheme to popularize and protect free enterprise," Manne concludes, "can succeed only if the free market is abandoned in favor of government controls. The game isn't worth the candle."

There seem to have been some cases in which "socially responsible" behavior has actually hampered business operations. California's Bank of America, upset and moved by radicals' demonstrations against it, went in some time ago for being socially responsible in a big way. It appointed an executive vice president, G. Robert Truex Jr., as custodian of social policy, and he is now dabbling with a social audit. The bank also set aside no less than $200 million for low-interest loans that would help provide housing for minority-group members and other underprivileged persons.

But the bank has found itself in a dilemma. The 2,500 loan officers in its thousand California branches pride themselves on knowing the credit-worthiness of people in their areas. Now many of these officers have been asked to lend money to people who had no conventional credit standing at all—indeed, they were being asked to *persuade* people to borrow. How, in these circumstances, do you preserve the loan officers' morale and esprit? The Bank of America is wrestling with that problem.

Some proponents of increased corporate responsibility have given high marks to Levi Strauss & Co. of San Francisco, maker of the famous Levi's and other informal apparel. As its many admirers note, the company contributes 3 percent of its net after taxes to carefully chosen social programs, does a lot of hiring from among disadvantaged minority groups, helps finance minority suppliers, and has established day-care centers for employees' children. At the same time, the company has done well. It has expanded sales from $8 million in 1946 to more than $504 million last year, and net income from $700,000 to $25 million.

Getting Their Money's Worth

But Levi Strauss is obviously getting a lot for that 3 percent. It does business in an intensely liberal city and has a market in which tastes are heavily influenced by young people. And so, whatever its top executives believe in their heart of hearts, their social-responsibility outlays would appear to be rather effective public relations. So far as an outsider can determine, these outlays cost no more than would conventional high-pressure public relations in a different kind of company.

Many of the costs associated with social responsibility, such as minority training and aid, are often marginal, out of proportion to all the time and talent that have gone into arguing about them. Behaving responsibly often means no more or less than acting humanely, treating employees and customers with consideration, avoiding ineptitudes and blunders, cultivating a sharp eye for the important little things, and knowing how to spend where the returns are high. In this sense, responsibility can accomplish a lot with relatively small cost.

But many other expenses of behaving in a socially acceptable way, such as the cost of meeting the escalating demands of the consumer advocates, will not come cheap, and might easily get out of hand. Heavy social involvements can also cost a company dear in terms of managerial talent. And so the impact of the corporate-responsibility movement on companies that must husband their resources, on the endlessly striving cost cutters, indeed on competition itself, is not yet clear. Americans can only hope that businessmen will retain enough of the old Adam Smith in them to keep productivity rising.

5
Epilogue

The Epilogue presents views of modern organized life from a quite different perspective: not from that of recognized poets and novelists, but from the perspective of career participants in governmental and business organizations. These practitioners have all studied the poetry and prose in *Business in Literature* and have been moved by these works to reflect on and share their own experiences. They do not claim the artistry of a Sandburg or a Frost, but in our view, they have made fresh and sometimes powerful statements that very much add to the value of the book. Their statements go beyond each chapter's Viewpoints, which tend to be scholarly positions about modern organized life. In the Epilogue, we have "front-line organizational operatives" who have stepped back from their jobs, to communicate various impressions in a moving, poetic way. Some of the works are whimsical, some biting; all are thoughtful and on-target in speaking to the book's themes. We can learn a great deal from these statements. Above all we can be glad we have contemplative persons such as these taking a hand in directing our modern organizations.

In the Essay section, Atlanta newspaper editor Jim Wooten observes a number of these young professionals in a graduate business class. They are involved in the process of organizational (and self-) examination that leads to works such as those presented in this Epilogue. He listens to their questioning and asks a question of his own. As with Socrates, the questions here may be more important than the answers.

POEMS

Mary T. Gentry

Lament for a Rush Hour Crowd

Stampeding herds
Lemmings moving to the sea
Propelled in channels eroded by time and habit
Eyes permanently focused to screen the unfamiliar
Radar set to exclude unknown blips
Ignoring warnings: think, know, care!

Recognizing their brotherhood,
Do lemmings smile as they plunge into the sea?

Ginny Sikes (1945–)

Prayers : 1964–1984

Lord, help me through this quiz,
so that I can make an "A" in this course,
so that I can bring up my grade point average,
so that I can get accepted into medical school.
So that I can finally make some money.
Then everything will be perfect.

Lord, help me through oral exams,
so that I can finish high enough in my medical class,
so that I can get a choice internship,
so that I can get accepted into a prestigious residency.
Then everything will be perfect.

Lord, help me through this presentation,
so that the residency faculty will give me recommendations,
so that I can get offers to join a respected practice,
so that I can finally make some money.
Then everything will be perfect.

Lord, help me expand my practice faster,
so that I can put money into my retirement plan,
so that I can quit before I'm sixty-five,
so that I can spend some time with my family.
Then everything will be perfect.

South-bound on 75

Hammers down and ears on
they shatter the night
jack-jawing on their C.B.'s
about bears, birddogs and beavers.
They swagger from the Waffle House
properly groomed with a toothpick and Vitalis . . .
One with their rigs,
C.W. trucks for Jesus,
Wayne's got a hot load,
and Ray's running a Pardon Special.
Pitying the man who doesn't haul,
their canon is "have a good one",
and they rejoice in their freedom.
Tonight they'll be loving, fighting, and getting home,
in some order.

Interstate Billboard

KOA CAMPGROUNDS
full hook-ups
hot showers
level pull throughs

> coin laundry
> swimming pool
> video game room
> Let your family enjoy nature with us!

Macon, Ga.

Change, being very disturbing—
they found the perfect way to do things
and the perfect families to do them
thirty years ago.
Then change became unnecessary.

But industries discovered Macon.
Industries with factories that pay taxes and create jobs
and have university-trained management.
Management that doesn't know how it's always been done
and says"sin"in one syllable.

The Chamber of Commerce is fascinated,
and scared.

JAMES L. STANFORD   (1945–   )

The Tyrant

Imperious it sits and stares vacantly
Its eyes, for the moment, gray and lifeless.
In an instant, at its own discretion,
its eyes will blaze insistently, incessantly,
and from its heart of cold-rolled steel
(or is it plastic now?)
Will come its cry.

Not even the day-old infant,
God's most self-centered creature
demands and commands such instant attention.

No matter the time or place,
No matter it interrupts a warm
reminiscence with an old friend,
a proposal of love, or the creative
musings of the solitary mind—
Solitude is shattered, and all attention
turns to the blinking, screaming Tyrant.

Perhaps we do not wish to talk.
Perhaps it screams in error—the result
of a number only half-remembered.
No matter! It must and will be satisfied.

After all, it is a modern wonder;
without it modern industry would fall
and yet, sometimes when my privacy is shattered,
my thoughts destroyed, my confidences broken
and my leisure interrupted,

Sometimes when consigned to that
Purgatory called Hold, or forced to converse
with a machine which times my thoughts
and cannot heed my questions . . .

Sometimes I wish that Watson had not heard,
or hearing had refused to bend his will to
that of the Machine. . .

But my phone is ringing. . .

Karen Eckert (1955–)

My Second Job

Friday night again.
What an affinity with Monday morning.
Time to dress for success; put on
    the finery, makeup, fascinating personality.
It's like most jobs.
Some nights are very productive and rewarding
    with arrangements made for future meetings.
Others drag on with endless blah blah.
Let's face it.
In this job one has got to be efficient
    when there's only a two-day work week.
The pressure's on to produce, show results.
It's an art form.
It requires well-developed interpersonal skills.
The job involves entertaining small talk
    with computer software and insurance salesmen.
Moonlighting is tough.
But some needs aren't met by my primary source of income.
The best investment opportunities there are unavailable,
    already committed to going concerns, too costly.
It's a risky enterprise.
Too much so now for only a short-term focus.
The operating environment has become treacherous
    with incurable disease a distinct possibility.
It's not all bad.
Even with maturity there are still surprises.
While the competition gets younger and stronger
    so do the new targets of my business strategy.
TGIF.
I have no intention to file for bankruptcy.
When my parents' friends ask when I'm going to
    settle down I say I'm working on it.

The Appointment

I know I'm supposed to meet someone
But I can't remember who.
It's so hard to remember everything
With so many things to do.

I know I'm supposed to be somewhere
I said so long ago.
Go to school, get a job, I told myself
To succeed, prosper, and grow.

I know I'm supposed to be happy now
Everything's going my way.
Good job, good home, good friends to call
But what is there to say?

I know I'm supposed to meet someone
If I miss her I know she'll be gone.
Yes, I remember the appointment now
It's with whom I'll some day become.

LINDA PODGER-WILLIAMS (1958–)

Don't You Know What You Want?

For your parents' sake:
    Grow up strong and clean your plate.
    Work hard in school and don't be late.
    Never get grounded and always meet curfews.
    Sunday mornings be found in the church pews.

For your spouse's sake:
    Always look like a million but spend like a pauper.
    Entertain friends and clients—be the first to offer.
    Stay fit and trim as the day you were wed.
    Fulfill every fantasy on a satin sheet bed.

For your children's sake:
   Read all that's available from every authority
   On how to raise children—it's your first priority.
   Vacation at Disney World year after year,
   And supply them the goods to stay up with their peers.

For your community's sake:
   Be the one to lend a helping hand,
   For fund drives to benefit the church and the band.
   Volunteer for every committee and task,
   They know you'll say yes—that's why they ask.

In the two minutes and fifty-eight seconds remaining,
Do something for yourself. Well, why are you waiting?

A ConglomeRation Of Nicknames You Most often Say

       You're the BMOC at UCLA
       Then get a job paying 50K.
       If you wanna play basketball, it's the ACC,
       Go to UVA if you got the SAT.

       If you're a YUPPIE, work for IBM.
       Buy a fancy house with an ARM.
       Drive a BMW with a prestige plate,
       Advertise SWM to get a date.

       The UAW is concerned about the MPG.
       I just wanna watch my MTV,
       Listen to music on my new CD
       And maybe try out some R&B.

       For the MBA take the GMAT,
       Maybe go on and get a Ph.D.
       Then start on your path to be the CEO
       Of AT&T or an HMO.

You don't have to be VP of the USA,
Just start out small with a local PTA.
Then work on the board at the YMCA,
But just make sure to always CYA.

I'm not quite sure how to end this poem,
This silliness could be endless, So I'm
Quitting now and you'll be left,
To sit and ponder until TGIF.

PAT BROWN (1958–)

I'll Be Home at Six
(a promise I will keep)

Today I made a promise
    the kind one keeps if sincere,
        broken when priorities lie elsewhere.

Some live by promises;
    others never enter into them.
I am the latter changing to the former.
    A most radical move; a forfeited risk.

My spouse utters ultimatums
    "On time, any time, you chose the time.
    but you're held to that time!" (or else?).
Most demanding, threatening, yet reasonable.

But the work deadlines disagree.
    They also utter ultimatums
"It must be done, time is of the essence,
    lost if late." (or else?)
Most demanding, threatening, yet unreasonable.

Timetables, some reachable, others out of grasp.
So unachievable, the homefront ones.
Reasoning holds that
> it shall be damned at six,
> returning home as vowed,
> a self-imposed schedule,
> my own chosen time.

And, I will hold to this pledge.
> I'll be home at six, dear,
> I'll be home at six, somehow
> I'll be home at six (California time).

SHIRLEY ADAMS (1946–   )

For You

We approached from two directions speeding
> recklessly out of the five-day snare.
Long cool evenings, languid mornings, hot afternoons stretched
> with gazes and smiles and satisfaction
We were apart from the rest; complete freedom
> complete possession. No interference from outside.
We give and take adulation but I feel powerful.
I *know* this game.

The talks are long and indulgent
> I know so well what you want to hear.
We were pleased to agree so completely
> or to argue so wittily.
You belonged to me. We were different.
I even began to relax into you; I was really important to you.
Nothing can compare.

I am leaving the weekend reluctantly, taking you with me
> into *my* week!

You leave me with the urgency of a phone call and a
   voice from 3,000 miles—an appointment and
     the next plane out.
     I watch you cradle the phone,
   Your eyes are darting to the ceiling, away from me,
Away from my leaving.
Your feeling dries into acumen. You transfer your passion from
    head to head and I am
   left wondering about my own singleheadedness.

You belong to something foreign to me. We are different.
Does it compartmentalize so easily: two days
    for passion and five days for profit?

John B. Farrow (1951–   )

Machine

You don't bother me
Though the poets all seem down on you.
You can pick more cotton and bale more hay than I could
   in a lifetime.
You can sew a thousand shirts or mill a million tons of steel.
You're all right.
You don't fight back and you don't go on strike.
When I quit working, you're still going strong.
The poets say you have no heart;
They can't stand your efficiency.
Well hell, of course you ain't got no heart!
If you did, you couldn't work the way you do.
And obviously you got no brain either,
Or you'd have killed us long ago.
You know, you built the hospital where I was born,
Helped the doctor,
Got the nurse there on time,

And in general you have made all tasks much easier.
I appreciate that.
When I die there will probably be a backhoe to dig my grave.
You'll be standing strong when I'm no longer here.
That don't bother me machine.
We've grown up together, you and I,
And each of us knows his place.
You'll never have a funeral and I'll never rust in the rain.

BONNIE GREER

Enlightenment

I used to complain
"There are no windows in my office."
   (Were the slits of glass
      cut so tall
         and narrow
           To please some cop-and-robber game players in Security,
           To accommodate some efficiency expert in Real Property,
           Or merely to manifest a meanness
               obscured within some architect's artistic soul?)
Never-ending redundancy of the same eight-hour days,
Never-ending redundancy of the same
     four walls
        caused the heaviness in my heart.

Now that I am more fortunate—
With my wall of glass,
And plaza of boxwood and begonias,
And dogwood and pine,
And mulberry,
  and hickory,
I am also wiser.

The four drab walls were my protection, as Security intended,
    and the architect was truly kind.

For now I watch the wind working silently to replace
    the clean hard blue of October sky
        with November's subtler dome of gray.
And I watch the leaves of gold and rust and brown, clinging
    ever-so-gingerly to the slender, baring black branches
        they share with bustling birds, balanced
            poised in mid-song—
            listening, waiting, testing,
                for the throatiness that tells them it is time to go.
Now I watch the swirling of seasons.

And my heart, once blissfully heavy,
    whimpers softly now,
        incessantly,
           refusing to die.

ESSAYS

Jim Wooten (1945–)

Finding Happiness in Work

At the age of 10 or maybe 12, Roy Clayton knew he would be a salesman, knew that as soon as he was old enough he would join the gregarious band of men who started out in Knoxville and worked their way down to his mountain home near Elijay.

Fun-loving, free-spirited, those were the men he would join, men whose satchels revealed the exotic new and whose imaginations regaled, delighted, amused, enthralled—ah, the tales they could tell of the places they had seen, the people they had known. That is what he would do with life. He knew that. Knew he would be a salesman. And he is.

"It worked out just like I'd planned," says Clayton, now 77 and still working. For 55 years he's been in sales, the last 31 as a salesman of textiles to hospitals, hotels, nursing homes and schools.

He could have retired, of course. If it had been a job, he probably would have. He probably would have left after the stroke two years ago; instead he only slowed, cut back his office and travel schedule.

At 77, Roy Clayton is able to reflect on his life at work and say what the young fear they will never be able to say: "I have done just what I wanted to do. If I had it to do over, I would do the same thing."

The young fear they will not be able to say it, and increasingly work is assigned a role less central to their lives. It is not so much a vehicle for enjoyment of life as a provider of the means to find satisfaction elsewhere. Accounts heard repeatedly of auto workers and others who refuse to work overtime, despite substantial pay incentives, reflect the changing attitude: Work is to afford leisure.

When viewed from that perspective, it is not surprising that today's young workers examine jobs much as they would autos in a showroom. What are its features? How fast does it go? How well is it designed?

At Georgia State University eight graduate students in business administration sit around a conference table discussing a text called "Business in Literature." The students are, for the most part, those who would be expected to spend careers climbing the corporate ladder, relocating when they are told, taking jobs assigned for corporate advancement. Most are in their late 20s or early 30s.

They are discussing not how to succeed without really trying, but how people relate to their jobs; how bureaucracies affect people; how writers through the ages view work and the workplace.

Listen to them talk and it is readily apparent that though the suits are the same, the hairstyles, the appearance; the corporate man in the gray flannel suit is no longer an extension of the corporation. He just looks the same.

Inside he is different. "There's a lot more to life," says one, "and I'd like to know about it." He, like many others there, expects that he will change jobs or even careers, sampling work like the offerings of a smorgasbord.

Will they be happier, happier than the boy of 10 who knew one job, accepted it uncritically, and imagined where it would take him?

SUGGESTIONS FOR FURTHER READING

NOVELS:

Balzac, Honoré de. *César Birotteau.* Translated by Frances Frenaye. New York: Juniper Press, 1955.

———. *Eugénie Grandet.* Translated by Ellen Marriage. New York: Dutton, 1968.

Caldwell, Taylor. *Captains and Kings.* Greenwich, Connecticut: Fawcett, 1976.

Camus, Albert. *The Fall.* Translated by Justin O'Brien. New York: Knopf, 1972.

Conroy, Pat. *The Great Santini.* Boston: Houghton Mifflin, 1976.

Dickens, Charles. *Bleak House.* New York: Oxford University Press, 1956.

———. *Hard Times for These Times.* New York: Oxford University Press, 1955.

Dickey, James. *Deliverance.* Boston: Houghton Mifflin, 1970.

Dreiser, Theodore. *The Financier.* Cleveland: World, 1946.

Ellison, Ralph. *Invisible Man.* New York: Random House, 1952.

Erdman, Paul. *The Last Days of America.* Boston: G. K. Hall, 1982.

Golding, William Gerald. *Lord of the Flies.* New York: Coward-McCann, 1962.

Hawley, Cameron. *Cash McCall.* Boston: Houghton Mifflin, 1955.

———. *Executive Suite.* Boston: Houghton Mifflin, 1952.

Heller, Joseph. *Catch 22.* New York: Simon & Schuster, 1961.

———. *Something Happened.* New York: Knopf, 1974.

Hersey, John Richard. *A Bell for Adano.* New York: Knopf, 1944.

SUGGESTIONS FOR FURTHER READING/**339**

Howells, William Dean. *The Rise of Silas Lapham*. Bloomington: Indiana University Press, 1971.
Huxley, Aldous Leonard. *Brave New World*. New York: Harper & Row, 1946
Knowlton, Christopher. *The Real World*. New York: Atheneum, 1984.
Koestler, Arthur. *Darkness at Noon*. Translated by Daphne Hardy. New York: Modern Library, 1941.
Lewis, Sinclair. *Babbitt*. New York: Harcourt, Brace & World, 1950.
———. *Main Street*. New York: Harcourt, Brace & World, 1948.
Norris, Frank. *The Octopus: A Story of California*. Garden City, New York: Doubleday, 1901.
———. *The Pit*. Columbus, Ohio: C. E. Merrill, 1970.
Orwell, George. *Animal Farm*. New York: Harcourt, Brace & World, 1954.
———. *Nineteen Eighty-Four*. New York: Harcourt, Brace & World, 1963.
Payne, David. *Confessions of a Taoist on Wall Street*. Boston: Houghton Mifflin, 1984.
Rand, Ayn. *Anthem*. New York: New American Library, 1946.
———. *Atlas Shrugged*. New York: New American Library, 1959.
———. *The Fountainhead*. Indianapolis: Bobbs Merrill, 1968.
Sinclair, Upton Beall. *The Jungle*. New York: New American Library, 1960.
Thomas, Piri. *Down These Mean Streets*. New York: New American Library, 1967.
Wells, Herbert George. *Tono-Bungay*. New York: Modern Library, 1908.
White, T. H. *The View from the Fortieth Floor*. New York: W. Sloane Associates, 1960.
Wilson, Sloan. *The Man in the Grey Flannel Suit*. New York: Simon & Schuster, 1955.
Wouk, Herman. *The Caine Mutiny: A Novel of World War II*. New York: Pocket Books, 1973.
Zola, Émile. *Germinal*. Translated by Havelock Ellis. New York: Dutton, 1948.

PLAYS:

Albee, Edward. *The American Dream*. New York: Coward-McCann, 1961.

Anouilh, Jean. *Antigone*. *Jean Anouilh: Five Plays*, Vol. 1. Translated by L. Galantière. New York: Hill & Wang, 1958.

Becque, Henri. *The Vultures*. *Representative Continental Dramas*. Edited by M. J. Moses. Boston: Little, Brown, 1924.

Brecht, Bertolt. *Mother Courage*. *Seven Plays by Bertolt Brecht*. Edited by Eric Bentley. New York: Grove Press, 1961.

———. *The Good Woman of Setzuan*. *Seven Plays by Bertolt Brecht*. Edited by Eric Bentley. New York: Grove Press, 1961.

Chekhov, Anton. *The Cherry Orchard*. *Best Plays*. Translated by Stark Young. New York: Modern Library, 1956.

Dürrenmatt, Friedrich. *The Physicists*. Translated by Gerhard Nellhaus and others. New York: Grove Press, 1965.

Giraudoux, Jean. *The Madwoman of Chaillot*. English adaptation by Maurice Valency. New York: Random House, 1940.

Hauptman, Gerhart. *The Weavers*. Translated by Mary Morison. New York: B. W. Huebsch, 1911.

Ibsen, Henrik. *The Master Builder*. Translated by Eva Le Gallienne. New York: New York University Press, 1955.

———. *Peer Gynt*. *The Collected Works of Henrik Ibsen*. Translated by William and Charles Archer. 4 vols. New York: Scribner's, 1911.

Kaufman, George S., and Marc Connelly. *Beggar on Horseback*. *Twenty-five Best Plays of the Modern American Theater*. Edited by John Gassner. New York: Crown, 1949.

Miller, Arthur. *Death of a Salesman*. *The Portable Arthur Miller*. Edited by Harold Clurman. New York: Viking, 1971.

———. *The Price*. *The Portable Arthur Miller*. Edited by Harold Clurman. New York: Viking, 1971.

Odets, Clifford. *Waiting for Lefty*. *Six Plays of Clifford Odets*. New York: Modern Library, 1939.

O'Neill, Eugene. *The Hairy Ape*. *Nine Plays by Eugene O'Neill*. New York: Random House, 1932.

Osborne, John. *Look Back in Anger*. London: Faber & Faber, 1957.

Pinter, Harold. *The Dumb Waiter. The Caretaker and The Dumb Waiter: Two Plays.* New York: Grove Press, 1960.
Rice, Elmer. *The Adding Machine.* Garden City, New York: Doubleday, 1923.
Roulston, Keith. *His Own Boss.* New York: Playwrights' Co-op, 1979.
Shaw, George Bernard. *Major Barbara. Selected Plays.* 2 vols. New York: Dodd, Mead, 1949.
Sophocles. *Antigone.* Translated by Richard Emil Braun. New York: Oxford University Press, 1973.
Van Itallie, Jean-Claude. *Interview. American Hurrah.* New York: Coward-McCann, 1966.

NONFICTION:

Agee, James, and Walker Evans. *Let Us Now Praise Famous Men.* Boston: Houghton Mifflin, 1960.
Bennis, Warren, ed. *Beyond Bureaucracy.* New York: McGraw-Hill, 1973.
Berkley, George E. *The Administrative Revolution.* Englewood Cliffs, New Jersey: Prentice-Hall, 1971.
Brown, J. A. C. *The Social Psychology of Industry.* Baltimore: Penguin, 1975.
Clance, Pauline Rose. *The Imposter Phenomenon.* New York: Bantam, 1986.
Chewning, Richard C. *Business Ethics in a Changing Culture.* Richmond: Robert F. Dame, Inc., 1983.
Deal, Terrance E., and Allan A. Kennedy. *Corporate Cultures.* Reading, Massachusetts: Addison-Wesley, 1982.
Donaldson, Thomas. *Corporations and Morality.* Englewood Cliffs, New Jersey: Prentice-Hall, 1982.
Ewing, David W. *Freedom Inside the Organization.* New York: McGraw-Hill, 1977.
Glover, John Desmond, and Ralph M. Hower. *The Administrator.* Homewood, Illinois: Irwin, 1963.
Golembienski, Robert T. *Men, Management and Morality.* New York: McGraw-Hill, 1965.
Handy, Charles B. *Understanding Organizations.* Baltimore: Penguin, 1976.

Heilbroner, Robert. *An Inquiry into the Human Prospect*. New York: Norton, 1974.

Jay, Anthony. *Corporation Man*. New York: Random House, 1971.

———. *Management and Machiavelli*. New York: Holt, Rinehart & Winston, 1968.

Livesay, Harold C. *American Made*. Boston: Little, Brown, 1979.

Loden, Marilyn. *Feminine Leadership*. New York: Times Books, 1985.

Maccoby, Michael. *The Gamesman*. New York: Simon and Schuster, 1976.

Mumford, Lewis. *Technics and Civilization*. New York: Harcourt, Brace & World, 1963.

Naisbitt, John. *Megatrends*. New York: Warner Books, 1984.

Naisbitt, John, and Patricia Aburdene. *Re-Inventing the Corporation*. New York: Warner, 1985.

Ouchi, William. *Theory Z*. Reading, Massachusetts: Addison-Wesley, 1981.

Pascale, Richard Tanner, and Anthony G. Athos. *The Art of Japanese Management*. New York: Warner Books, 1981.

Peters, Thomas J., and Robert H. Waterman, Jr. *In Search of Excellence*. New York: Harper & Row, 1982.

Pugh, D. S., D. S. Hickson, and C. R. Hinings. *Writers on Organizations*. Baltimore: Penguin, 1975.

Reich, Robert. *Tales of a New America*. New York: Times Books, 1987.

Riesman, David. *The Lonely Crowd*. New Haven, Connecticut: Yale University Press, 1964.

Schein, Edgar H. *Organization Culture and Leadership*. Washington: Jossey-Bass, 1985.

Schumacher, E. F. *Small is Beautiful*. London: Blond & Briggs, 1973.

Servan-Schreiber, Jean-Jacques. *The World Challenge*. New York: Simon and Schuster, 1981.

Sheehy, Gail. *Passages*. New York: Bantam, 1977.

Skinner, Burrhus Frederic. *Beyond Freedom and Dignity*. New York: Knopf, 1971.

———. *Walden Two*. New York: Macmillan, 1948.

Stewart, Rosemary. *The Reality of Organizations.* London: Macmillan, 1970.
Toffler, Alvin. *The Third Wave.* New York: Bantam Books, 1980.
———. *Future Shock.* New York: Random House, 1970.
Whyte, William Hollingsworth. *The Organization Man.* New York: Simon and Schuster, 1956.